CW00662583

Adrian Tame was born in Luton, Engla [...] twice and has three adult children, D [...] spent twenty-five years in journalism i [...] North America (1966–1967) and Austr [...] Australia with his family in 1973, and [...] After resigning as news editor of *Truth* [...] of them as a director, with IPR, Australia's largest public relations company. He and his wife Ann moved to rural Victoria in 1994, where they live today. Adrian is the co-author of *Maralinga: British A-bomb, Australian Legacy*, published by William Collins in 1982, and the author of *A Fruitful Life, A Biography of Bill Montague*, published in 1996. In 1981 he scripted *Thunderground*, a cinema release feature on the Hell's Angels Motor Cycle Club; and in 1983 he scripted and researched *Street Kids*, an award-winning Channel Nine documentary on homeless youth. His interests include bush walking, books and music.

The
Matriarch

The Kathy Pettingill Story

Adrian Tame

PAN
Pan Macmillan Australia

First published 1996 in Macmillan by Pan Macmillan Australia Pty Limited
This edition published 2002 in Pan by Pan Macmillan Australia Pty Limited
St Martins Tower, 31 Market Street, Sydney

Reprinted 2002, 2003

National Library of Australia
cataloguing-in-publication data:

Tame, A.S. (Adrian Sanigear), 1944– .
The matriarch: the Kathy Pettingill story.

[Rev. ed.].
ISBN 0 330 36387 5.

1. Pettingill, Kathy. 2. Criminals - Victoria - Biography.
I. Title.

364.374092

Typeset in 11/14 pt Palatino by Midland Typesetters, Maryborough
Printed in Australia by McPherson's Printing Group

This book is dedicated to my wife, Ann

Acknowledgments

TO GEOFF FLATMAN, CHRIS DANE, PHIL DUNN, BILL MORGAN-PAYLER, PAT TEHAN, BOB VERNON, CHARLIE NIKAKIS AND BERNIE AHEARNE, with thanks to each and every one of you for legal assistance provided

TO NUNZIO LAROSSA, who comforted me when I was feeling down

TO LEO, who kept me going at court when I was in dire straits

TO LILLIAN LIEDER, QC, for comforting me in Lonsdale Street

TO STEVE AND HIS WIFE, who never let our family down under any pressure

TO MY TWO SONS, who conducted themselves in the dock during the Walsh Street trial like gentlemen

TO DEBBIE, for being there with me at the verdict, and who is still with me with her two young sons

TO HUGH RIMMINTON, who sat with me through the verdict

TO SALLY GLUYAS, who was kind when the jury were out

TO ROBIN AND THE TWO DEBBIES, who came to Fairlea every fortnight for our great barbecues

TO PAT from Venus Bay

TO RAY, JANE AND PADDY, who supported me in my court case after having known me at Venus Bay for only two months

TO THE UNKNOWN PERSON who wrote to me at Venus Bay and let me know she felt for us

TO DENNIS, my first-born, despite all the violence and fear he created

AND TO ADRIAN TAME, for having the guts to write this book

KATHY PETTINGILL

TO WARREN BARKER, for inspiration

TO JOHN GRANT, for introductions and memories

TO LEON GETTLER, for invaluable advice

TO TOM NOBLE, for generous assistance with research, and permission to quote from his excellent books

TO JANE (for reading) and GEOFF (for listening) McDONNELL

TO PETER HILL and VIRGINIA KONG, for comments and safe-keeping

TO ANDY WALKER, for research and wise counsel

TO ROBERT MACOLINO, for his thoughts

TO *THE AGE* and *HERALD-SUN*, Melbourne, for allowing me to use their library facilities

TO THE CORONERS' OFFICES in Melbourne and Adelaide, for research

TO CHARLIE NIKAKIS, for reading the manuscript

TO MY EDITOR, AMANDA HEMMINGS, for her enthusiasm, insights, patience, and sharing of a strange obsession.

ADRIAN TAME

Contents

Chronology

1935	March 27	Kathy born to Albert Kemp and Gladys Lee
1937		Kathy's sister Wilma born
1939		Kathy's sister Barbara born
		Albert enlists in army and goes to war
1941		Albert dies
		Kathleen Shields takes over care of girls
1945		Family moves to St Kilda
		Barbara dies
1950		Kathy starts work in clothing factory
1951		Kathy meets Dennis Ryan
	Nov 7	Kathy's first child, Dennis, born
	Dec 14	Kathy marries Dennis Ryan
1952	Sept	Dennis Ryan goes to fight in Korean war
1953	Jan 25	Kathy's second child, Peter, born
	Feb	Kathy meets Billy Peirce
1954		Gladys takes over Dennis and Peter
	Aug 11	Kathy's third child, Vicki, born
1956	July 8	Kathy's fourth child, Shelley, born and taken into care
1957	July 15	Kathy's fifth child, Stephen, born and taken into care
1958	Nov 11	Kathy's sixth child, Victor, born
1960	Jan 7	Kathy's seventh child, Lex, born

xi

1961		Kathy meets Jimmy Pettingill
	July	Kathy's eighth child, David, born and taken into care
1963	Dec 18	Kathy's ninth child, Jamie, born
1965	Feb 1	Kathy's last child, Trevor, born
1967		Kathy breaks with Jimmy Pettingill
		Kathy moves family to Olympic village and starts work at Sentimental Bloke Hotel
1968	Sept 16	Billy Peirce dies
	Dec 8	Dennis's first conviction (wilful damage)
1969	Nov	Dennis learns Kathy is his mother
1970		Jason Ryan, Kathy's grandson, born
1971		Kathy has heart attack, recovers, then goes into massage parlours
		Family moves to High St, Northcote
1972		Jimmy Pettingill dies
1973	Oct 17	Dennis and Peter go on rampage in Sandringham
1974	Aug 1	Dennis sentenced to ten years gaol, Peter fourteen
1975	March 11	Kathy's first charge (indecent language)
1976	June 25	Kathy gaoled for fourteen days for harbouring escapee
1978		Dennis released
	Oct 1	Kathy loses eye in shooting incident

	Dec 18	Dennis gaoled for three months for harbouring Jamie
		Family moves to Ross St, Northcote
1979	July 20	Dennis gaoled for four years for parole breach
1980	April 22	Dennis given two months' sentence for aiding escapee
1981		Dennis marries Heather (Sissy) Hill in Pentridge Gaol
		Dennis's and Sissy's daughter Lindy born
1982	June	Kathy buys house at 108 Stephenson St, Richmond
	July	Dennis released and joins Kathy
1983	May 27	Greg Pasche last seen alive
		Dennis's and Sissy's daughter Jade born
	Sept 14	Tom Wraith murdered
	Nov	Victor Gouroff disappears
	Nov-Dec	Dennis buys three more houses in Richmond
1984	July 23	Operation Cyclops launched
	Aug 11	Wayne Stanhope shot dead
	Sept 18	Lindsay Simpson shot dead
	Oct	Six Cyclops raids on various houses
	Oct 24	Dennis buys five houses in Cubitt St, Richmond
	Nov 8	Helga Wagnegg's fatal visit to 108 Stephenson St
	Nov 27	Victor and Trevor charged with trafficking in heroin

	Nov 29	Jamie bashes undercover policeman
1985	Jan-Feb	Further Cyclops raids
	May 9	Coroner's Court bombed
	May 14	Dennis allegedly sends 'Miss X' to Sydney to collect heroin
	May 14	Jamie dies from overdose
	Aug 6	Peter released from gaol
	Sept	Dennis threatens roadie with gun
	Sept 4	Shots fired at Prahran Police Station
	Nov 6	Anton Kenny murdered
1986	March 5	Anton Kenny's body recovered from Yarra
	April	Peter raided and remanded in custody
	Aug 27	Sissy suicides in Pentridge Gaol
	Dec 10	Vicki Ward murdered
1987	Mar 11	Dennis charged with Stanhope murder
	April 13	Dennis dies in St Vincent's Hospital
	April 13	Inquest into Sissy's death
1988	April	Kathy moves to Venus Bay Peter gaoled for thirteen years
	Oct 11	Graeme Jensen shot by police
	Oct 12	Two police constables murdered in Walsh St, South Yarra
	Oct 31	Jason charged with policemen's murders
	Nov 1	Anthony Farrell charged with policemen's murders
	Nov 17	Jedd Houghton shot by police

	Dec 30	Victor charged with policemen's murders
1989	April 9	Gary Abdallah shot by police
	May 18	Peter McEvoy charged with policemen's murders
	July 15	Wendy Peirce enters witness protection
		Kathy's lost children contact their mother
1990	Feb 22	Victor, McEvoy and Farrell committed
	July 9	Trevor charged with policemen's murders
1991	Jan 21	Wendy's about-face
	Feb	Vicki enters protection
	March 26	All four accused acquitted
1992	Dec	Kathy moves to Rowville to look after Victor's children
1993	April	Victor gaoled for eight years on drug charges
	May	Gladys dies
	Sept 16	Operation Earthquake raid on house at Venus Bay
1994	May	Kathy released from gaol
1995	March	Trevor gaoled for five years on drug charges
1998	March	Trevor released from gaol
	April	Victor released from gaol
1999	July	Peter released from gaol
2002	May 1	Victor murdered in execution-style shooting in Port Melbourne

Kathleen Gorrie

De facto relationship with ? Fraser

Pearl, Maggie

Married ? Shields

Norman, Gladys, Lou, William, Mona, Bertha

Married Rowdy Mason

Jacky, Billy, Bobby, Pearl (Mickey), Lorna

Married ? Lee

Gladys

Married Albert Kemp

Kathleen (Kathy), Wilma, Barbara

De facto relationship with Harry Allen

De facto relationship with Billy Peirce

Vicki

Shelly (Adopted, married, one child)

Married John Brooks

Jason, Mark, Lee

Stephen (Adopted, married, two children)

Victor (Deceased) (married, two children)

De facto marriage to Wendy Peirce (four children)

Lex (married, two children)

David (Adopted)

Married Dennis Ryan

Dennis Allen (Deceased)

Married Sissy Hill

Lindy, Jade

Peter Allen

Two de facto relationships bearing him five children

Second de facto relationship with Jimmy Pettingill

Jamie (Deceased)

Trevor (Married, two children)

Introduction

Kathy Pettingill is at the wheel of her old brown Falcon, her head of grey, curly hair barely visible, as she heads down the main street of Venus Bay. She and her car are a familiar sight in this tiny holiday resort on the remote southeast coast of Victoria. She's on her way to pick up the mail, and the paper, or maybe to check the refuse tip for treasures like the fridge or settee she salvaged there last year. If it's a Wednesday she'll be heading further afield— another thirty kilometres into Inverloch for her beloved bingo. It's been eight years since she moved down here and, with a few exceptions, the locals have stopped referring to her as 'that wicked woman'. Their conversations no longer come to an abrupt halt when she walks into the local store; one or two have even been inside her modest, spotlessly clean cottage hidden behind the dunes, and sampled her famous boiled fruit cake.

Kathy's sixty now, and her memories of murder, heroin dealing, prostitution, torture and betrayal are just that ... memories. Before age fades them for ever and they drift out to sea with the mists that sometimes swirl over the village, she needs to marshall them together one last time: line up the ghosts and exorcise them once and for all.

Because that's what this is all about—the re-examination of a life that has juxtaposed unspeakable brutality with deep loyalties, that reveals occasional glimpses of a nature so callous that there should be no place for the irrepressible humour, warmth and sheer resilience of the other Kathy Pettingill. Let there be no mistake—here is evidence of all the depravity that earned her the nickname 'Granny Evil', but equally of an uncrushable spirit which instinctively leaps to the defence of the weak and oppressed.

THE MATRIARCH

The public perception of Kathy Pettingill, gleaned from decades of newspaper headlines, courtroom battles and vindictive gossip, sees her as the matriarch of a family steeped in vicious and often lucrative crime. Local legend has it that when she bought her cottage at Venus Bay she opened the boot of her car and thrust the asking price in a bundle of crumpled notes into the arms of the town's real estate agent. The truth is she paid a $20 holding deposit.

So where do public perception and private reality diverge? What is it behind those eyes, one glass, the other fiercely alive, that has created the legend? In simplest terms there are two catalysts for the reputation Kathy and her web of relatives have earned as possibly the most infamous criminal family in Australian history. The first is her son Dennis Allen, and the second is the execution of two young police officers in a crime that has become known as the Walsh Street murders.

Dennis was Kathy's first-born son and, depending on whose version is believed, he murdered between five and thirteen people. He also built a drug-dealing empire over a five-year period which earned him an estimated $70,000 a week; he was linked with names like New South Wales's notorious rogue policeman Roger Rogerson; he tried to blow up a coroner's court building where an inquest was being held into the death of one of his victims; he used a heavy calibre automatic rifle to try to shoot a police helicopter out of the sky when its night lights annoyed him; he flew the Jolly Roger outside his inner suburban home, and he once dismembered a Hell's Angel with a chainsaw.

But these are not the only reasons a cult following has grown around Dennis's memory since his bizarre death in 1987. The delicious shudders that mark the raising of his name in after-dinner discussion around the candle-lit dining tables of South Yarra and Toorak have more to do with the legends surrounding his black, sadistic humour. There is a story, possibly apocryphal, that halfway through chainsawing Anton Kenny's legs from his body, Dennis wiped the bone and gristle from his brow and mimicked the words of a popular television commercial for the State's favourite beer, Victoria Bitter ... 'Matter of fact I've got it now'. What the ad, and Dennis, referred to was a raging thirst earned by 'pulling a plough'. Certainly it's true that Dennis broke off from his work with the chainsaw to quench his thirst with a couple of beers before finishing the job.

In an age where Hannibal Lecter and his serial killing peers have replaced James Bond and similarly wholesome figures in our celluloid fantasies, a fascination—some would say an unhealthy obsession—has evolved around the subject of evil. Dennis has his place somewhere in this obsession, but evil, like all things, is a question of degree.

Most of us would agree that the ultimate evil of our time was the system of death camps created by Hitler's Nazi Germany. It has been said that when the Allies finally extinguished the ovens and ended the slaughter at Auschwitz, they found the birds had stopped singing and the grass wouldn't grow. The evil wouldn't go away. Well, the birds sing and the grass grows profusely on the vacant lots in the back streets of Richmond where Dennis committed his murders and sold his heroin. So how much further down the scale of evil does he take his place?

Certainly somewhere well below those monsters of twentieth century mass murder like John Reginald Halliday Christie, or the Yorkshire Ripper, Peter Sutcliffe. Each of us probably has a different idea of men like Christie and Sutcliffe. Brett Whiteley, for instance, captured the evil of Christie in a series of unforgettable canvases. But I gained an insight into the psychology of the mass murderer when I was still quite young, from Ludovic Kennedy's book on Christie, *Ten Rillington Place*.

I felt that the essence of Christie's evil wasn't that he had intercourse with at least three of his victims while they were dying, or even that he cut off their pubic hair and kept it, long after their deaths, in a tin box. Illogical as it now seems, I was most repulsed by the image of what lay behind the wallpaper in the charnel house that was 10 Rillington Place in West London. A new tenant had moved into the house on 24 March 1953, a month after Christie moved out, leaving behind the bodies of six of his eight victims. The unfortunate newcomer was checking the walls when he came across what seemed like a hollow spot. He peeled back the wallpaper to reveal a broken cupboard door. With the aid of a torch he peered through a hole in the wood and found himself staring at a naked human back. That was my first realisation of pure evil, that glimpse of flesh through a hole in the wall of a grimy West London slum. After the police had dragged the bodies out from behind the walls, under the floorboards and in the garden, the house was pulled down and the street renamed Rustyn Close. But for me that image of evil would never go away.

Does a place become evil? Whether it is a room, a house, a street, or even a geographic feature, what is it that transforms it forever into something stained by the horror and suffering inflicted there? Sometimes it is not the place itself that comes to represent the legacy of that horror. It can be something else altogether, like the shadowy security camera shot of two eleven-year-old boys leading two-year-old James Bulger by the hand from a Liverpool shopping centre to his brutal death on a railway line.

Or it can even be something someone said. When Peter Sutcliffe, the Yorkshire Ripper, was being questioned by police about Helen Rytka, one of his thirteen victims, he described how he had hit her from behind with his favourite weapon, his ball-pein hammer. Helen was an eighteen-year-old prostitute who sometimes used an old woodyard to conduct her business in some pathetic semblance of privacy. After repeatedly smashing her skull with the hammer, Sutcliffe dragged her, still alive, into a far corner of the yard, where he propped her against a wall and raped her as she was dying. It is hard to think of a more explicit expression of evil than the way in which Peter Sutcliffe described the experience to police: 'She just lay there limp. She didn't put much into it.'

The level of obsessive self-absorption demonstrated by these words provides a glimpse of something even more chilling than the view through the hole in the wall at 10 Rillington Place.

So where *is* Dennis's place amid all this horror? It should be said at the outset that he was a criminal first, and a murderer second. He killed because of his lifestyle. Life around him was cheap—deaths from drug overdoses were commonplace. He always had a loaded gun on hand—if it had been a set of knuckle dusters or a cosh, perhaps his victims might have escaped with maimings or severe beatings. He was almost permanently in a state of drug-induced paranoid rage—he generally killed because of some perceived threat or insult. Where Christie and Sutcliffe killed alone and in the dark, Dennis did his slaying in front of an audience in broad daylight. Christie and Sutcliffe preyed on the weak, choosing either sick or defenceless woman as their targets; Dennis's victims included a Hell's Angel and convicted thugs known for their brutality.

None of this, in any way serves as a justification for his awful record of violence and death. It merely puts it into perspective, and perhaps helps to explain why his life and deeds contributed so much to the aura surrounding Kathy and those close to her.

It's almost beyond belief that one family could spawn a multiple killer like Dennis and then, only eighteen months after his death, find itself the focus of Walsh Street, the most callous crime in Victorian history. These two factors combined to create a public perception of the family as something beyond evil.

In October 1988, two police officers in their early twenties were executed in cold blood in Walsh Street, a leafy by-way in one of Melbourne's most affluent suburbs, South Yarra. It was an atrocity that would change the way the criminal justice system operates in Victoria. The involvement of two of Kathy's sons, a daughter, a grandson and a daughter-in-law in events surrounding the murders earned the family a permanent place among the nation's most feared lawbreakers. Not even Ned Kelly and his gang inspired the same hatred among the state's police force as Kathy's boys. And yet this infamy was achieved despite her two sons, Victor and Trevor, securing acquittals on charges of having shot down the two young police officers in cold blood.

It is perhaps the ultimate price Kathy and her family have been forced to pay for Dennis's misdeeds that his brothers' innocence is today seen as almost irrelevant. The result of their trial was somehow not the point. It was the sequence of events leading up to the verdict, the treachery and betrayals by blood relatives and the allegations of brutal, uncompromising warfare between the family and the police that captured and then repelled public interest.

During the two and a half years of Walsh Street, between crime and acquittal, Victorians peered in fascination and horror through a window into a world beyond their worst imaginings. These were people who had not merely placed themselves outside the laws and customs of normal society—they had simply failed to recognise the existence of any such bounds.

Just as Walsh Street intensified the enmity between the State's police force and the underworld, it split Kathy's family into two irreconcilable camps. On one side were Victor and Trevor, charged with the murders; on the other were their sister Vicki and her son Jason as the prosecution's two key witnesses. Victor's wife Wendy fell somewhere between the two. She began as the prosecution's brightest hope of securing convictions: her evidence at the committal hearings condemned Victor out of his own mouth and, as a bonus, unveiled all the horrors of Dennis's evil reign in Richmond. But after eighteen months, $2 million and countless hours of police time guarding her since she entered the witness protection scheme, Wendy did an about-face and refused to repeat her evidence at the trial. Today Wendy is back within the family, and Vicki and Jason are lost and gone forever.

At the end of the $30 million debacle that Walsh Street became, there was only one of three conclusions to be drawn. Firstly, the acquittals represented an appalling miscarriage of justice caused by a combination of Wendy's duplicity and the subsequent inability of police to put together a convincing case, thus allowing four guilty men to go free. Secondly, as is Kathy's unshakable conviction, the police decided within hours of the crime that her family and their associates were responsible, set out shaping the facts to fit the theory and, in the process of failing to do so, destroyed the lives of a number of innocent individuals. The third possibility is that, based on their early enquiries and their previous knowledge of the four accused, the police genuinely believed they had caught the murderers.

Whichever version prevails, the nature of the crime and its implications for both the police and the underworld in Victoria ended once and for all the subtle checks and balances that keep ongoing hostilities between the two sides from brimming over into outright warfare. And if that sounds extravagant, consider the following: when the jury returned after six days of deliberation, delivering their findings in favour of Victor, Trevor and their two co-defendants, a message went out across all police radio channels:

'The verdict in the Walsh Street trial was all four not guilty, repeat not guilty. All units are warned, keep yourselves in control.'

However justified and even necessary this admonishment may have been, given the circumstances, it does not preclude the asking of one simple question. How, exactly, did the broadcaster of the message expect his listeners, custodians of law and order, to react?

And what of the call, by then State Premier Joan Kirner, for the community to remain calm in the wake of the verdicts? Warning against a 'frenzied reaction', Kirner said:

> Vendettas are not appropriate. This is a time for calm reflection, and that's what I would be expecting the Police Minister to be doing. It must be hard for the whole community to come to grips with the very long trial, long deliberation, and no result. Either you've got faith in the justice system or you haven't.

More recently, in November 1995, seven years after the murders, the state's chief commissioner of police, Neil Comrie, put Walsh Street into historical perspective. Speaking at a press conference called after the latest in a series of police shootings which were beginning to erode public confidence in a police force long regarded as the least corrupt and most stable in the country, he said about Victoria's criminal underworld:

> It's an environment that has existed in this state, which perhaps hasn't existed elsewhere. The fact of the matter is that from 1985 to 1988 there were a series of events in this state that involved such things as the Russell Street bombing, the Walsh Street execution of two young constables, the Queen Street and Hoddle Street massacres, and a number of other serious assaults and shootings of police officers. Had that trend continued there is no doubt that the criminals would have taken over this society, because they were in no fear of the police, and no fear of the law, and were prepared to murder and do whatever else was necessary to push their cause.

One month later, on Christmas Eve, 1995, there was talk of re-opening the whole Walsh Street saga with an inquest into the deaths of Constables Tynan and Eyre. The families of the two men had reportedly held meetings with the coroner's office seeking such a step. No inquest had been held previously because of inquiries the then coroner, Hal Hallenstein, had been making into police shootings.

If, then, Dennis and Walsh Street represent the public face of Kathy's notoriety, what is the private nature of the woman herself, and what are the milestones along the road that led her to the sleepy sanctuary of Venus Bay?

I first met Kathy Pettingill in 1974. She was a mother of ten children battling, more often than not on the wrong side of the law, to keep intact what was left of her family. What crime she was involved in was small-time, her days of infamy and fortune still a decade away. I was a journalist on Melbourne's *Truth* newspaper, then owned by Rupert Murdoch. Kathy's tale of police harassment of two of her sons, Trevor and Victor, seventeen years before their acquittal of the Walsh Street murders, had an all too familiar ring to it. But it was a story, and I wrote it anyway.

Kathy rewarded me with much more significant leads—like the exclusive telephone interview she arranged for me with another of her sons, Peter, at that time officially Victoria's most dangerous criminal and on the run from a fourteen-year gaol sentence for rape, shooting at police and the wounding of two men. There were other stories and other memories—an exclusive on the bombing of a Richmond massage parlour, a whirlwind car trip around Victoria's country gaols with introductions to the prisoners' wives living in local caravan parks, inside information on the pecking order in Pentridge Prison, conducted tours of Fairlea Women's Prison, and so on.

When I moved away from journalism and crime reporting in the mid-1980s Kathy and I lost touch. She was in the middle of her decade of tragedy and terror; I was mired in the grey-flannel heartland of corporate Melbourne as a director of a public relations company. In 1993 I re-established contact with a phone call, the first time we had spoken for more than half a decade.

'Kathy?' I said as her unmistakable 'Hello?' came down the line.

'Is that you, Adrian?'

I was amazed. 'You've got a great memory, Kathy.'

'Why wouldn't I?' Only Kathy could have injected that precise mixture of humour and cocksure defiance into the question. I knew immediately that notoriety hadn't changed her.

As the planning for this book began certain friends asked me if I had considered the possible effect of prolonged exposure to the mind and memories of 'Granny Evil', the legendary criminal matriarch; others simply counselled against the project. Grasping the nettle of what they perceived to be a tangible evil was all well and good, until you tried to let go. That's when you got stung. And so on, and so on.

I ignored the advice, well meant as it was, and the interviews began in July 1995 at Kathy's seaside hideaway cottage, and continued well into the following year. Our sessions generally ran for four hours at a stretch, and as I went deeper into Kathy's past, and began to learn more of the private woman behind the public facade, a series of contradictions emerged.

There were things she dredged up which shocked and appalled me—like her anger over Dennis's burning of her new vacuum cleaner after he'd used it to remove the splattered brains of one of his victims from the carpet. How could she care about the destruction of an inanimate object while remaining seemingly indifferent to the brutal murder of a human being?

Then there was the terrible business of the tracksuit trousers. Dennis and his minders were in the process of bludgeoning some innocent youth to near death when Kathy noticed his nearly new clothing. 'Save the trousers for Jamie' (another of her sons), she urged them. Such callousness was tempered only slightly by the additional information that she eventually helped the youth escape.

But then there was the other side of her that began to emerge simultaneously. How at the age of fifty-nine she engaged in a vicious fight with a woman half her age, in defence of a frail and elderly victim of prison brutality. Or her decision at the age of fifty-eight to leave the sanctuary of Venus Bay and return to Melbourne to look after three of her young grandchildren for nine months when their parents landed in gaol.

And there was the way she would waltz into the opulent reception area of her long-time Melbourne solicitor's office, not waiting to be announced but hollering: 'Charlie, I'm here, where are you?' as she passed the gaping receptionist. 'And why fucking not?' she responded when I mentioned it. 'Dennis's fees paid for that foyer.'

Probably the most important thing I've learned about Kathy is that she doesn't change for anybody. She is utterly unaffected by rank or fame, as incapable of airs and graces as she is of disloyalty.

Now it's all over, and I've seen her tears and witnessed her rage, one factor emerges—I still like Kathy Pettingill as a person, and I still regard her as a good friend.

I also happen to believe that in a different world she could have been someone special. And not for all the wrong reasons, this time.

CHAPTER ONE

Seeds by the
_ Wayside _

THE THREE SISTERS WILL NEVER MEET AGAIN. THE YOUNGEST, Barbara, is minutes away from death. Her polio-racked body and its withered left arm will go, shortly, into the ground. A lifetime of salt baths and traction is nearly over.

But Barbara doesn't know this. At six years of age she has little concept of her mortality. Her life has been a dwindling form of death, anyway, and now the pain is blurring her awareness. She is cradled in the arms of a man carrying her out through the front door of an enormous house, on the first leg of her journey to hospital.

As Barbara's vision wavers over the garden for the last time she takes in, without registering it, the forms of her two elder sisters, standing silently by the tall, iron gate. Wilma is eight, and Shirley-Temple-gorgeous. Kathleen is very different. Two years older than Wilma, she has an air of sullen resentment.

The object of the two girls' attention is a car parked outside the gate on Beaconsfield Parade in wartime Melbourne. It has running boards wide enough for a game of cards. Elliot Ness should be at the wheel, but he isn't. Instead a covey of murmuring relatives gaze out through the car windows at the man walking towards them through the gate.

1

He reaches the side of the car and, as the rear door opens for him to place Barbara inside, she suddenly stiffens in his arms. There is one clenching convulsion followed by a series of fluttering lesser seizures throwing her head back across his arm. The light in her eyes goes out.

'It's too late, she's gone.'

'Take her back in the house.'

The words mean nothing to Kathleen. She hears them, but as with Barbara's last sight of her sisters, the message doesn't get through. All she can think of is what she has just seen. Her head feels light and airy.

'She just died,' she says, taking Wilma by the arm. The grown-ups have climbed down from the car and gone inside, too preoccupied to notice the girls. Kathleen leads Wilma through the gate to the edge of the pavement. They stand together watching the trundling parade of carts, trucks and cars.

'Stand on the road, Wilma,' says Kathleen, guiding her sister towards the traffic. 'Now you can be dead, too.'

Barbara's death is not the first Kathleen has witnessed. There has been one before and many will follow. Four years earlier an elderly relative dies in the Brunswick house where Kathleen is living. His body lies in its coffin, mounted on a trestle in one of the rooms. Kathy wanders in and is instantly drawn to the open cask and the withered face of the elderly man inside. Why is he sleeping, and why is he in a box, not his bed?

The six-year-old reaches over the side of the coffin towards the still face. Small fingers force their way past the dry lips and lock onto the upper teeth. The dentures come loose inside the mouth, and the little girl twists them back out through the lips. She pauses briefly to examine them before placing them inside her mouth. They feel big. She removes them, pushing them carefully back from where they came.

Dead man's teeth in a little girl's mouth.

Kathy was born on 27 March 1935. Her parents were Albert Frederick Kemp, a twenty-year-old timber worker, and Gladys Grace Lee, aged nineteen, who had married on 17 May of the previous year. Kathy was their first-born. They lived in a tiny single-fronted, two-bedroom terraced house in Gold Street in the Melbourne suburb of East Brunswick.

Four weeks after Kathy's birth, on April 25 1935 a one-tonne tiger shark began behaving strangely in Coogee Aquarium in Sydney. Shocked visitors to the Aquarium backed away from the pool as the monster went berserk, threshing the water into foam, and vomited up first a bird, followed by a rat, and then a human arm. A tattoo of two boxers on the arm led to identification of the victim as James Smith, a small-time criminal. Today, sixty years later, the murder remains unsolved.

So what sort of a world was Kathy born into? Frenzied sharks and severed arms apart, the Australia of the mid-1930s was, like much of the rest of the globe, preoccupied with what historians invariably describe as the storm clouds of war gathering over Europe.

Under the heading 'Berlin Talks: Hitler Holds The Floor; What Germany Will And Will Not Do', *The Age* of 27 March 1935 detailed a six-hour marathon summit taking place at the Chancellery in Berlin. Sir John Simon, Anthony Eden and Ambassador Sir Eric Phipps, representing Britain, emerged hoarse from their discussions with 'Herr Hitler', Baron von Neurath, and Foreign Minister von Ribbentrop. Closer to home 17,000 Victorians went on strike, refusing to work for 'sustenance' on unemployment relief schemes. The *Sun News-Pictorial*, cataloguing the various locations where strike action was most disruptive, declared with

3

a complete absence of irony: 'The half-castes of Framlingham aboriginal reserve, who are working for sustenance, stopped this morning, declaring the work black.'

Robert Donat was starring in *The Count of Monte Cristo* at the Armadale Kinema, and Eddie Cantor in *Kid Millions* at the Regent. Appearing in a real-life drama at the Melbourne District Court was a woman called Alma Claire Ritcher, charged with the murder of her son Allen Carl, aged nine. She had, the court heard, mutilated his head and neck with an axe.

Kathy's earliest memory is of a loose brick in the wall of the house in Gold Street, where she was still living at the age of four. It appealed to her instinct for secrecy and soon she was depositing pennies and ha'pennies in her own private vault. Not all were obtained honestly, and there was other naughtiness—often demonstrating less guile. Her mother, Gladys, had acquired a sweet shop nearby in Gold Street.

> *I remember there was a piece of wood that you could stand on to open the display cabinet for when they gave the order and my mum could get the lollies out, right? So, I used to stand on it and get the clinkers and bite them in half and put 'em back. I didn't eat the whole evidence, right? So I got a belting for that because they worked out it was me. Who else'd put them half back? I told them it was the fairies.*

The environment in which Kathy spent her early years was less than stable, and threw up two significant contradictions. Firstly, loyalties between family members were fiercely held— yet marriages were scarred by frequent 'domestics'. And secondly, certain branches of the family were proud of their rebellious, anti-establishment view, while others, like Kathy's great-uncle Norman Shields, served for six years on the local

Brunswick Council and had a reserve named after him.

It was, however, the dysfunctional nature of marriage within the family that was to have the greatest influence on Kathy's life. Even the earliest family legend deals with a breakdown in relationships. Kathy's great-grandmother, Kathleen Shields, was first married to a ship's captain, who had transported the last of the convicts to arrive in Australia. She so valued her independence that, when he returned to home port on one occasion, she moved all the furniture from the front of the house to the rear and erected a 'TO LET' sign on the front fence, hoping he would be misled into believing she had moved away.

Kathy's earliest experience of the family malaise came in the same lolly shop where her taste for clinkers had got her into trouble.

My second memory of that shop is of my mum and dad fighting. Maybe it's because my dad enlisted. They used to have packets of dummy chocolates on the wall—advertising— only cardboard or something in it, whatever. I'm sitting on the counter, my mum is putting her lot of lollies there beside me, my dad's doing the same. They were asking me: 'Who do you want to stay with?' My mum would say: 'Do you want to stay with me?' and put more lollies beside me. I didn't know they were false boxes, I thought they were real. I can remember where they were standing. I'm sitting on the counter, my mum was there, my dad was there, and the chocolates were coming from everywhere. I just remember that. I was bewildered. And that's the only memory I've got of my dad. I must have been four.

When Albert was sent over to the Middle East after enlisting in the 2nd AIF on the outbreak of war, Kathy's relationship with her father ended for ever. A card bearing the words 'To my three darling daughters' arrived from Egypt, with a wrist watch for

Kathy. She broke it not long after in a fall, and was devastated. The next message was that Albie had died, on 13 February 1942, and had been buried in Gaza. The family was told he had fallen victim to a disease. In fact he had lost his mind and committed suicide. Many years later one of Kathy's children applied under the Freedom of Information Act for details of Albie's death. The finding was not what Kathy wanted to hear.

> *They said he went mad with sand fever or something, and shot himself.* I don't want to know that story, I don't believe that story. I wanted to believe the best. If he'd come back it probably would have turned out different. He'd probably have taken us to the other side of the family with him. I might have turned out different. But Wilma's still all right. I mean there's nothing ever wrong with Wilma.*

With Albie away in the war, his wife Gladys began to enjoy her freedom, and eventually her preference for a good time over the needs of her three daughters came to the notice of the authorities. Kathy and Wilma were found walking the streets on a particularly cold night wearing little more than singlets and, along with Barbara, were made military wards.

> *Because my dad was away in the War, my mum was playing up. She was having a good time. I think it's because she was so young, I'm not making excuses but she was so young to be tied down with three children.*

---

* During the writing of this book Kathy learnt from Wilma, who visited and photographed their father's grave in Gaza, that he had committed suicide, not through illness, but because of hate letters he received, almost certainly from Gladys. Wilma had known this for some time, but kept it from Kathy, who was deeply upset by the news.

It was now obvious that Kathy and her two sisters had to be removed from Gladys's negative influence. Their grandmother, Bertha Mason, who also lived in Gold Street, had her hands full with her stormy relationship with her husband Rowdy. So it fell to the girls' great-grandmother on their mother's side, Kathleen Shields, to do something about the rapidly disintegrating mess that Gladys and Albie's family had become. Despite being seventy years old, Kathleen let Gladys know she was taking the three girls in and effectively assuming the role of mother to them. Kathy doubts Gladys would have put up much opposition, although she does recall one half-hearted 'kidnapping' when Gladys took her three daughters off to Stawell, 250 kilometres northwest of Melbourne. It wasn't long before they were back with their great-grandmother, however. Kathleen transformed the girls' environment from a little backstreet hovel to a palatial home called Green Court in Sydney Road, Brunswick. Here food was never scarce and there was a world of long corridors and hidden rooms to explore. On one occasion shortly after the girls moved in, Barbara went missing and the local fire brigade was called in to search some of the less accessible parts of the mansion. Hours later she was found, curled up fast asleep in the folds of one of the luxurious red velvet curtains which hung in the main rooms.

Kathleen Shields was to remain a major influence on Kathy, long after her death at the age of ninety-five. Gladys's removal from the scene was almost certainly a blessing. Kathy and her sisters saw her only at irregular intervals and as time wore on even became unsure of their exact relationship with her. This was when Kathy and Wilma began referring to her as 'that lady'.

For Gladys, the death of Albie and the virtual loss of her three daughters was the catalyst for a series of bigamous relationships, generally with merchant seamen. Much later in life she admitted to Kathy she had married as many as six, largely for their pensions. A number died, and because of uncertainty over dates and the order in which the 'marriages' had taken place, Gladys was never prosecuted. Many years later there was to be a sordid little sequel to her cavalier attitude to the sanctity of marriage. Kathy's two eldest sons were under investigation by the police, whose inquiries had begun to widen. Although Kathy's underworld reputation was still undeveloped, her manner, even over the phone, was enough to intimidate corrupt policemen.

This copper was investigating the family, and he told my mother that if she had $500, he'd call at her house at Ascot Vale and they could do a deal. She told me she'd married about six, but they couldn't work out who had died first or who she'd married first, and so they couldn't prosecute. The copper found out they'd never prosecuted, and he was threatening to do something about it.

So here she is sitting in the house at Ascot Vale with the $500 in her hand. So I rang the copper. I said: 'Don't you dare blackmail my mother. She's sitting there a nervous wreck with fucking $500 in her hand. It's not on.' So he didn't come. I threatened him.

The Sydney Road house provided another vivid childhood memory involving death—only this time Kathy didn't see the body. Her two-year-old cousin Robin had climbed inside a buggy hitched to a horse standing in the long driveway. The horse bolted and Robin was thrown out, either the wheels or the horse's hooves running over his head.

I remember my uncle Willy leading the horse along the drive-way afterwards. He was taking it to the zoo to be killed. I always see the horse with its head going up and down, because he was so angry, my uncle. He had hold of it so tight with the

*reins from in front, and he wasn't a tall man. He took it to the
zoo to be fed to the lions.*

By now the ties between Kathy and Wilma and their mother
Gladys were becoming increasingly tenuous. The situation
wasn't helped when one of Kathy's two aunties, half-sisters of
Gladys, had a birthday party. All the presents had been left on
a sideboard while the family went out to celebrate. Gladys broke
into the house and stole the presents. By this time, because of
her general contrariness, various relatives had begun telling
Kathy: 'You're going to grow up bad, like your mother.'
Although this verbal abuse of a young, impressionable mind was
to go on for years, it had little effect on Kathy at the time.

*I took no notice of it. It didn't bother me, because I didn't know
what they were talking about. At that stage really I didn't know
for sure who my mother was. Before this I do remember my
mum going to gaol for theft, and she came to the Sydney Road
house wrapped in a blanket, because she didn't have any
clothes. She was in Pentridge Prison and I remember her telling
me you only got a tin of jam a month and a packet of tobacco.*

Nevertheless, photographic evidence suggests the dire prophe-
cies of her relatives may have been having some effect on the
young Kathy after all. A shot taken of her and Wilma around
this time shows Kathy with a sour, resentful expression, while
Wilma is doing her adorable Shirley Temple impression.

Apart from the widening gap between her and her mother,
Kathy had another sorrow to nourish her resentment—Barbara's
deteriorating health.

*She caught polio, and besides that she was born with a slightly
withered arm. I can remember her laying in traction, in this
big iron contraption that was on the floor. That's the reason*

9

we moved to Beaconsfield Parade—so she could have a sea bath to get her joints going.

I can remember this contraption where she was strapped in. It was along the floor, and her head was down a bit lower, trying to straighten her out, like you do with straitjackets. I didn't have much feelings about it because I didn't know what was happening to her. Why was she in it? Nobody told you about infantile paralysis at the time. It was raging. I knew she was sick.

Kathy's memories of Barbara's death—'I saw her go stiff; it was like she had had a big convulsion'—are not as strong as her recollection of the immediate aftermath, and her attempt to get Wilma to walk into the traffic.

She wouldn't do it. I said: 'Now you can be dead, too.' To me it was a game. I was curious. Wilma must have known something. She wouldn't do it. It was nothing against Wilma—I just wanted to see another death to see what it was really like.

Within weeks of Barbara's death Kathy and Wilma were travelling alone on the tram across the city from St Kilda to Carlton to visit the grave.

I used to pull the bell every stop and I got told off something shocking. I didn't care. When we got to the cemetery I used to pinch Wilma to make her cry to get some money. There were people around that were tending to graves on the weekends, and I'd make her cry, and they'd say: 'Why are you crying?' and I'd say: 'It's our baby sister.' If we got two bob we were rapt. We'd go straight over the road to a shop—we'd have the big ice cream and everything. We had a good rort going, her and me. We used to go once a fortnight for a couple of years. I did miss Barbara. But I didn't really understand, I knew she wasn't coming back, but that's all I knew. We took flowers— we might have only picked geraniums or something, but we took them.

At this stage Kathy was attending St Kilda Park School. Along with thousands of other Australian school children, she found the influence of war creeping into the classroom. She was issued with her own tin helmet, and remembers the air raid shelters just outside the school building—'trenches with flimsy wooden floors'.

Much more exciting than attending school was the opportunity to see more of the world when running bets for her great-grandmother. Kathleen Shields liked the odd two bob each-way on a horse, and would wrap the money in a piece of paper, and send Kathy off to Gold Street on the tram, where she would give the bets to her 'Nan' (Gladys's mother, Bertha Mason). As a special treat Nan would occasionally take Kathy to the ladies' lounge, a little snug in the local pub, for a soft drink. The resident SP bookie used to pin bets on a wooden fence down a lane by the side of the pub. On one memorable occasion Kathy was asked to keep nit, or act as the bookie's 'cockatoo'. She received a double-header ice cream for her trouble, even though she had no idea what she was supposed to be guarding against.

This is how cluey I was even then. Sundays I'd go round to the horse trough at the front of the pub, 'cos the blokes'd either wee in it or vomit in it, and they'd spill their money. I often used to get a couple of pennies or a two bob out of it. Even then I was enterprising. I used to sell geraniums to the Yank servicemen for chewing gum. I'd stand outside the house on Beaconsfield Parade until I'd got the letter box full of chewing gum, all different flavours they had, then I'd go in.

These outings to Gold Street often involved Kathy staying overnight at her Nan's house—another opportunity for her to witness first-hand the battleground of marriage. Rowdy Mason, Bertha's husband, was renowned among neighbours for the frequency and volume of his rages.

> They'd leave the pub, and then there'd be a blue, and I could hear the neighbours saying, 'The Masons are at it again.' I always remember on Saturdays my nan used to polish the sideboard and put a bunch of fresh flowers there. Every Sunday morning when I got up it was tipped upside down. He did it in a drunken rage. I used to sleep with two of my aunties—one that got her head cut off later on. I'd be in the middle, and when it was cold they used to pile all the coats on top, that's what they did in the old days. And the bloody dog, a little Australian terrier named Chooka—named after Chooka Howell, the Carlton champion—was down the foot of the bed.

It was Aunty Mickey Mason who was virtually decapitated in a road accident when Kathy was twelve. Mickey and her husband were returning along the Hume Highway from New South Wales where they had celebrated their honeymoon with another couple, when their car ran under a truck, killing Mickey, who was in the front, and the male friend in the back. For the third time in her young life Kathy was about to encounter a corpse.

> The coffin was at home—by now we were living in a two-storey house in Parkville—and they had all gone to visit Mickey's husband in the hospital. He had a split tongue. There she is lying in the bloody coffin again, isn't she? I was left in the house alone with Wilma.
>
> We knew Mickey's head was cut off, we'd overheard them talking about it. She's got a lace cap on the top of her head, and I said to Wilma: 'I wonder if she really did . . . ?' because there again is the mystery. How did they put it back? She was

lying there, and the head looked normal. I said: 'Wilma, if she's got her head on what happened? How'd they put it back?' I wanted to pull the lace thing off to see how the head was stuck back on. But Wilma wouldn't stay, and I didn't do it.

She looked so peaceful, but the mystery to me was how they put the bloody head back.

By now Kathy and Wilma had been separated from Gladys for six years. They had little sense of loss—they knew their great-grandmother, Kathleen Shields, as 'Mum', and only rarely saw their real mother. When they did there was always a veil of uncertainty around her identity.

Kathleen Shields, after whom Kathy was named, was one of the few adults to see she was starved for affection compared with the more outgoing Wilma. So Kathleen always tried to ensure Kathy got her share of kisses and cuddles. She was a stabilising influence for the girls, and her various homes always represented a sanctuary from the destructive rowing and near-poverty of other branches of the family. Gladys was simply becoming 'this lady'.

I used to see this lady at the park over the road from Beacons-field Parade, and she always introduced some bloke to me as Uncle. I went to Coles and bought a threepenny rouge, and I gave this present to the lady. Somewhere I must have known something because I cared for her, or I wouldn't have bought her the rouge.

Then I used to get beltings off my aunties, because instead of going to the cemetery to visit Barbara, we'd get picked up from somewhere by this lady instead. And the flowers I used to pick for my sister, I'd give to this lady. Nobody ever told me it was my mum. Just the aunties telling me I'd grow up bad like my mum. She was just very friendly, she kept cropping up all the time.

The contradictory effect of their early lives and their mother's influence on Kathy and Wilma is most apparent when the pair are together. Wilma is an urbane, well-spoken and immaculately groomed woman in her late fifties, with none of Kathy's rough edges. There is an obvious bond between them, however, and Wilma has her own theories as to why they have turned out so differently:

> I believe our mother, Gladys, has a lot to do with it. She was a terrible influence, an entirely negative influence. We were brought up by her to perform. She saw us as ornaments. She didn't want any responsibility for us, just to show us off. Basically my own mother frightened me. I would often refuse to go with her, while Kathy would.
>
> Having said all that, I don't think Kathy can blame everything that has happened to her on our mother. Kathy has made her own decisions in life, and these have shaped her destiny.

Wilma, however, is a staunch supporter of another side of Kathy. 'She is, deep down, a very Christian woman in a strange sense. She has always helped people she perceives to be weak or in need. There is tremendous good in her.'

By the age of twelve Kathy had more pressing issues than the influence of her mother with which to contend—her first period was looming. Like most young girls in the 1940s, she was totally unprepared for it, reacting with a mixture of shame and fear. She sat on the toilet, convinced someone had made a bizarre attempt to kill her, and that her life's blood was draining away.

Even when one of her aunties took pity on her and gave her some primitive form of sanitary pad, she received no instructions on its disposal. So the frightened Kathy began hiding the pads under her mattress, where they were finally discovered by her great-grandmother. But her awakening sexuality was not all blood and tears. When she was thirteen one of her favourite aunties, Lorna, would take her to the weekly dance at Moonee Ponds Town Hall. It was here she first realised the delicious power she could exercise over adolescent boys, and even men. In the end Lorna became disenchanted with continually being left seated while Kathy was invited onto the dance floor.

I felt a bit shy because all the others were older than me, and I couldn't dance. Lorna would dress me up really great, and put make-up on me just before we went. So I must have looked young and fresh. I wasn't supposed to wear anything like that. She even lent me a pair of shoes that made me a bit taller. First time I wore heels I had to stagger around.

One of Kathy's first boyfriends was Bobby Sedgman, brother of Frank Sedgman, the famous tennis player. She and Bobby were both fourteen.

Bobby was a good-looking boy. We'd walk up to the fish shop through the lanes hand in hand. Buy sixpenn'th of chips. And then one day he put a box of chocolates in my letterbox, but it didn't go any further than that. He was my special boyfriend at school.

Kathy spent most weekends with a group of local boys who used to ride bicycles to Mount Eliza and back, a round trip of around 100 kilometres. Her main ambition at this time, outside her burgeoning social life, was to be a chemist. Kathleen Shields had moved with the two girls to Darebin, a northern suburb, and Kathy was attending Princes Hill High School in Carlton.

It was where everybody went that was any good. I was a horrible kid at school, but I loved it. I was very popular. There was this poor French teacher. He was shell-shocked in the war, and I used to love to get him going, 'cos the veins'd all stick out in his neck, and he'd go purple. He'd say: 'Kathy Kemp, stand outside in the passage,' and I'd say: 'You can't make me do that.' And I loved it.

Kathy had a serious accident during this period, smashing a number of front teeth when she landed on her head after jumping over a wall to retrieve a ball. Partly because of her great-grandmother's dislike of doctors, she never received proper treatment for her injuries and her mouth became septic and hideously swollen. The pain became so intense she spent her daily one-shilling lunch money on painkillers, and would sit in class sucking on aspirin.

By the time she was fifteen, a year after she left school and was working in a local clothing factory, Kathy was beginning to enjoy the early stirrings of a healthy sexual appetite. No guilt, and no strings attached. And then, quite suddenly, this freedom was snatched away, almost as unexpectedly as it had begun. Kathy met the first of the three men who, between them, were to father her ten children and shape much of the next sixteen years of her life.

The first of the three, and the only one still alive today, was Dennis James Ryan, who made his entrance astride a gleaming Triumph motorcycle. Dennis was four years older than Kathy, but more than that, he worked on a farm at outer suburban Reservoir, and the farm had haystacks ... The 650 cc motorcycle, with Dennis in the saddle, entered Kathy's life one sunny day in Royal Parade, a broad, tree-lined boulevard close to the centre of Melbourne.

He was riding past where I was sitting on a wall, and I whistled him, and he came back, and that was it. I think it was the bike that got to me first. He took me for a ride and I loved it. I put

16

*my arms around him and that felt good, too. I didn't have
anyone else that I used to be able to cuddle. And I used to nick
off to the farm, and sleep in the haystack and whatever ... I
had no sex education whatsoever, but I was a bit cheeky. Dennis
was nineteen, but he didn't know what he was doing, either.
He must have been a virgin, too. First time was in the haystack.
I didn't know what had happened. It wasn't that special. It was
just a bit of a bloody nuisance because I was bleeding. Later on
it got better—that's why I was always nicking off to the farm.
Later on when we got married, when we were in bed he used
to put the blankets over his head and light a candle and have
a look, so he didn't know much.*

Within three or four months of their first meeting Kathy became
pregnant. She confided in an older girlfriend, Dolores, that she
hadn't had her period, and her worst fears were confirmed.

*I was terrified. I didn't know what to do. In those days abortion
was out. I didn't know how to tell my family and so me and
another friend, Marion, ran away to Sydney. We caught the
train. We only had about four shillings between us when we
got off. We went to a pub and got a job, on the corner of
Castlereagh and Park. I was a waitress and she was a house-
maid. The owner wanted me to iron his shirts, and I scorched
them all. I put the best one on top, and that's when we left. I
rang my great-grandmother, and I said: 'Mum, I'm coming
home, but you're not to go crook at me because I'm pregnant.'
She sent me the money to come home.*

Typically, Kathleen Shields hid her anger and disappointment,
leaving another member of the family, Kathy's Uncle Jacky, to
confront Dennis. Jacky took Kathy, and a shotgun, to the Reservoir farm. Officials at the Melbourne Royal Women's Hospital,
where the pregnancy had been confirmed, had told the family

the matter would be reported to the police, because of Kathy's age. Dennis knew he was to be charged with carnal knowledge, but despite this—and the shotgun—refused point blank to marry her.

> With my great-grandmother there was no hint of adopting out the baby. She had eight children, and this one was going to be ours. There was no way in our family that you gave up kids. They were family, and there was a big family of us. That was the love she had for me, see. Actually Dennis didn't want to marry me. I went to church with him at St Mary's Star of the Sea in West Melbourne. We went for counselling first—'and marriage is for the conception of children' and all that shit . . .then the first time we were going to get married he never turned up. I was waiting at the altar. My aunty had dressed me up in a nice light tan coat with a hat and flowers. The wedding was due to take place about seven. There was just me and a couple of aunties. It wasn't a full church or anything. When he didn't turn up I didn't know what to think.
>
> I didn't think he was a bastard or anything. I was more disappointed. I think he went up to his parents' at Sea Lake on the coast to stay and see if the baby was born alive, because then he wouldn't have had to muck up his life if the baby was born dead. Just nicked off on his bike. Maybe he couldn't cope. We were both young and had nowhere to live. Well, after that I had baby Dennis on the seventh of November, and to stop the court case on the carnal knowledge charge he married me on the fourteenth of December.

Kathy's revenge was precisely what would have been expected from the child she still was. The second time around she lingered in the bath, delaying the ceremony and keeping everyone waiting in the church. 'I'm thinking about it,' she told Dennis when he asked her for the tenth time if she was going to get out of the bath. But then, arriving late at the altar has always been a bride's prerogative, and at least Kathy, unlike Dennis the first time, eventually did put in an appearance.

And so did Dennis junior. Kathy's delivery, at sixteen years of age, took place in the Royal Women's Hospital shortly before midnight on Tuesday, 7 November 1951—Melbourne Cup Day. Dennis shared his birthday with Captain James Cook, Leon Trotsky, Billy Graham and Joni Mitchell. He was to make his mark on the world in a somewhat different way from all of them.

CHAPTER TWO

— Roots of Evil —

KATHY AND HER BABY SON ARE GOING VISITING. THE PROUD sixteen-year-old mother wants to show off Dennis to her Nan, Bertha Mason. Having travelled halfway across town to Bertha's home in West Brunswick, Kathy is tired and wants to sit by the fire. Only there's somebody already there. It's 'that lady', the woman who is always turning up unexpectedly, always making a fuss of Kathy and Wilma, introducing them to a series of men she refers to as 'uncles'. But this time there's something different.

Why is 'that lady' sitting by the fire in Nan's house? Kathy isn't left wondering for long. 'Meet your new grandson,' says Bertha, looking at 'that lady' and gesturing towards the bundle in Kathy's arms. The meaning of Bertha's words sinks in instantly, and leaves Kathy's heart pounding, her mouth dry and her mind whirling. 'That lady' is her mother. Maybe it's something she's subconsciously suspected all along. But to be confronted by it so suddenly, so casually . . . Almost defensively, Kathy hugs Dennis a little tighter. He's hers, her very own, and she knows it. No uncertainties, no rude surprises. Nobody can change that.

It's eighteen years later. Baby Dennis has become a man in a prison cell. He's doing time in Pentridge for the latest in a series of violent outrages that have brought a rapid escalation through the punishment book of juvenile crime—probation, fines, supervision orders, boys' homes, and now adult prison. Dennis has just received a letter, and the familiar handwriting on the envelope tells him it's from his sister, Kathy. She's a regular on visiting days, and writes constantly. But there's a time bomb ticking inside this particular letter, primed to explode in Dennis's head. The first few lines are unusually affectionate and form a declaration of love and, for some reason, guilt. Then he reads the words: 'Dennis, I'm not your sister. I'm your mother, and I love you.' Something snaps inside him and his head spins . . . just as Kathy's did eighteen years ago by the fire at Bertha Mason's.

This process of children being reared by their grandparents or great-grandparents has happened in Kathy's family for three generations now. It began with Kathleen Shields taking Kathy, Wilma and Barbara away from their mother Gladys. Then Kathy became a mother at a ridiculously young age and was unable to cope. So Gladys stepped in and took Kathy's first two sons, Dennis and Peter, away from her. Kathy's children, particularly Peter, also became parents at an extremely young age, and lost their children. Peter was a grandfather at thirty-five, making Kathy a great-grandmother at the age of fifty-two.

During the later stages of her pregnancy Kathy found work, performed at home for a card manufacturing company, earning four shillings and fourpence a gross for tying ribbons around the cards. The first item she bought from her earnings was a cradle—'I used to look at it and line it up, this cradle. It was like I was waiting for a doll of my own.'

Childbirth for a frightened sixteen-year-old was a mixture of mystery and terror.

I was petrified. My water broke and I got the shakes, all cold and trembly. My aunty took me to the Royal Women's, and they shaved me and got me ready. There were a lot of wogs screaming in the labour ward. In those days it was just one big room with sliding curtains, no private rooms. I was outside waiting to go in, and I could hear all this screaming and I'm thinking: 'Is that what you have to do?' But I shut up anyway. Labour wasn't a long time—three or four hours. And they did come in and tell me I was a good girl, because I was so frightened from all the screaming. But that's not me. They gave me the mask and I kept putting it over my mouth and taking big gulps. Then they laid you on your side, it's not like today. They put one of your legs in the air, and the baby comes out. It was worth it when I saw him. I thought he looked beautiful. They didn't give them to you straight away, like on your breast nowadays. They took them away and washed them and swaddled them up real tight. All you could see was their head. When I got him on my own I undid the blankets to see if his ten fingers and toes were there, naturally, like any mother would. I just felt he was that beautiful, I had waited that long. I had something of my own to love. It was like my own doll. Before he was born I used to go to the cradle and look at it and think: 'Soon I'll have a baby in it.' But I didn't know it was going to be a boy.

Today, examining the first photograph taken of baby Dennis at a few weeks old is a strangely unnerving experience. The overriding impression is of an almost startling alertness about the eyes. Are they simply impish and mischievous? Or would a subscriber to the theory of original sin detect a glint of something

more sinister? For Kathy there was no doubt. She loved Dennis
without qualification.

*He was beautiful. He was beautiful. Oh yes I loved him. Dennis
was my first-born, and I loved him most of all. But if it hadn't
been for Dennis a lot of the things that went had wouldn't have
happened. We're all still paying for Dennis.*

The young mother and child left the hospital five days after the
birth and went home to Kathleen Shields.

*I didn't know how to bath him or do anything, and my great-
grandmother I can remember putting on a big apron, taking
hold of him. She'd lay him on the towel, soap him all over first.
We had a baby's bath, and then she'd put the towel around him
and do his head first till he was all soaped up, and then after
his head was dry she'd put the rest of his body in. That was
the old way of doing it.*

Kathy remained with her 'Mum' for the five weeks between the
birth and her marriage to Dennis Ryan. She then moved with
Dennis senior and junior into Dennis's sister's and brother-in-
law's home in the inner suburb of Albert Park. There were
already six people living in the two-storey house, and the Ryans
were confined to a small bedroom.

Dennis was an otherwise unexceptional baby, but he had
problems getting off to sleep. Kathy devised an unusual but, as
it turned out, oddly appropriate method of soothing him. She
used to visit an uncle and aunt at a shop they ran in Union Street,
Brunswick.

*My uncle was a wag. He was a Pom, and he had the police
radio playing all the time in his car, and we used to have to
drive Dennis around to put him to sleep. That was his lullaby,*

the police radio. We'd get to the scene of the crime before the police.

When Gladys became involved with little Dennis, there were far-reaching consequences. It was only when Gladys first saw the baby that Kathy finally learnt the truth—'that lady' was her mother.

I was round at my Nan's and that lady was there for some reason. Well, she nearly fell of the bloody chair, me Mum, she didn't know I'd had a baby, and I didn't know she was my mum until she told me that day. I was stunned. There was no embracing, none of that. I suppose I hid my emotions. I do a lot of that. I dunno why. So I kept everything in. I just cuddled my son tighter, he was mine. I had something of my own. I didn't need anyone else. It didn't make me feel any less about Kathleen Shields. My great-grandmother was always my Mum to the day she died, and still is today. She was my life.

There was animosity between me and Gladys. Later in life we had a fist fight. One time we were sharing the same kitchen and I was getting Billy off to work, and she was getting her Harry off. There were two stoves, and she wanted to use the one I was using, and that's when I started on her. I got to know her later on when she was dying. I tried to do the right thing by her. I'd take her meals round, and she'd say: 'They're too bloody spicy.' She didn't want them. She always had a freezer full of food, and she'd say: 'Find something to take home with you,' but the things were always out of date by years. She gave me a packet of mixed fruit to make a cake, and it was walking.

Whether or not Gladys had designs on Kathy's husband Dennis is uncertain, but one incident around the time of Dennis junior's birth aroused Kathy's suspicions. Gladys was living on board an old rust bucket scow moored on the banks of the Maribyrnong River where Kathy and Dennis came to visit her one day. Dennis took Gladys for a ride on the Triumph—and didn't come back. Several hours later Kathy was left to beg her fare home from the man with whom Gladys was living on the boat.

> It was one day when me Mum had put red dye in her hair, and I thought her head was bleeding. Then the next thing I know Dennis has disappeared with her. Most probably she fancied him. If she could have taken him she would have. He was young and I didn't matter.

Dennis duly came back and shortly afterwards Kathy, still only seventeen, fell pregnant with her second and last child by him. Peter was born on 25 January 1953, again in the Royal Women's Hospital.

> I'm on the trolley outside the labour ward, right? Well, he was in such a hurry to come he nearly fell off the bloody trolley. I was in the passage ready to go into the ward and he wouldn't wait. I thought: 'God, he's going to fall off.' There was no nurse there. When they came out I said: 'He's born.'

Dennis senior had left to serve in the Korean War when Kathy was five months pregnant and was still away when Peter was born. In retrospect Kathy thinks he joined up more out of panic than patriotism. Lack of money and a fear of being tied down in his early twenties with two children were his main motivation, she believes. But his going off to Korea reminded Kathy of her last links with her own father and his fatal involvement in World War II.

> My grandfather on my Dad's side worked for the military. He

25

was pretty high up. I had gone to see him to get my dad's medals and the stuff left when he was killed. When I saw my grandfather in his office, he told me how he had won his money in a lottery, and given all his grandchildren this and that. I said: 'Who the fuck am I, you old bastard? I'm your fucking granddaughter, too, and so is Wilma.' He was nonplussed because we'd had nothing to do with him after dad died. He didn't want to know us, we didn't exist.

Meanwhile Kathy was learning all about life as a young single mother.

The local policeman used to ride around on his push bike, he only lived up the street. His daughter was on the cover of Post magazine, and she was up herself. And I was walking Dennis up the street to get the paper, and she walked past me, and she's la de da and everything and she said to me: 'He's nothing but a little bastard.' I was angry, I wanted to bash her. I did smack her face, and then I went straight and told her dad, and she got a belting. He was a typical old policeman, the old style—kick you up the bum.

Later on in years to come I met her at a wedding. She said to me she had been jealous of me, and here she is on the cover of Post and that. I dunno whether she was jealous of me having the baby or what.

Peter was just three weeks old when Kathy met the second of the three men who fathered her children—William George Peirce. She believes if she had stayed with Dennis Ryan and never met Peirce, her life would have been conventional and law-abiding, but ultimately boring.

I had no intentions of having a boyfriend or anything because my husband was in Korea. And this bloke's ran out of the pub

and said to me something about how I looked beautiful. I think
he had a suit on with the wrong colour shoes. Well, I didn't
know what he was on about, because I looked a good sort, he
reckoned. He was a good-looking bloke, a bloody lady killer. He
followed me, and then it evolved from there.

'This bloke' was Billy Peirce, and a few months after they first met he moved in with Kathy and the two boys who, because of Dennis Ryan's absence, were back with Kathleen Shields. Over the next eight years Kathy was to have six children by Peirce. She sums up their time together in just one sentence—'He was good-looking, and he loved a drink and a fight.'

It was Billy who introduced Kathy to the world of crime, and his influence on her behaviour gradually made the more conventional Wilma ashamed of Kathy and her young family. So much so that she paid Kathy twenty pounds to stay away from her wedding to avoid any embarrassment on her big day. Predictably, Kathy accepted the money, spent it, and turned up anyway. 'Wilma didn't say a word to me, but I behaved myself,' she laughs.

The awkward question of how she would tell Dennis Ryan on his return from Korea that she had found a new man never arose. Dennis simply didn't bother looking up his wife and two children. This didn't particularly worry Kathy, as she was so deeply involved with Billy Peirce. Kathy and Dennis's divorce, thirty years later, was almost as farcical as their wedding. In the early 1980s Kathy had started to acquire property and was concerned her long-lost husband might make some claim on her, so she filed for divorce.

The reason I did it was because I owned a house, and I didn't
know how he'd turned out, and so I had to cover my skin. I
said to the judge, 'I haven't seen him for thirty years, Your
Honour', expecting to have to wait a month after the decree

27

nisi, right? He made it absolute straightaway. And then I found out Dennis had already divorced me, and I'm blueing with myself because it's cost me $400 to get divorced from him.

Kathy and Dennis met only once during those thirty years—on a bus, of all places—but still managed to end up in bed together.

I was alone for Christmas dinner. I'd caught the bus. I had burnt my bra years before everybody else, and I'd dyed my hair blonde and had this black top on, with no bra, and I saw Dennis about to get off the bus. I said: 'Excuse me, would you mind getting off the bus. I want to talk to you.' He looked at me stupid, and I said: 'I do happen to be your wife.' He shit himself. Got off the bus. Then we went out to my aunty's house, and I had a cold sausage for Christmas dinner, and he stayed the night. We had a lot to talk about—the letters he sent me from Korea. He was impressed with the way I dressed. Then we never saw one another again.

In the early stages of her relationship with Billy Peirce, Kathy's two young sons, Dennis and Peter, were more often than not living with Gladys in Monbulk in the Dandenong mountains on the outskirts of Melbourne. After her series of bigamous marriages Gladys had finally settled into a relationship which was to last for the best part of half a century. Her partner was Harry Allen, from whom Dennis and Peter took their surnames, although Dennis was buried as a Ryan. Unlike Gladys, who died in 1993, Harry is still alive.

Harry worked in a sawmill and one of his legs had been crushed in an accident, for which he'd received very little by way of workers' compensation. So life wasn't easy for him and Gladys.

Billy Peirce had a job in Hughesdale, halfway between the city and the Dandenongs, working as storeman in a clothing

factory and there were prospects for Kathy there too. By now
Gladys's relationship with the two boys had evolved into a form
of semi-permanent guardianship, which had come to suit Kathy
and Billy Peirce. Their plan was to pay Gladys and Harry from
their wages for the upkeep of the two boys. Kathy hotly denies
that Gladys had taken on the boys out of a sense of guilt at
having forsaken her three daughters and wished to atone by
bringing up her two grandsons.

> It was nothing to do with that. She and Harry needed the
> money. My idea was if Gladys minded them I'd send her
> money. But I never got 'em back. It was supposed to be short-
> term. I used to pinch Dennis and my Mum used to kidnap him
> back, so in the end I gave up. I'd go to school to pick him up,
> and she'd already collected him early.

This allowed Kathy and Billy, who was still in his early twenties—only five years older than she was—the independence to
enjoy the blossoming of their love.

> We lived in a house in Drummond Street, Carlton, and we
> were dearly in love. We used to run down the street together
> hand in hand all the way to Flinders Street, skipping and
> jumping. That was one of my happy times. We'd spend hours
> lying on the beds just reading together and talking. There were
> three single beds in the bloody room!

Kathy was prepared to leave the two boys with Gladys and
Harry partly because she had been told that if she went onto
social security they would be taken from her and put into care.
So the Monbulk arrangement, painful as it was for Kathy, came
to be accepted. She would visit the boys at least once a week
and was always with them at weekends. Monbulk was not an
easy place to reach by public transport, and Kathy had no car.

The problem was alleviated when Gladys and Harry moved with the two boys to Carrum, another outer suburb, but more accessible by public transport than Monbulk.

Billy Peirce didn't have a car either, but considered public transport beneath him. So each weekend he found a different means of getting to Monbulk or Carrum.

He bloody stole cars, didn't he? I got in this one car with him, and we were on the way to Monbulk. By the time we got to Gladys's I was hanging onto his tie, because the doors were gone. They fell off. He bloody well hit trees and God knows what. Then one day I was already up there and in the night he came up in a green Met bus. Gladys said, 'I don't know what's coming into the yard, but it's got bright lights,' and it got bogged so they got the timber jinker to get him out. There was a cliff up there, and the next thing the bus goes over the bloody cliff.

By this time both Dennis and Peter were starting to call Gladys 'Mum' and regarded Kathy as their sister. Kathy felt if she told them the truth it would have an adverse effect on their relationship with Harry and Gladys. This didn't stop her feeling guilty, either then or now. As with Kathy's relationship with 'this lady', the subterfuge continued for many years. Until he was eighteen Dennis was never sure exactly who his mother was. The manner in which he found out the truth may well have had some bearing on the way his character developed in later years.

He thought I was his sister for years. Gladys told Dennis she was his Mum and I was his sister, and he believed that. By then I had other children, and I was still going down to Carrum to see him, and I did, I did try and steal him back. Many times I wanted to tell him the truth. He was running around unsupervised, and he started to get into trouble. I visited him

when he was in Turana and Malmsbury, the prisons for kids.
I thought he had enough on his plate without me telling him
this. When he was eighteen and in Pentridge I'd had enough,
and I wrote to him and told him I was not his sister, I was his
mother, and I loved him. I had guilt, the guilt was all mine. I
couldn't tell him to his face, I could only put it in a letter. It
must have been hard for him to be in there and read it. I think
by then he had an inclination, because I was always at
Pentridge at the weekends. I dunno.

In the end, before he died, he didn't know who the fuck I
was, because he used to brandish guns at my head, too. Half
the time I think he thought I was his girlfriend. There was only
sixteen years' age difference between us. There were a couple
of girls that he went with that were like me to look at. I've got
a photo of one of his girlfriends that later had her head shot off,
and she looks like me in the picture.

But when Kathy visited Dennis in Pentridge after writing the
letter, they both found it difficult to raise the subject. 'We didn't
talk about it,' she says. 'Didn't mention it. We don't show emotions in our family.'

That didn't mean Kathy was incapable of showing Dennis
affection. To most people, particularly Gladys, Peter was the more
lovable of the two brothers, reminding Kathy of the way her own
sister, Wilma, had always received more attention than she had.

Gladys and Harry showed Peter the love and affection. He was
like my sister, Wilma. He had naturally curly hair; Dennis was
more like me, the surly one. But it was Dennis I gave my
cuddles to.

There was no doubting, however, that Gladys, Harry, Dennis
and Peter were a family that did things together—like the time
they buried a car in the backyard.

There was a big tree where nothing grew. I don't know why they wanted to get rid of this car. So they decided to dig this hole, and I go out into the garden and I can't find them. I could hear the voices, and they're right down this hole. It's big enough to put I don't know what in. A car, anyway. The four of them had dug it, and the next thing I know the car's been put in there and covered up. And I thought they were fucking idiots. I don't know who bought that house later—they must have had some surprises.

As Gladys and Harry raised Dennis during his formative years it could be argued that it was their influence or lack of guidance that started him on the wrong path. But Kathy prefers not to confront this question, although for some time she incorrectly believed Peter blamed Gladys and Harry for his life of crime.

It was after Gladys died in May 1993. Peter put a death notice in the paper the day after I put mine in. He wouldn't put it in the same day. It just said: 'You made me what I am.' He didn't mean it in a wrong way, but I misconstrued it as meaning she had made him the criminal he was.

Kathy and Billy Peirce were, by financial necessity, living apart in August 1954, when their first child—Kathy's third—was born. Kathy was working in a boarding house in Bairnsdale, 250 kilometres east of Melbourne, while Billy was woodcutting in a nearby timber town. He made it to the local hospital for the birth, but wasn't of much assistance to Kathy—'I had her on my own, he was too busy chatting up the nurse. The baby was snuffling and sneezing, but there was nobody there to clean her up.'

The baby was called Vicki-Jean, and is generally believed to be Kathy's only daughter. That doesn't take into account her three 'lost' children.

Most media accounts of Kathy's life have wrongly stated she

had only seven children. In fact, she had ten, but three were taken from her and placed in care shortly after they were born. Six of the ten were born to Kathy and Billy Peirce during the eight years they were together from 1953 to 1961. They were Vicki, born 11 August 1954; Shelley, born 8 July 1956; Stephen, born 15 July 1957; Victor, born 11 November 1958; Lex, born 7 January 1960; and David, born in July 1961. Of these six, Vicki, Victor and Lex stayed with Kathy; Shelley, Stephen and David (names Kathy uses for them to protect their real identities) were taken from her. It is only during the last six years that Kathy has re-established contact with two of her three 'lost' children—Shelley and Stephen. David's whereabouts are still unknown.

Shelley and Stephen traced Kathy through Freedom of Information and other sources, discovering one another in the process. Their reunion with Kathy came just before a legislative change which now protects natural parents from being confronted by fostered children without agreeing to see them. Although Kathy would not have denied Shelley and Stephen the opportunity of meeting her, and is glad they did, she wishes she could have been prepared for the event, instead of it occurring in circumstances she remembers as especially traumatic. The two 'lost' children' had travelled to Melbourne to find Kathy without any prior warning.

It was in 1989. I was staying with relatives at the Carlton Housing Commission flats during the committal hearings concerning Victor and then Trevor over the Walsh Street killings. I had enough on my mind with this, and I was walking to the court every day from Carlton, and walking back. Gladys and Harry were living at 49 Cubitt Street in Richmond, and Gladys phoned saying she wanted to see me urgently.

It was a Sunday morning and Trevor's wife Debbie and me came out of the flats and there was a bloke downstairs fiddling with his tow-truck. Debbie's cheeky, and she says: 'Give us a lift down to Richmond.' We hop in the tow-truck, and I've got a mink coat on, full-length mink, mind you. And we're talking and laughing, and we get out, not expecting anything. And I go into the house at Cubitt Street, and there's a girl standing beside Gladys's bed, because she was bed-ridden then. Gladys said: 'This is your daughter.' And with that, this voice behind me said: 'And I'm your bloody son.' It was Stephen. He was angry because I'd let him go, and the reasons why. Shelley was scared of me, my reaction. I was shocked, and then I cried, didn't I? I'll never forget it. Shelley didn't come near me. She was too scared to talk. I believed them straight away because Stephen looked so much like Dennis, and Shelley looked like Gladys.

There was no doubt. And I'd always known they'd come to light some day. But I was angry, because they should never have sprung that on me like they did. Later I took them by the arm and we walked around and I showed them 35 and 37 Stephenson Street in Richmond, and I said: 'That's where we lived.' I said: 'If you'd stayed with me, and you'd been down here with the rest of us, you'd either be dead or in gaol. I did the right thing.' How would they have got a chance if I'd kept them? But they both said: 'We'd still rather have been with you.' Later that day I took them straight out to H Division in Pentridge to introduce them to Victor. He wasn't impressed. Because he didn't know anything about them. He didn't want anything to do with them. Since then he spoke to Shelley on the phone, and he saw Stephen on several occasions.

Kathy has no doubt, however, about the wisdom of allowing the three children to be adopted. Meeting Shelley and Stephen forced her to come to terms again, as a loving mother, with the realisation that the only chance those children had for a normal life was if they were taken from her at birth. Being re-united with

Shelley and Stephen helped Kathy confront this awful truth—
probably the most damning indictment of her turbulent life. She
had ten children, three of whom were taken from her shortly
after they were born. Of the seven she reared, three are dead;
two have recently been released from gaol; one is lost to Kathy
forever, living under the witness protection scheme, and has not
seen or contacted her mother for four years; and the other has
also spent time in gaol for crimes of dishonesty.

The two children with whom she has re-established contact
have both been living useful, well-adjusted lives. Shelley owns a
pet shop in north Queensland, and is happily married with a
teenage daughter. Looking at a family portrait of Shelley, her
husband and daughter, the sheer wholesomeness of their appearance shines through. It is difficult to avoid the obvious, painful
comparison between this photograph and one of Kathy's other
family portraits—guns, tattoos and all.

Stephen is a professional chef living in Victoria, and is also
happily married, with two children.

*How does that make me feel as a mother, that my only suc-
cessful children are the ones that got away? Terrible: terrible
now, and terrible at the time. It's not meant as an excuse for
letting them go, but most of the time around then I had five
children with me, and Billy Peirce in and out of gaol.*

The circumstance of the first of the three adoptions was, in itself,
highly irregular. Kathy has more than a suspicion that someone
made money out of her and her 'lost' daughter. An assistant at
the Royal Women's Hospital, where Shelley was born, made the
arrangements and, Kathy believes, was later the target of an
investigation into her activities.

*With Shelley I was introduced to a young couple, then we went
to a solicitor's office, and they offered me money. I said: 'No.'*

I wasn't going to sell her. I'm not that much of a Granny Evil. They told me the baby would have a good home, would have this and that, nothing to ever worry about.

I didn't see any of the three of them. They take them away from you straight away. You don't even get to hold them. They're gone. If I'd seen them I wouldn't have been able to give them up. What you don't see you don't miss, terrible as that sounds, but I thought her life would be better. I remember the assistant, she was shifty. She arranged everything for the first one. Because I knocked back the money, maybe she got it.

Stephen was taken in by a children's home in Broadmeadows, an outer Melbourne suburb. When they were reunited Stephen asked Kathy if his father, Billy Peirce, had bashed her.

I told him, yes, but when I was heavily pregnant it was only on my back and that. And Stephen was born with bruises. Dennis Ryan and James Pettingill, the fathers of my other two kids, never bashed me. Only Billy Peirce. Mostly when I was pregnant, out of frustration, I suppose. The funny thing was I seemed to always be going into hospital after a bashing on his fucking pay day. He was usually drunk, but it was fists and all. I couldn't fight back, I had to cover myself up. One time I was talking to my friend Dolores and he was making eyes at her or something, and I said something, and I got two black eyes. I went into hospital to have Victor with black eyes.

When I came home to my great-granma's place two days later I went straight upstairs so she wouldn't see my eyes, but she said: 'I'd like to see the baby,' and she saw my eyes then. Five minutes after it happened he was apologetic, but it was too late. I stayed with him because I still loved him.

When Billy was serving time in Bendigo prison for burglary, Kathy regularly stole tobacco from the milk bar where she was working. She would take it up to Bendigo and attach it to a rope hanging over the prison wall. Billy would haul it up and over, and enjoy the benefits of being the prison's tobacco broker. When he was in Pentridge he would hide the tobacco in hollowed out cabbages in the prison garden.

Before Kathy fell pregnant to Billy Peirce for the sixth and final time she enjoyed a brief relationship with another man. Billy was in gaol, and this unnamed lover provided Kathy with something she found difficult to cope with from a man—kindness.

> That was one of the boys from my childhood that really did love me. He was so good to me, I couldn't live with him after Billy Peirce. He was too kind to me, and I'm not used to that. I couldn't, because he was too nice. Buy me flowers, and do this and do that. I couldn't cope. I dunno why, I couldn't get used to it.

As usual Billy Peirce was in gaol for burglary for most of the time Kathy was carrying David, their sixth child. Unknown to Kathy, Billy was out for long enough to get married to another woman between the births of Lex and David. Since then Kathy and Billy's legal wife, Valerie Peirce, have got to know each other and occasionally meet.

Kathy's pregnancy with David didn't stop the third man in her life, Jimmy Pettingill, from falling in love with her. Kathy still more often than not refers to him as 'Mr Pettingill', an oddly quaint expression of her lasting respect for him. 'I met Mr Pettingill when I was pregnant with David,' she says. 'He was willing to take me, pregnant and all, but I didn't think it was fair for him to have to bring up someone else's child.' So David was taken into care.

During the early stages of Kathy's relationship with Jimmy

Pettingill, Billy Peirce made an attempt to win back the mother of his six children, despite being legally married himself.

> *We were living in this little house in Brunswick, and the kids went to school at Albert Street Primary. Vicki happened to tell me about how this man used to pick them up and buy 'em ice creams, which was Billy Peirce. He was out of gaol. So he came to my house and said he wanted me back. I told Mr Pettingill and he left for the night and Bill moved in. They confronted one another in the passage, and I warned Jimmy: 'Don't turn your back on him for a start.' But the next morning I thought to myself: 'This is not on.' One night was enough, I couldn't go back to the old ways. And I begged Jimmy to come back.'*

Jimmy Pettingill remains something of a mystery figure. When he and Kathy met in 1961 he was already married with a family living in South Australia, and was quite open with Kathy about this. What he didn't tell her was that he had a third family living in remote central Australia.

There was no question of bigamy—Pettingill was married only to the mother of his children in South Australia. But throughout the six years he and Kathy were together he maintained regular contact with both his other families. Strangely his legal wife and his two de factos were all called Kathy—'No wonder if he talked in his sleep it wasn't any problem,' Kathy comments wryly.

One of the reasons Jimmy could successfully juggle these three separate lives was his job as an interstate truck driver. But the strain of the long hours and overnight trips told. 'He would just get in the house and fall asleep against the front door,' Kathy recalls. 'And I couldn't take it no more, because I never had him there.'

Jimmy Pettingill was to father her last two children—Jamie, born 18 December 1963, and Trevor, born 1 February 1965. Kathy remembers him as a kind man, an opinion not shared by Lex, her fifth child by Billy Peirce. Lex describes his stepfather as a 'mongrel' who tortured him as a child, inflicting serious physical and emotional scars. According to Lex, Jimmy broke both his arms on separate occasions. Nevertheless, Kathy maintains she didn't know about his 'sneaky' brutal treatment of Lex. 'He was a truck driver, and they use pills, hallucinate and that,' she says. 'Maybe that was it. But he must have been remorseful, because he killed himself in the end.'

There was an element of the bizarre about the deaths of Billy Peirce and James Pettingill, like many of those who came into contact with Kathy from the time she was a little girl. Billy was the first of the two to go, on 8 December 1968.

He was in a cave-in at a building site in the late 1960s at Clayton. He was digging drains. Trevor had slammed his thumb in a door, and we were in a friend's car, driving to the children's hospital. While I was in the hospital it came over the radio in the car and the friend heard. Hal Todd was the announcer, and he cried. One of the men was pulled out, and as for the other one, well, the trench caved in again. The chap that drove me to the hospital, he knew it was Billy from the radio. So when we got back home with Trevor he suggested I take all the kids and put them to bed. And I was thinking: 'Who's he to tell me what to do?' He said: 'I've got something important to tell you.' So I get rid of all the kids, and then he explained to me that Billy'd been buried alive. Well then I watched the news and saw his tattooed arm coming out of the grave, I saw the mud that had fell on him. It was close to Christmas because I had stuff on the lay-by for the kids. So I got the stuff off the lay-by to buy clothes to wear to his funeral. I had a go at the cops after he died. 'You'd be fucking happy he died,' I remember the police had come for him one night and as he was being taken away to the lock up, I said to them: 'There

39

doesn't want to be a fucking mark on him either when he comes home.' You know what they did? They put him in a locker and turned him upside down in it, and they put a bucket over his head and hit him through the bucket. That's where I learned about police.

Unknown to Kathy, Billy had had a premonition about the manner of his death. The day before the accident he told his wife, Valerie, he was worried there would be a cave-in at the building site, and said: 'I think it will be me.'

At his inquest, on 11 June 1969, Coroner Harry Pascoe heard how Billy and the foreman, Jack James, had both been buried when the three-metre-deep trench in which they were working caved in. Their fellow workers thought Billy had scrambled his way to safety, so concentrated their efforts on freeing James, whom they dug out after forty minutes or so, still alive. When James's head was pulled clear of the mud he said, 'Where's Bill?' By then it was too late. It took another half-hour before they uncovered Billy's body. His legs were doubled up underneath him and there was no sign of life.

James Pettingill died in 1972, five years after he and Kathy split up, but she didn't find out about it for another seven years.

Mr Pettingill killed himself. I don't know whether it was because he knew the kids were in trouble. I think it was in Mt Gambier. Jamie used to run away to South Australia all the time when he was young. I think he was looking for him. Jamie was young in Pentridge when we found out his dad had died, and I went out there with the priest. Jamie said, 'Who's dead?', thinking it was one of his brothers. I said: 'Your father.' He said: 'Well, I'm not bloody worried about him.' I didn't get told officially because I was the de facto.

James Pettingill's adoptive father, Mr F.J. Pettingill, is still living in Mt Gambier. He is reluctant to speak of his adopted son, but confirms that he had taken his own life in 1972. 'James was happily married as far as I'm concerned. He never said anything to me about this family in Melbourne, and I don't want to hear about them.'

The Coroner's Court in Adelaide failed to turn up any record for the death of a James Pettingill during the 1960s or 1970s.

After Kathy's six-year relationship with Jimmy Pettingill ended in 1967 there were other men in her life, but no more children—a tally of ten was somehow pre-ordained.

But you see, years ago when I was a kid, and not having anyone, I made a vow. When I walked along those air raid tunnels to school, I said to Satan: 'Give me ten children.' I didn't know anything. I read the Bible a lot, we had a great big family Bible, and the thing that stuck in me mind was that wise King Solomon, when he cut the baby in half. I don't know why I said it, I must have read something about Satan being the evil one, the Prince of Darkness that tried to get God to come down to his kingdom. And I thought he must be more powerful than God, because he was trying to get him down there. I couldn't get pregnant after ten.

CHAPTER THREE

When I'm Asleep
— It's Still Open —

KATHY AND DENNIS ARE STANDING ON THE STAINED AND LITTER-strewn concrete floor outside the locked door to a housing commission flat in Wellington Street, Collingwood. It is around 8.30 in the evening of 1 October 1978. It is already dark on the street outside the block of flats and there is a chill in the air. Dennis is drunk and Kathy is angry because of the $300 she has in her hand. It's money to settle a debt owed by her daughter Vicki to a woman called Kim Nelson. Kathy doesn't like her family being in debt, least of all to a person like Kim Nelson. Nelson is a thirty-five-year-old prostitute who, eighteen months earlier, had gained considerable notoriety for her behaviour in court while appearing as star witness in the trial of five senior Melbourne policemen on conspiracy charges. For some years Nelson and Kathy have maintained an uneasy form of friendship based on the mutual respect of two tough and uncompromising women. At this moment Nelson is on the other side of the door from Kathy and Dennis. With Nelson is a second woman, Keryn Jean Thompson, aged twenty-three, of Port Melbourne. And a loaded .22 calibre rifle. But Kathy doesn't know this. Suddenly the stream of abuse and insults coming through the door is drowned by the sharp retort of a firearm. At first Kathy doesn't feel a thing; then comes a roaring inside her skull, and a warm, sticky trickle down the front of her face. She looks across at Dennis, her vision blurred. Gazing back at her, smeared across the chest of his white T-shirt, is a human eye.

Kathy's gradual climb to the highest echelons of the underworld went back to the time as a small child when she ran bets for her great-grandmother in Brunswick. Watching the SP bookies in action with her grandmother Bertha Mason gave her a first glimpse of something excitingly illicit. Little more than a toddler, she was somehow aware the grown-ups were up to something naughty.

Billy Peirce was the next stage in Kathy's criminal evolution. Although only a small-time criminal, he had a wide circle of underworld acquaintances and their larrikin behaviour was instantly attractive to Kathy. By the time she was visiting Dennis and Peter in gaols like Pentridge and Beechworth she felt strongly that the adrenalin rush and occasional fear of a life on the wrong side of the tracks was infinitely preferable to the boring expectations of ordinary society. And she rarely missed the opportunity to shine in front of her growing circle of influential criminal acquaintances. She vividly remembers one visiting day in Pentridge where prisoners' wives and children were gathered around one of the two donated swimming pools inside the gaol grounds.

Arthur* was there, and he was captured by a policewoman of all things, which we thought was pretty hilarious. He'd shot someone and done a lot of things. Anyway I saw this baby

---

* A major player in the underworld. He once gave evidence on Victor's behalf saying: 'Your honour, I wouldn't lie for Victor Peirce, but I'd kill for him.'

crawling towards the swimming pool. And there was nobody watching it. And it was getting closer and closer, and I said: 'Arthur, the baby.' And he got up, and I said: 'Not now.' So we waited 'til the baby falls in and I scream out: 'Arthur, the baby.' And he's dived in, all his clothes on, and got the baby. And he got three months off. I saw it as a good opportunity. Afterwards he was stood up as a hero.

Another incident involving an unwanted set of weights didn't do Kathy's growing reputation any harm. She decided to donate them to the gym at Pentridge but she was unable to lift them. So she worked at it until she was able to hoist them aloft with ease.

I walked into the gym with them held above my head and the screw said: 'Have you got permission?' I said: 'Yes, I have.' And he goes to take 'em off me and he drops 'em straight to the ground. Can't lift 'em.

Years later in 1988 when convicted murderer Alex Tsakmakis was beaten to death by Russell Street bomber Craig Minogue with the 2.25 kg weights in a sack, Kathy was to wonder whether she had unwittingly supplied the murder weapon.

Around 1967 Kathy and the family moved to a house in Liberty Parade, West Heidelberg, the site of the 1956 Olympic village. Despite its auspicious origins the village was a hard, tough neighbourhood, not at all a pleasant place to live or grow up in—as the children soon discovered. Kathy, with no other means of support, found work for the next four and a half years as a barmaid at The Sentimental Bloke Hotel in nearby Bulleen, a regular haunt of local police.

Despite the long hours she worked, she was determined to give the children, Vicki, Victor, Lex, Jamie and Trevor, a loving home and a place where their friends would feel welcome, as well as her two older sons. But the sixteen-year-old Dennis was already showing signs of the violence that would become his trademark.

The backyard was always full of kids. They had a swimming pool, one of those above ground ones, and a pool table in the bungalow. Of a night I'd sit the kids on the couch and I'd count them, before bathing them, and I'd hear the balls clicking out in the bungalow, and I'd know someone was missing. Dennis and Peter used to come and stay, and one night me boyfriend was there playing with them, teaching them how to bite noses off. Well, Lex has come in, and he's had a fight, and we all go out. It was a Sunday night, we must have been poor, we only had sausages for tea.

Well, Dennis bit me boyfriend's nose off. They all scarpered, right, and the police come, and this bloke's nose is all dripping blood, and I said: 'You're not bringing him in here, I've just bought a new fucking carpet.' Dennis bit off his nose. He was just getting taught how to do it.

A myth has evolved around this period that Kathy became close to a number of both uniformed and plainclothes police through serving them drinks. One of them has said that Kathy would appeal to her 'mates' in the force to let Trevor and Victor off when they began to get into trouble in the village. Kathy hotly denies this, saying she had already formed her negative opinion of the majority of policemen because of the violence inflicted on Billy Peirce. (Besides, she had her own method of inflicting discipline on the boys. Because they could run faster than her, she would wait until bath time when they couldn't escape, and flog them with a length of garden hose for the day's misdemeanours.)

All the police drank for free at The Sentimental Bloke. There was a lady over the road from me with ten children. This day she's in the lounge at tea time drinking with a copper, while her kids are left at home. And I said to my boss: 'That woman's got fucking ten kids at home, and they're scabbing for a meal. Are you going to give her and that copper a free meal, while her kids go hungry? Because if you do, I'm walking out.' I could do every job in the joint. I worked the bottle shop, I could do the large bars single-handed, make him quids. He said: 'No, I'm not.'

There was another time when there was some do for a superintendent or someone, and they had the function room, and they'd approached the boss, and said: 'Whatever you do, don't let Kathy work that night.' It was a Sunday night and they were all there with their wives. But he let me work, he was funny like that, having a go. And I'd be putting the jugs on the table and smiling saying: 'Are you having a nice time?' and you could see them squirm, because I knew all their girl-friends. There was an Ascot Vale crime car squad bloke there, and I introduced him to my girlfriend, and later she broke up with her husband and had a baby to the copper.

The Sentimental Bloke's entertainment lounge regularly drew crowds several hundred strong to see stars like Kamahl, Johnny Farnham, Johnny O'Keefe and Warren Mitchell. And occasionally the audience itself included a celebrity, like the night Charmain Biggs, wife of Great Train Robber Ronnie Biggs, sat at Kathy's table. Kathy formed a quick opinion of the big-name visitors.

The one I hated the most was Warren Mitchell. He was an utter pig. He was an arrogant pig. It was the way he spoke to you, and he had a fetish for always washing, showering and washing. He was ill-mannered, gruff and said: 'Who are you?' and everybody was beneath him.

But Johnny O'Keefe I'll never forget. It was about three

o'clock in the morning, and I had Victor and Lex at a table.
Charmain Biggs and her bloke asked if they could sit at the
table, and I said 'Yes.' I can always remember Johnny shaking
Victor's hand and Lex's hand. They were very young. And he
said: 'When you shake a man's hand, you look him in the eye,
and you say: "How ya goin', mate?".'

So we're up at the manager's office, and Johnny O'Keefe's
trying to get through to his wife at the Southern Cross, and
he's saying, 'I am Johnny O'Keefe,' and they're saying: 'Oh
yeah, we've heard that one before.' And apparently they'd can-
celled his concert at Pentridge the next day, so he was getting
on to the people, and standing over them, and saying: 'I am
doing the concert.' Well, he did do the concert. And I couldn't
believe that a man in his position was so determined to do a
concert for Pentridge; I thought it was good of him.

John Farnham was fun. He was only twenty. I was singing
'Sadie the Cleaning Lady' and the boss said to me: 'You love
that song, don't you?' And I said: 'Oh, yeah.' And he said:
'Well, how about scrubbing?' I thought: 'You fucking cunt.'
Here I am out the front with this other sheila scrubbing these
white chairs.

Kamahl was a proper gentleman. When he went on I had
to keep the lights out till the drum roll, and they built it up a
bit, you know, and I said to him: 'Listen to me, can you smile,
because I can't see you.' He just laughed. Well I've got his
autograph there.

The head waiter at The Sentimental Bloke was also a part-time
choreographer at Channel Nine and talked Kathy into being
filmed in her hair curlers and dressing gown for a station promo,
dancing in front of the camera as she collected a bottle of early
morning milk and the newspaper from her front doorstep.
Drinkers at the hotel would mimic her dance steps as they
approached the bar to order a drink.

The strain of the long hours she was working, combined with the trouble her children were beginning to get into, began to tell on Kathy. On one occasion Trevor stole a car and sideswiped two pursuing police vehicles off the road. When Kathy arrived at the police station he was sobbing and complaining bitterly that one of the officers who finally caught him had put a gun to his head. One policeman involved in the chase took Kathy aside and said: 'Get that kid on a racetrack. He's a natural.' Trevor was just eleven years of age.

The result was that at the age of thirty-six in 1971, Kathy had a heart attack. Peter was at home at the time and probably saved her life by rushing her into intensive care. By the time she had come out of hospital and was well enough to resume her job her boss had been sacked, so Kathy decided to go elsewhere. She began working in the lounge bar of a Heidelberg hotel, but after a few weeks a high profile criminal identity known to Kathy began drinking there.

The owners of the hotel said to me: 'What's more important, him or your job?' And I said: 'Well, actually him.' Because he was a friend and he was paying for his drinks—I wasn't giving them to him. So I left there. Then I went to the Union Hotel in Ascot Vale part-time. And I knew a girl in a massage parlour down in Park Street, South Melbourne, The Black Rose. And she said, 'Come down one day.' So I went down, and she said: 'Go and do a massage,' and I didn't know what a massage was, and I'm bang, bang, bang, chopping down on this bloke's legs and back. And he gives me $40, and all I did was massage him. So I do another one, and I've earned $80. That's a whole week part-time at the pub. So I thought: 'Fuck that.' Later I had sex with some of them for money. It didn't worry me—not for $1,500 a week. I told the boys at home in High Street, North-cote, where we were living by this time and they didn't like it. They didn't approve. But next thing was: 'Mum, will you bail so and so out? Mum this and that.' It didn't bother me, the sex. I used to think of paying the bills.

I was always faithful to Dennis Ryan, Billy Peirce and Mr Pettingill, when I was with them. But I didn't have anybody at this time. But the money was there. I never saw so much. I went blank, and you'd get into brandy, that's what you've got to do to stop yourself thinking. The girls get into pills, heroin, anything because they can't stand what they are doing. Go through the motions, lay there and think of the bills. A lot don't come in for sex, just companionship. I don't even remember the first one, it wasn't a big deal. The second day I was at The Black Rose one of the girls said: 'Rip it off.' And I'm thinking: 'Rip what off?' She meant: 'Don't put the money in the book.'

So it took me a week to learn how to run a parlour. I used to work ten in the morning till six. Not many drunks, and you didn't go with ones you didn't like the look of.

The bloke who ran the parlour got his car blown up, and lost his appetite for the job. All that was left of his Mustang was a wheel. Next morning I come in, and the next minute I'm slammed down the fucking passage by the South Melbourne jacks [detectives]. 'And where were you last night at such and such a time?' And I could see the operator with his arm in a sling. I got thrown from one end of the room to the other. The operator got out and within that week I took over as manager-ess. There was this bloke called Menzies who owned the building. We used to pay him the rent.

Those were interesting days in the parlours. We had speciality girls that would help out with the men that used to come in wheelchairs. I don't know what they used to do in the rooms, it was none of my business. But they used to be looked after. The girls were kind to them.

In another parlour at the back, I can't remember the name, there was this big fat girl, and she had a bloke about eighty, and she comes running over, and she says: 'He's dead!' So we *ring South Melbourne police, and they were very good. They dressed him and they put him down the lane, so it didn't look like he died in the parlour. So they get in touch with his relations, and they say: 'What's Dad doing over in that part of town?' He was supposed to be at some old people's home, playing cards or something. But I bet he died with a smile on his face.*

There was this girl, she was an Australian, and I'm walking past the door and I hear her sing in some sort of language, and I thought, 'What's she bloody well up to?' And she said to me later on: 'I do that to annoy them, so they'll go quick.' It was to give the clients the shits and hurry up and get out.

In 1978, after Kathy was released from Fairlea, the family moved from High Street, Northcote, to another place in Ross Street, not far away. Before long they were surprised to find the street in a virtual state of siege, with residents operating under a self-imposed curfew and rarely venturing out after 9 p.m. Houses wore 'For Sale' signs everywhere, and Kathy still couldn't work out why.

Well, I happened to be up in Sydney. I got a phone call, there'd been a shoot-out in Ross Street. Russell [Russell Cox, one of Victoria's most notoriously successful armed robbers, was a close friend of the family and a one-time lover of Kathy's] *and Tommy Wraith, who was on with me daughter Vicki, had come to pick her up to take her to a motel down in Rosebud on the Mornington Peninsula. Vicki's standing on the pavement talking to them, and the next minute a police car's there, and there's shots fired. Tom's swung the wheel and drove into the brick wall, and he's knocked himself out. Russell gets away across the Merri Creek. Tom's pinched, and Vicki's up at the Northcote Police Station, and I'm in Sydney getting all this in me ear. So Vicki's up there, and they went to hit her with the typewriter, and she says: 'If you think for one minute that you've got trouble with my mother and her boys, well I'm her only daughter.' They said. 'Oh, fuck, get her out.' That shoot-out started it all with the neighbours.*

A famous party Kathy held in Ross Street didn't help.

We had this Christmas party. I sat up all night and I set up the tables and chairs and I had a present for everyone. We had a tree inside and everything. I had prostitutes, criminals, anyone who didn't have anywhere to go.

After The Black Rose Kathy took over another parlour in West Melbourne known as Vampirella's. A friend in Beechworth gaol made a sign, complete with vampires, for the front door. The next parlour was on Victoria Street, East Melbourne.

And all my friends used to come there on the Sundays, and we'd all get in the big sauna. We'd get blind drunk, and the Crown Lager was as hot as anything, right? So they're listening in on the intercom this day, and there's this beautiful girl there, and this bloke says to her: 'I'll give you $20 to whip you.' And one of my friends went out and said: 'I'll give her $20 not to get whipped.' Oh God there was a lot of funny things went on. I'll tell you now, they were all Australians wanted whipping. One time I worked for a Jewish woman. She only did enemas, to blokes who'd been to the private schools.

Kathy's experiences in the seamy world of prostitution and massage parlours led her deeper into the underworld. Her sons regarded her newfound wealth as the means to bail out their friends, and this widened Kathy's circle still further. During the period she was managing a number of establishments, Melbourne's parlour scene was being run by four main operators. Fabulously rich men with wildly expensive imported sports cars, these four overlords ruled their empires ruthlessly and often violently. Stories of cars and even parlours being blown up in the middle of the night were commonplace.

Life for the girls, with few exceptions, was miserable. This was before heroin became the standard method of forgetting the grime and grind of daily existence, and alcoholism was rampant. A regime of petty fines imposed by the owners—$10 for more than two butts in an ashtray was an example Kathy remembers— ensured the owners profited further from the girls' labours.

Charges varied from as little as $10 for a couple of minutes, to as much as the punter would wear. But the girls who charged the least often had to work the hardest. A friend of Kathy's in a parlour in Fitzroy would see up to forty clients in one shift. And the milk of human kindness hardly flowed freely among the four bosses.

One girl came in with Vick's Vapour on, she had a chest cold. The boss made her have a cold shower, and locked her clothes in the boot of his car to get rid of the smell. Made her do extra to get her clothes back.

Kathy had a better reputation than most of the madams. An ex-prostitute nicknamed The Talking Bone who she employed in her parlours for three years speaks warmly of her generosity. 'Most parlours were on a fifty-fifty take in those days, half for the girl, half for the boss,' she says. 'Kathy only charged us $10, or $12 at the outside, for however long. She was straight down the line and she looked after you if there was trouble. Dennis, too. I remember one guy decided to strangle me on the bed, and Dennis threw him out on the street with his pants down.'

The big difference between today's underworld and that of Melbourne in the 1960s and 1970s is drugs. Before the 1980s armed robbery was the quick route to a fortune and instant respect from other criminals. Today wealth and prestige in the underworld is enjoyed by those who sell the most smack (heroin) or speed.

There's no honour now. Not now, not much. They're all sniv-elling junkies, not good crims. The good crims are the ones that don't take it. It's a very small club left at the moment, they provide for one another. If you look after somebody you get repaid in kind. A debt is not forgotten. A relative of mine named John looked after someone in the remand centre, spoke to him nicely, just looked after him, a first-timer, and when the bloke got out, John didn't think any more about it, but the bloke bought John's wife a washing machine for over $600.

When my friend Anthony Farrell's grandmother Patsy was arrested on a big drug raid, and I saw her on the news dragged into Russell Street in the middle of the night, I got Victor's wife Wendy to ring up the gaol and tell them that Patsy was coming in, and she was a friend of mine. Then I wrote straight-away to a girl named Irene who was doing a lot for a murder up at Moe, the gaol where Patsy was going, and she looked after her there. Well Patsy can't believe that she was looked after so well, and she owes me, she says. She was scared stiff and worried.

But scores were not always settled for positive reasons. When a friend of Kathy's had his car shot up for 'mucking around with a boxer's wife', Dennis evened up during a forty-eight-hour leave from Pentridge. 'They hit this flat in Northcote where the boxer lived, and the boxer ran down the street in the nude to get away,' Kathy recalls with a chuckle. 'Dennis went back to gaol and nobody knew about it.'

53

THE MATRIARCH

Kathy could always look after herself, and her kin, physically. Her younger boys were beginning to get into trouble and by November 1975, and with his seventeenth birthday approaching, Victor was in Turana Boys' Home, but escaped to celebrate the occasion with the family at home in High Street, Northcote. Kathy was unable to join in the festivities as she had had a minor operation on her foot that morning. She was lying in bed upstairs when suddenly bedlam broke out in the street below. She hobbled down with her foot swathed in bandages to see four men in suits—obviously detectives—standing over Victor and his brother Lex, one with a gun at Victor's head.

She only has a dim memory of a girlfriend handing her a cloth handbag containing a large bottle of perfume, but a moment later she was out in the street and striking the man with the gun a crunching blow over the skull. As he slumped to the ground, his head split open, blood gushing, Lex felled one of the other detectives with a chop of his hand and Victor bolted down the street to safety.

Blood streaming down his face, Kathy's victim got to his feet and stamped viciously on her bandaged foot, then began tearing wildly at her clothing. 'I'm putting you in the morgue, you fucking arsehole,' he screamed, as another detective pulled him off.

Some months later Kathy was taken in for questioning over Victoria's most celebrated armed hold-up, the Great Bookie Robbery. As she was hustled into the squad office she spotted the man she'd bashed grinning at her from behind his desk. 'Don't smirk at me, you dog,' she yelled. 'You would've been fucking dead if I'd wanted to kill you.'

As Kathy tells it, the room went suddenly quiet. The first person to speak was the detective leading her in. 'Yeah, believe it,' he said. 'She could have.' No-one argued.

At age sixty, as she straightens up at the front of the oven from where she has just removed one of her famous boiled fruit cakes, Kathy looks at me across the room in her ocean-side hideaway cottage. I've just asked her whether one of Dennis's soldiers (bodyguards) with whom she fought was a big man. 'No,' she says, as if I should know better than to ask. 'But he was taller than me. Anyone's big who's taller than me.' She has a point. At five foot nothing with her grey hair and glasses, Kathy looks about as deadly a streetfighter as the Queen Mother. But appearances are misleading. A lot of good men, and women, have underestimated her to their cost. Not that Kathy is particularly proud of her reputation as a brawler. It's just a fact of life, like prison. 'There's nothing special about fighting,' she says. 'It's just something you sometimes have to do.'

Remembering the victim of the perfume bottle, now no longer a police officer but a prominent figure in legal and sporting circles, Kathy has this to say:

I split his head open when he was a D [detective] in the armed robbery squad, and he has to live with that forever. Everybody thought it was a gun in that bag, but it was a dirty big bottle of perfume. I got charged and I got a $200 fine. When I see him I have a giggle because he's got to live with the fact that a five-foot woman put him down.

But it wasn't only Kathy's sons who were getting into trouble. In 1970 Vicki, her oldest daughter, had her first child, Jason, at the age of sixteen, and a second, Mark, a year later, thus continuing the family tradition of mid-teen motherhood.

Jason was to play a role of almost unthinkable significance in the family's history as he reached adolescence. But back in the early 1970s it was his mother Vicki who was becoming a problem for Kathy.

THE MATRIARCH

Vicki ran away with three of my boyfriends. The first was a bloke I fell in love with from West Heidelberg, when we were living in the village. The next was a bloke I was going out with for nine years, but I never lived with him, because he was a mummy's boy, and he barracked for Collingwood, and I can't stand Collingwood. He had a Collingwood bedspread, Collingwood carpet, Collingwood curtains. We used to go on their family picnics, and in the end I got fed up, bloody Collingwood.

The third one was much later, one of Dennis's soldiers in Richmond. He was much too young for me. He had been in gaol and asked me to come to his welcome home party. So after I shut the drug shop* for the night, I just went up there in my casual gear, and there was a lot of young girls there, and their hearts were all beating and that, and he's come straight up to me, and I'm thinking what the hell's going on here? I got a bit flattered and carried away, and then he became one of the soldiers. With that—I'm always the last to know about it—Vicki started to live with him. But I was glad to get rid of him—he was too young. I was just flattered. Anyway he used to bash Vicki, and that's the reason why Jason ran away and come to live in Richmond.

However much Kathy resented Vicki's behaviour over her boyfriends, it paled in comparison with her reaction to a series of events in the late 1970s. It was Vicki who was unwittingly responsible for Kathy losing an eye in a celebrated shooting incident in October 1978.

Unknown to Kathy, Vicki had been arrested and charged over a dubious cheque while shopping in the outer suburb of Doncaster. A friend of sorts of the family, Kim Nelson, heard of Vicki's plight, drove to the police station and handed over the

---

* Premises in Richmond from where Kathy and her family trafficked in drugs.

$300 bail to secure her freedom. Next morning Kathy went to Kim Nelson's house in Otter Street, Collingwood, and was surprised to find Vicki there, thinking she was still under arrest. Kim told her: 'It was only three hundred, and I got her out.'

Months passed without Vicki repaying the debt and Kim Nelson understandably became annoyed at her cavalier attitude. Then on 1 October Kathy went to visit her son Lex in a block of Housing Commission flats in Wellington Parade, Collingwood, accompanied by Dennis. On the way Dennis told her that Kim Nelson and another woman, Keryn Thompson, were in a flat elsewhere in the building, where Vicki was staying with friends. He also mentioned that Vicki had not yet repaid the $300, and Kathy decided to call in and give Kim Nelson the money on her daughter's behalf.

What neither Dennis nor Kathy knew was that the two women were actually lying in wait for Vicki with a .22 rifle belonging to Kim Nelson which had been used in a shooting incident at the Gasometer Hotel in Collingwood a few weeks previously. The weapon had been confiscated by the police, but then returned to Nelson by an officer who subsequently left the force. According to Kathy, 'he went white when I accused him about it later.'

Unsuspectingly Dennis and Kathy made their way to the flat.

The lifts were out, and we walked up a flight of stairs, and I knocked at the door. Kim and Keryn called out: 'Who is it?' 'It's me, Kathy, I've got the money for you.' I had it in my hand. I hear: 'Is the safety on?' and I'm thinking they mean the door. I'm standing facing Dennis, and I had a pair of wedgie shoes on, maybe if I hadn't had them on, it might have gone over my head, or it could have gone right into my brain. And I feel the hit. It's a quarter to nine at night. And I look at Dennis and say: 'I've been shot.' He said: 'Don't be fucking stupid.' I can see my eye on his shirt, his T-shirt. I can feel the blood pumping out of my head. I know enough about first aid, having had all those kids, to lay down, keep quiet, keep calm. With that Lex came, he must have heard the shot from the next floor up. Somebody must have rung the police and the ambulance. The ambulance came and they spoke to me and said: 'What's your age, date of birth and all that?' and I told them, and then they put me out.

Before that Lex is going crook at the police: 'Leave my mother alone.' And they thought I was going to die anyway. Kim and Keryn were waiting for Vicki to come, to shoot her, because she hadn't paid back the $300. They didn't believe me when I said I'd brought the money, so they shot me anyway. I got to know who pulled the trigger. It was Keryn, but it was Kim Nelson's gun. They meant to shoot someone through the door, it didn't go off by accident. Anyway, they hid the gun under the baby's mattress in the cot. I'm within minutes of death in the hospital, and all that shit. And I had about six different operations, plastic surgery to do up the hole. I had a piece of chicken tendon to keep my eye stitched to my head, because when I'm asleep it's still open.

While she was waiting to be operated on after being rushed to hospital, police were at Kathy's side. 'I don't know what I said to them,' she claims, 'but it was a dying statement. Then Lex told them to piss off.' Whatever it was Kathy said, Nelson and Thompson were soon arrested and appeared in court charged with attempted murder and other offences. During one of her court appearances nine days after the shooting, Nelson caused a furore in court when she was refused bail. 'Okay, so I'm a known prostitute, but that doesn't mean I can't have bail,' she said, adding that she had a seventeen-year-old daughter, a dog and a cat to look after at home. Magistrate Alexander Vale still refused her request. 'Thanks for listening, you mug,' she screamed from the dock. 'I hope you rot in hell.'

Between surgery, Kathy lay in state in her hospital room, decked out in floral splendour.

Painters and dockers used to bring in flowers, out of respect for my sons. Every time I came back from an operation the room was full of flowers. There was a rort on with the flowers. I'd hate to have died because it was like a big bloody funeral parlour, every bloody room I was in. 'Cos they looked in the phone book, get a name, you could do it in those days, get away with it, send flowers under false names. They did it every day, the prostitutes, everybody I knew.

Kim's and Keryn's fellows had come in and brought flowers. The minute I could get out of bed I went to the phone with the drip in my arm and I rang the gaol and said to tell the girls they're sweet. I just wanted them to know I was alive and well, and everything would be sweet. That was our code. And that gave them a chance to get bail. If I was to die they wouldn't have got bail.'

Kathy remained in hospital for a fortnight before signing herself out, still so sick she had to go back in for further treatment. Despite this she drove her car to a hotel in Preston to visit friends. 'The minute I walked in with my head all bandaged, they all stood up and clapped. It was a crims' pub. They were just glad to see me alive.'

Kathy lay low during the lengthy period between the shooting and the attempted murder trial. She knew she was the main prosecution witness, but hoped to avoid appearing. She later realised how naive this was.

I was in and out of the parlour in Stephenson Street, Richmond. I'd go in the front and out the back and they'd come looking for me to go to court.

While I was waiting for the trial I flew back from Sydney

and Mad Dog Murphy [ex Victorian police officer Brian Murphy] *was on security duty at Tullamarine. He said: 'I'll give you a lift home.' I said: 'You don't know where I live.' He drove me right to me fucking door. I shit myself. Here I am thinking they don't know where I live. I finally got to court and I said to Kim: 'Tell the barrister not to put shit on me for being a prostitute and all that fucking shit, and you'll be sweet.' Then I saw the police photos of myself laying there, and all that blood. God I got a shock. I didn't say much in evidence. I was all for them. I said it was just an accident. I got 'em off. They were both acquitted. Afterwards Kim Nelson said to me: 'And now I'll have the $300.' And I said to her: 'I fucking paid, cunt. I paid.'*

What happened next provides an insight into Kathy's thinking and the unspoken criminal code by which she lives. The prospect of informing on Nelson and Thompson in court was unthinkable: it would have destroyed forever Kathy's reputation in the underworld. But that didn't mean she had to lie down and accept what had happened to her.

Some years later, in a house in Richmond owned by her son Dennis, she had a confrontation with Thompson where she sought to even the score. Dennis, his younger brother Jamie, two men and Thompson were together in a room when one of the men, nicknamed Snaggles, put a gun, albeit playfully, to Dennis's head. Jamie didn't see the funny side, and shot the second man in the leg, causing Snaggles to drop his gun saying: 'Fuck this, youse play for real.'

At this point Kathy walked into the house, saw Thompson and attempted to wrestle the gun from Jamie.

I said: 'Jamie, gimme the gun, gimme the gun, gimme the gun.' It was my opportunity to get even. But she was too fat. We

would've had to cut half of her off to get her into the barrel.*
I couldn't have stood up in court and said: 'This fucking bitch
shot me,' but I could have shot her. We would have got rid of
her. That's the code we live by.

As it happened, Jamie refused to hand over his gun and Kathy
lost her chance. But losing an eye was something she eventually
adapted to, although eighteen years later she still occasionally
misses the sink when washing up and drops a dish on the floor.
But then, as she says, she never experiences double vision after
drinking too much. She received $5,000 compensation for her
injury, but even that didn't help her to forgive Keryn Thompson.

---

* A reference to the disposal of the body of Anton Kenny, one of Dennis's murder
victims, in a barrel.

CHAPTER FOUR

Stone Walls
— Do Not ... —

THE DAY THE MINISTER COMES TO FAIRLEA PRISON FOR HIS inspection they move a bunk into the woman's cell. Previously she has been sleeping in her nightdress on the cold stone floor of the punishment block. As soon as the Minister leaves, so does the bunk. Kathy has found out and, ever the champion of the underdog, is up before a senior prison official, articulating her rage. The prisoner in question has a medical condition, causing a hormonal imbalance. According to Kathy, she shouldn't be in prison at all. And the reason she stabbed the sewing teacher had more to do with her condition and general mistreatment than any particularly malicious intent. That's just the start of the harangue. 'And what about handcuffing her behind her back, and keeping her in her cell twenty-three hours a day? You can't do that, the Geneva Convention . . .'

The senior official looks up coldly at the warder standing beside Kathy, her voice knife-edged with contempt. 'How long has she been down there?' Kathy doesn't allow the warder time to respond. 'Four fucking months, to my knowledge.' The official stands up behind her desk. 'Come with me, I'll fix that.' The trio, official, warder and Kathy troop through the corridors, waiting as doors are unlocked, and stop outside the solitary confinement cell. The official peers through the bars, and orders the warder to unlock the door. 'Get outside!' The woman, vulnerable and frightened in her nightie, steps gingerly across the threshold of the cell. 'Now, back in there.' As the woman, cowed and obedient, does as she's told, the cell doors clang shut again. The official turns to Kathy, her eyes glinting: 'Right, she's been out, hasn't she? Happy now?'

Kathy's internal controls go into overload. She's a whisper away from launching a physical attack on the official. Instead she spits at her feet. Her words come out like sharp-edged flints dipped in venom. Her voice is trembling and hoarse with emotion: 'You fucking thing. You get fucked every day by your fucking dog. Up the arse.' That's for now. For the next sixteen days Kathy goes on hunger strike, doesn't eat a morsel, and loses over twelve kilos. And for the rest of her stay every time she passes the board bearing the staff list of prison officials, she spits squarely on the woman's name. Today she says: 'The rat, the fucking dog, she'll never forget me.'

For a woman of her reputation and standing in the underworld, Kathy has spent remarkably little time in prison—less than two years in total. The first forty of her sixty years of life, in fact, were spent as a cleanskin. She has no real horror of losing her freedom; she regards imprisonment as 'just another part of life', and counts among her happiest memories the good times she has shared in Fairlea and Pentridge Prisons.

The individual cell in which Kathy, like all prisoners, was locked each night provided her with a sanctuary, and clearly represented a form of peace and privacy from the outside pressures of Dennis and the family.

I was so pleased I had been in Pentridge. I was so pleased I had been through what my kids had been through. Now I know

what it's like. Much better than Fairlea. You get locked up at
twenty past four. The door closes, you're on your own, you've
got your own room, your own TV. I used to think it was
grouse.

It was while she was working in the massage parlours that Kathy
first came before the courts. In March 1975, at the age of thirty-
nine, she was fined $40 for indecent language, but both the
conviction and sentence were quashed on appeal six months
later. As she recalls the episode:

Well the constable or who ever came said something, and I went
to close the door and he kicked the door and it hit me in the
knee, and I swore: 'Fuck you!' So, indecent language, right,
and he puts me in the van. I appealed against the $40 because
I was in the end flat of the block and how could people have
heard? It was quashed.

So it wasn't until she was forty that her criminal record began.
By this time her son Dennis, sixteen years her junior, had already
amassed convictions for rape, assault and a multitude of lesser
offences. He and his brother Peter were then in prison serving
sentences of ten and fourteen years respectively.

Kathy's first real conviction came in February 1976, when,
under the name Lee Kirk (one of her many aliases) she was fined
$60 for using premises (The Black Rose) for prostitution. Four
months later she received her first prison sentence—three
months for harbouring a known criminal, Joe Tongalini.

I knew Joe Tongalini from when he was in Beechworth gaol, a
good bloke, staunch. I don't know what he was in for, you never
ask that, you never, it's bad form unless they're willing to tell
you. He used to mow the lawns at the gaol, and he told me he
wanted to see his parents 'cos they were old or something, very

ill. I had the parlour in West Melbourne, and he come there, and I sent him down to the butcher's shop, and he got some osso bucco. I cooked that, and then the cops kicked the door in.

Today she has no memory of fear or shame at the moment sentence was pronounced. The three months was reduced, on appeal, to two weeks, and she served just nine days in Fairlea.

Okay, I didn't know what to expect when I first went into gaol, but I wasn't scared. The message had already gone into Fairlea from Dennis and Peter to look after their Mum. As soon as I got in there a big tall thing in overalls, I didn't know if it was a man or a woman, came up to me and said: 'Have you got any weed?'

'No,' I said, so she got me a packet, and I tried to roll a cigarette, but I didn't smoke. She said: 'You ain't smoking cigars now, Kathy.' And she rolled me a little skinny cigarette, we used to call them greyhounds. By the end of nine days I was able to give her everything back she'd given me.

The same year, 1976, she faced other charges of unlawful possession, unlicensed driving, assault, hindering police and using premises for habitual prostitution. The offences arose from an incident when she and a friend without a driving licence were picked up while he was driving Kathy's car. 'Yeah, I probably hit the cops, but they always throw that in anyway,' she laughs.

The following year, 1977, she was back inside. This time the offence was obtaining property by deception, involving a cheque book and $4,000. She received fourteen months, with a minimum of two months. Six years passed before Kathy's next prison term, but in the interim period she was fined $125 on charges of indecent language and using premises for prostitution. In March 1983 she received twenty-eight days for five charges of assault and assault by kicking, but the prison term was reduced on appeal to a fine.

I was a bit drunk and we went to the Whittlesea swimming pool right on closing time. They accepted our money and Vicki jumped in the pool with her clothes on. Next thing there was a whistle and this butch lesbian and a couple of blokes that looked after the pool comes down. So that was it. The police handcuffed me and had me in the office. They nearly broke my arm putting the handcuffs on behind me back, because I was kicking 'em with bare feet.

The cops put me in the divvy van, and I screamed out to everybody coming out of the pool: 'That lesbian in there attacked me.' I said it was PMT [pre-menstrual tension] because that had just come out. The jack [detective] laughed and he said: 'I'm not putting that down.' I said: 'Well, it's true.' I got to the court case, right, and I said: 'Where's the old bloke that I'm supposed to have kicked nearly to death?' The jack said: 'He's in hospital, he's had a heart attack.' By the time it come to the case he was dead, not from me. They only give me four weeks because I had to mind Lindy and Jade [Kathy's granddaughters].

In March 1984 she was fined for possession, as a prohibited person, of an unlicensed pistol, a magnum, and three months later she was fined $150 for assault on police.

The Enforcer [Dennis's principal minder] was there at Stephenson Street sitting on a gun, and I'm ironing, right? And Victor and Trevor's there. Well there was a raid and the police tipped The Enforcer's chair up, and the bloody thing falls out. So I'm waiting for someone to take it. Well Victor and Trevor didn't step forward, and neither did The Enforcer, and the cop said: 'Your house, your gun, you're going.' And I'm ironing.

So Victor comes in and bails me out for $500. Trevor'd hit someone over the head with the gun in the morning, and forgot to tell me, and they've run in at lunchtime and arrested me.

She was sentenced twice in 1986 for possession of a firearm, and drug offences. She and Trevor were charged with possession and trafficking of eight ounces of heroin, with a street value of $200,000, dug up by police in the backyard of 35 Stephenson Street, Richmond, one of a number of houses purchased by Dennis from the proceeds of his drug dealing. When the cases came to court, the trafficking charges were dropped, and Kathy received an eight-month gaol sentence, and Trevor, then aged twenty-two, was sent down for seven months. Each time she spent five months of her sentence behind bars.

Three years later she was on committal on charges of conspiring to traffic heroin, trafficking in heroin, and possession of heroin. Police had kept the Stephenson Street houses under surveillance during January 1988 and as a result raided the premises, allegedly finding heroin and cannabis. Trevor, who was living there with Kathy at the time, was also charged.

When Kathy came before the Magistrates Court for the committal in March 1989 all charges against her were dropped. The magistrate sitting accepted there was no evidence against her.

Most recently, in 1993, Kathy faced fifteen charges, including six of trafficking in a drug of dependence and possession of a pistol. These were eventually whittled down to one count each of trafficking in heroin, amphetamines and cannabis. She received an eighteen-month sentence, half of it suspended for two years. She served the remainder.

So, despite being a relative stranger to the system, Kathy enjoys respect both from inmates and, in many cases, from prison authorities, from governor level on down. This attitude is caused by her prevailing optimism:

Look, you see it was easier for me 'cos I was older and I didn't have to worry about children. That's the real killer, not knowing what your kids are up to. I didn't have that. The other thing, what's the good of being morose and sad. You can still have fun in there.

The other positives Kathy has on her side are her pride in any work she is given behind bars, and her consistent support for the vulnerable—the weak or elderly who are all too often seen as fair game and preyed upon by other prisoners.

This is illustrated by her last physical encounter in 1994, when she was fifty-nine. Kathy has never denied she has a fearsome temper, and that her lack of ability to control its periodic outbursts has consistently caused trouble for her and considerable suffering for those on the receiving end. But sometimes that suffering can be deserved.

Margaret Raby was one of the more tragic cases to come before a Victorian court in recent years. On 22 November 1994, fifty-one-year-old Raby was sentenced to gaol by Mr Justice Bernard Teague, sitting in the Supreme Court, after a jury found her guilty of stabbing her husband to death. The charge was manslaughter, and the circumstances leading to Raby's decision to end her forty-six-year-old husband's life came after weeks of physical, psychological and sexual abuse at his hands.

Raby, a state registered nurse from Keilor, had originally pleaded not guilty to murdering Keith Raby on 6 October 1993. But when the charge was reduced to manslaughter she was convicted and gaoled for twenty-eight months with a minimum of seven. Because of time already spent behind bars awaiting trial, she was ordered to serve only an additional fourteen days.

Raby had been married to Keith for only eleven weeks, but

his previous wife gave evidence of twenty years of abuse at his hands. Starting on their honeymoon, Raby raped, beat and tortured his second wife, Margaret, on an almost daily basis. Despite this Margaret Raby loved her newly wed husband 'more than anything in the world.'

So by the time she went into Fairlea awaiting her trial on a murder charge, Margaret was middle-aged, terrified, grief-stricken, and entering an environment about which she knew nothing. She also weighed a little over forty kilos and was four feet ten inches (147 cm) tall. 'I was on my own, I didn't know why I was there,' she says. 'Prison is a world within a world, it's so alienating. I didn't know what to do. There was not much kindness.'

Like other prisoners Margaret was supplied with two pairs of tracksuit pants and other prison garments. But this didn't stop her trying to maintain some brave semblance of life on the outside. She insisted on washing one pair of tracksuit pants every day, so she always had a clean pair, and she refused to wash her clothing in a machine being used at the same time by other prisoners. This, inevitably, led to trouble.

Margaret was taking an educational course from 9a.m. to noon at the time, and one morning had her clothes in the wash when the course started. A young prisoner called Linda agreed to her request to put them in the drier for her when they were finished. But when Margaret returned from her lessons her clothing was still in the washing machine. Unwisely she made a derogatory comment about Linda, not realising she was within earshot.

'She was in a cubicle and heard me. She jumped me, grabbed me by the throat, and threw me up against the door. That's what my husband used to do. She thumped me and yelled and swore. All I could do was to run out and hide in the kitchen under the table. I crouched down.'

Later Linda overheard Margaret talking on the phone to her

lawyer, mentioning the attack. The result was a second beating. By now Margaret had been in Fairlea for a month, and unknown to her, Kathy was about to join her. 'Kathy was so gentle. She said: "I'll look after you. We'll show them, love." I was in a cottage with Kathy to look after me. Nobody ever questioned Kathy. It wasn't so much that they were frightened of her, I think it was respect for her. She grew ten foot tall if she was provoked. It put me off limits to people like Linda, it was well known, and it made me feel a lot better. I didn't do much without Kathy, she taught me who was okay to talk to.'

Kathy was aware Linda had been standing over Margaret, and let her know the violence must end. Linda ignored this and assaulted Margaret again. Then she sent a message to Kathy which became the final straw. Kathy's cooking was popular with prisoners, and their favourite dish was her corned beef and cabbage with mustard sauce, which she generally prepared for Sunday evening's meal. Linda's messenger told Kathy the girls were fed up with her corned beef and didn't want it. Kathy snapped, and launched a vicious attack on Linda, who was half her age, and much larger and fitter.

Me brain snapped. I'd put up with months of this tart, and I ran down from my bedroom, and I jumped over the couch, how I did it I don't fucking know.

I took a running leap down the passage. Well, I got stuck into her and I blacked out, and I remember the girls pulling me off. I knew she'd done that to Margaret. If the girls hadn't pulled me off her I wasn't finished with her. I wouldn't have killed her, but I would've given her the best hiding she'd ever had. And I said to the thing: 'My fucking name's not Margaret Raby either.'

Well the next morning on the muster line she's got a big black eye. I give it to her, but I got pulled off. So this lady screw says to me: 'Do you know who gave Linda a black eye?'

I said: 'No.' She said: 'Well, pat 'em on the back.' And I never said another word, but the whole gaol knew.

Kathy and Margaret were together for six months in Fairlea, but later, when Margaret served her last two weeks, Kathy had been released:

> She used to write to me, and send cards telling me: 'Keep your chin up, it's not for ever, you will be home soon.' When she was on the outside she always made a point of making sure people got cards at their birthdays and Christmas.
>
> I think she is the most wonderful person. She guided me the right way, she told me what would happen at the trial. When I went to court, or even the dentist, she would come to the gate with me, and see me through the gate. She was like a mother. I love her like a mother, a friend, and everything else.

Another point Margaret remembers about Kathy was that she always found out when a new prisoner was due to arrive, and would make contact early on and, if they were newcomers to gaol, would offer to teach them the ropes.

Kathy's hunger strike in 1977 over the treatment of the prisoner in solitary confinement was an incident that won her widespread approval among inmates, and, unofficially, among a percentage of prison officers at the time. The author visited Kathy at the end of her period without food, and can testify to the extent to which it cost her, both physically and emotionally.

But it wasn't the discomfort that finally came close to breaking Kathy. It was the loss of privileges, or one in particular—the right to see her children.

THE MATRIARCH

*This Mothers' Day, in particular, I wasn't allowed to have
visitors, and I could see them coming with the flowers and that.
As you know you could bring flowers in those days, until
people started to put the smack and that in them. And I'm left
there in this dormitory and there's nine beds in it. If I could
have got a sheet over that beam I would have hung meself that
day, I was that upset. Because I couldn't see me kids.*

In 1986, the year Kathy finally made it to Pentridge, the Federal
Government instituted a drive against social security fraud. A
number of recently arrived immigrants, who had attempted to
gain illegal payments shortly after their arrival in their new
country, were flushed out and convicted, and ended up in the
women's division at Pentridge.

*I get called up to the office, and I think: 'What have I fucking
done now?' And the chief is there pulling his hair out, and he
says: 'They're [the social security frauds] all yours.' And I
said: 'What do you mean they're all mine?' He said: 'You look
after 'em.' I said: 'I don't have to, but all right—I want eight
new mop heads.' He said: 'Eight new mop heads?' I said: 'All
right, you mind 'em yourself.' So I get the eight mop heads, fix
'em on the handles and give 'em out to the new ones and stand
'em in a row and say: 'Come on, let's make out we're an army.'
I get 'em in a kitchen and we scrub the floor and things like
that. And we'd have a lot of laughs, it wasn't all sorrow, right?
You had a lot of fun.*

After the dole cheats, the next new arrival to come under Kathy's
wing was a Chinese girl convicted of bringing a kilo of heroin
into Australia. She couldn't speak a word of English, and Kathy
instantly felt sorry for her because of her treatment at the hands
of customs officers who had removed the heroin from where it
was taped to her body. 'She was still red raw. My heart went

72

out to her.' Kathy christened her Suzi Wong and embarked on her education.

The first word Suzi learnt was 'screw'. Kathy took one from the hardware section, showed it to Suzi and mouthed the word, and then pointed to the nearest prison officer. There were hitches, however, as Suzi began to pick up the language. Kathy had insisted she stand up for herself, and not jump when the prison officers summoned her. So, for weeks, every time an officer spoke to her, Suzi would respond fiercely: 'What do you?' 'No, no, no, Suzi, "What do you WANT?" ' Kathy would shout in the background.

Kathy preferred Pentridge to Fairlea.

At Fairlea you have to listen to everyone else's problems. I mean you have girls come in screaming all night. They'd be screaming and knocking on the doors. The screw would sing out: 'What number?' and we'd all be listening, 'cos we had a rule: after you got your medication that was it . . . go to sleep. So we'd hear: 'What number?' and they'd sing out. And next morning we'd get 'em. Give 'em a biffing.

It was while she was in Fairlea that Kathy received some unusual medical advice.

Olivia Newton-John's brother was there. So he's told me to get my frustrations out by standing on the football field and screaming out. So I used to. I'd stand there and scream out: 'Vegemite!' at the top of me voice. Well screws would come running from everywhere with their walkie talkies. They didn't know what was going on. When I was leaving they said: 'Why did you do that?' I said: 'Because Dr Newton-John told me to.' They said: 'I wish he'd fucking told us.'

Possibly Kathy's proudest prison memory of all is of the time

73

during her last spell inside, in 1993, when she brought close to 100 Fairlea prisoners out on strike.

> We got a message over the loudspeaker about 3.30 that the shop wouldn't be open for cigarettes, and we were all without. So I said: 'I've had enough of this, I'm calling the whole gaol out.' And my girlfriend Julie, she said to me: 'They won't go out.' So I went around to all the houses and cottages and everything, and I said: 'Listen, we're having a strike until we get our cigarettes, right?' With that every one of us sat on the road [running through the gaol linking buildings] *even the ones that didn't smoke, and we wouldn't get locked up.*
>
> So we're all sitting in the road, and everybody came from everywhere, and even Julie was astonished that I had the power to bring everybody out. So little Margaret Raby's sitting next to me, and the next minute an officer who's pretty reasonable comes down, and he says: 'What's the problem?' and I said: 'Well, you told me you'd see what you could do.'
>
> And the next minute I felt meself bodily lifted up, the girls got behind me and I was the spokesperson. So the officer and I walk towards the front and on the way to the office I said to him: 'Listen, I'm not going down the slot for this am I?' And he said: 'No way, Kathy.' He said: 'This is an honest request.'
>
> So in the meantime the girls have been locked up. I thought to myself: 'The top governor, Governor Moreland, I'll let him stand over me.' So I sat in the seat in his office and he said: 'Why are you all congregated downstairs looking up here?' and I said: 'The officer told us to wait there.' He said: 'Well I was in a meeting.' And then he said: 'Well, it's my fault. Give 'em all a packet of Peter Jackson.' The officer would have given them to us anyway, if Moreland wasn't on.
>
> So with that I go back, I knock on every cottage door, and I said: 'We're getting the smokes.' And big cheers went up and everything, and I get inside, and little Margaret Raby said to

me—who's killed her husband, right?—she said to me: 'It's the most exciting day of my life.' I thought to meself: If that's all . . . you know, the poor thing.

Among Kathy's most prized possessions from her days behind bars are what are probably the only two surviving copies of *The Fairlea Arrow*, a weekly magazine named after Queensland's legendary country and western singer.* At least a dozen editions of the magazine were published, each with Kathy's name as editor, on the front cover. Complete with recipes, horoscopes, weather forecasts, crossword puzzles, beauty tips and letters, the magazines have an over-riding flavour of optimism. Somehow they seem to sum up perfectly Kathy's attitude to life in gaol.

---

* Fairlie Arrow was a little-known Gold Coast nightclub singer who sprang to national prominence in December 1991 when she faked her own abduction. Fairlie, then twenty-eight, was fined $5,000 and ordered to pay police the $18,000 costs for their investigation into the bogus kidnapping.

CHAPTER FIVE

– Going Down –

JUST ANOTHER NIGHT AT THE GASLIGHT MASSAGE PARLOUR AT 108 Stephenson Street, Richmond. The usual collection of half-drunk, middle-aged desperates queuing for an empty. Exchanging their last few crumpled dollars for the promise of the unknown. Not romance, not love. Just the unknown, undiscovered flesh and unsmelled scent of a stranger. 'Fucking thrillseekers,' Kathy grins to herself as she watches through the evening as they shuffle out afterwards, the inevitable shroud of disappointment and disillusion hanging over them. But then Kathy can afford to grin. She's the madam, and only rarely takes a tumble herself. She's responsible for neither the illusion that brings them there, nor the disappointment that always marks their leaving.

It's 1 a.m., and time to lock the doors. As she passes through the front gate and walks briskly up the dark street to her home at 35 Stephenson Street, she decides to drop in nearby at 86 Chestnut Street to see what Dennis is up to. It's still relatively early, and he's been up speeding for days; he certainly won't be in bed. As Kathy lets herself in, unlocking the front door with her key, the normal wall of sound, Bob Marley jacked all the way up, hits her like a warm, sticky breath of Jamaican air. As she heads for the kitchen she first catches sight of the young boy who had called round at the parlour earlier in the evening. Couldn't be more than twenty-one, and not bad-looking. Said he was a mate of Dennis, and it was okay to get a freebie with one of the girls. But he isn't looking so cocksure now, lying on the kitchen floor.

Apart from the stainless steel meat cleaver embedded in the back of his head and the dried blood congealed around his hairline, he is half-naked and curled in a foetal position. Kathy knows she's going to throw up if she doesn't hit the bathroom quickly. As she turns sharply back out of the kitchen doorway she feels her stomach heave involuntarily. In through the bathroom door, groping for the light switch and there's the toilet. Her skin feels clammy as she rests her elbows on the porcelain lid, propping her head on her fingers. And then she takes in her surroundings, and the churning in her stomach erupts into the bowl beneath her. The walls, floor and even part of the ceiling are a crimson tapestry. 'Fucking abattoir!' The words come out involuntarily between the heaving, panting breaths she is taking. The screen on the side of the bath is shattered and shards of glass litter the floor. Mechanically, and without thinking further than the need to do something about the mess, Kathy leaves the room to return moments later with a mop.

As she begins to wash up and down the walls, she knows two things beyond doubt. One is that this is Dennis's handiwork, and the other is that she won't get out of here until it's over. He loves an audience at times like this.

The bathroom walls are as clean as they're going to be tonight, and she heads back towards the kitchen to get a brush and pan for the broken glass before she tackles the worst of the gore smeared across the floor. As she passes the boy's inert form she notices his tracksuit trousers crumpled beside him on the kitchen floor. She remembers them from earlier when he visited the parlour. They'd looked like new. She knows what's happening. Dennis and a couple of his 'soldiers' are in the lounge drinking and shooting up speed. They're going to knock [kill] the boy, they're just taking their time, having a drink in between.

Kathy opens the door to the lounge, and without looking at Dennis tells him: 'Don't burn the tracksuit. I'll wash it out and give it to Jamie.'

Not long afterwards Kathy hears Dennis and the soldiers grunting and cursing in the kitchen, as they lift the boy to his feet and drag him to the bathroom. She steps into the hall and asks one of the soldiers what is going on.

'He spied on Den having a fuck a coupla hours ago. We're making sure he won't do it again.'

Must have been after he left the parlour, Kathy thinks to herself, spotting the bloodied meat cleaver where it lies in the hall. At least that's not going into the bathroom. This time the beating continues for the best part of half an hour. From the sounds coming through the closed door they're using their fists, or maybe gun butts. When it's over and they've left the room, Kathy goes in again, tries hard to ignore the boy's moaning, bubbling sounds, and starts to mop the walls and floor again.

By now it's three in the morning and the anger is building inside Kathy. She's had enough, but knows better than to challenge Dennis at a time like this. Instead she pulls the boy half-upright and splashes cold water from the bathroom sink onto the raw meat of his face. Somehow she manages to get him out, past the closed loungeroom door on the other side of which the soldiers and Dennis are drinking and talking. She half-drags him into the kitchen, opens the back door and pushes the boy into the yard.

'Get out,' she hisses in his ear. 'Get going. Or else you'll be dead.'

She can see he's never going to make it across the yard unaided, let alone out into the alley. He's dressed only in underpants, but there's no time to worry about that. Once again she pushes and carries him in the direction of the gate, pulls it open and shoves him onto the hard bluestone cobbles of the alley.

A nd how he got home just in his underpants, I don't know. But I didn't want him to die. I saved one. And Dennis and the two soldiers didn't see me. So for about an hour they didn't miss him, and they never did find out it was me let him go. By this time I don't know what happened to him. And then I got told later on that he'd become nearly a vegetable. He could still walk and that, but his mind was gone. And I was pleased that I let him go. To me it was stupid, stupid. I know he came from Ascot Vale. Probably an acquaintance of Dennis, or maybe a boy that just got out of gaol or something, I don't know.

Dennis had been having sex in his bedroom and the boy was spying on him through the door. That was it. I felt sick. To me I was disgusted. And that's when I started to turn against him. I didn't say anything. Every few minutes he was injecting himself with speed, and you can't comment on someone when they're drunk and on that, no you can't. There was one occasion when he tried to shoot me, because he didn't know who I was in his mind. He was even going to shoot a crossbow into Victor. And he didn't pull the trigger. Mental. And that's when I decided to kill him. I said that when they interviewed me on A Current Affair.

The events detailed above, horrific as they are, were nothing out of the ordinary during the years between July 1982, when Dennis moved to establish his empire in the back streets of Richmond, and his death in April 1987. Kathy's life at Richmond revolved almost exclusively around Dennis. Their relationship had had many aspects—mother and son, brother and sister, partners in crime—but it was always intense and almost claustrophobically close.

This four-and-a-half year period marked the flowering of pure evil within Dennis Bruce Allen. The term mass murderer has rarely been used in reference to him, but that is what he became. Once Kathy asked a homicide squad officer if he believed Dennis was a serial killer and he replied: 'Not really, there's no pattern, Dennis just killed when he felt like it.' Nobody is sure how many killings he was responsible for; the police have claimed as many as thirteen, Kathy believes there were less. The real truth will certainly never be known.

Taking into account as many of the facts that can still be assembled, there were probably five or six slayings for which Dennis was directly responsible, and another four or five in which he was involved—either as an accomplice or simply by paying for someone else to take care of business.

Then there were the ones that got away, like the boy Kathy helped to escape. There seems little doubt that Dennis enjoyed inflicting pain on others and often turned the procedure into a form of ritual—beginning the torture and then breaking for a drink or another hit of speed before resuming. People, women and men alike, were sometimes kept chained for up to four days, during which they were systematically tortured.

Possibly the only point to be made in mitigation, the only faintly redeeming feature in this litany of violence is that Dennis chose most of his victims from within his own peer group. Reggie and Ronnie Kray, London's infamous twin founding fathers of violent, standover crime, always boasted that their unspeakable cruelties were inflicted only on other members of the criminal classes. If he were still here today, incarcerated forever in some Australian equivalent of Broadmoor where Ronnie ended his days, Dennis could justifiably have made the same claim.

So what made him the monster he had become by the early 1980s when the killings started in earnest? And what were the influences leading to his decline.'

Harry Allen, whom Dennis knew as a father from the age of

three to eighteen, is a frail, sweet-natured man in his seventies and has never recovered from the heartbreak of losing his partner Gladys three years ago. His memories of Dennis are coloured by the love he still obviously feels for him. That and a bewildered sense of disbelief that the young boy he brought up could have become a sadistic killer. It's not that Harry can't accept the dark side of Dennis's nature, just that he can't come to terms with other people's refusal to believe there was a gentle, loving child somewhere in there as well. He clings to the good memories and, initially at least, there were many.

> Dennis was about three when he first come to us, and he lived permanently with us all the time from three on. He was a good boy when he was little, very affectionate. We always had a good Christmas for 'em. Kathy and her other kids would come. They always had plenty for Christmas. They got bikes one year, footballs and things like that, cricket sets. He'd come and give you a hug. We were a close family, very close.

Harry would take Dennis ferreting in the paddocks at the back of Carrum. They had two ferrets, and if the rabbits escaped from the nets placed across their burrows Dennis would chase them across the rough ground. 'He'd catch 'em, more often than not. That's how fast he was.'

When Dennis first started to get into trouble, Harry refused to believe it. 'The police come around to the house, and I reckoned it must have been someone else they were on about. He would have been about twelve or thirteen, I suppose.'

Dennis's earliest troubles involved minor, petty affairs including assault, wilful damage—his first conviction in September 1968—indecent language, unlicensed driving and stealing from local schools. But there was an almost instant escalation. His reputation as a violent streetfighter was spreading. He was soon stealing cars, then he recorded three drunk driving convictions in one twelve-month period in Frankston, Sunbury and Footscray, and still later he was bashing people who tried to stand in his way, and finally he was caught in possession of a firearm.

The response of the courts was, understandably, to increase the penalties imposed each time. After fines and probation came the boys' homes, Turana and Malmsbury, and then Pentridge by the age of eighteen. When he was there he was attacked and savagely beaten with an iron bar by three men, including Jimmy Loughnan, who was to die in the fire in the Jika Jika wing of the prison in October 1987. Then shortly before his twenty-first birthday he narrowly avoided conviction on a rape charge, the lesser offence of unlawful carnal knowledge of a girl under sixteen earning him a two-year good behaviour bond. The fourteen-year-old girl involved, who cannot be named for legal reasons, later became involved in a de facto relationship with him and bore him a son.

His early problems stemmed from an obsession with cars. When he was as young as twelve or thirteen he would help out in nearby Frankston at a panel beating business, a job that Harry remembers made him as 'strong as an ox'. He would work late and take a car for a run after his co-workers had all gone home. He received his first custodial sentence, in October 1969, for unlicensed driving. Says Harry:

> We had a go at him over it, but they put him in Turana. I think that was pinching cars. It never helped him any, in there, to tell you the truth. He was a boy, let's put it this way, he couldn't be locked up. When he come home he told us about the hours they used to lock 'em up and that. He was a bit of a wild boy, like, he liked his freedom. He used to jump off the Carrum bridge into the Patterson River, about forty feet, just to prove he could do it.

As Dennis moved into his mid-teens, the darker, more violent side of his nature began to emerge. His problems with the police were becoming worse, and both Gladys and Harry began to suffer.

It knocked the wife around a lot, upset her, his troubles. I used to get into him about it, but he was that big of a boy he'd stand up and fight me. Gladys used to give him a bit of a whack with the broom stick. From about fourteen on he stood up to me. He put me in hospital once, about a fortnight I think. I was black and blue. I tried to stop him from going out, actually. I said: 'You're not going out.' He just turned around and he said: 'I effin' well am.' And I went to grab him, like, to take him inside, and that's when he took to me, punched me about and kicked me. When he come down and seen me in hospital he said: 'I'm sorry I done it to you, Dad.' I still loved him, I thought the world of him. I let it by. It was more or less temper with him. He had a vile temper.'

One bizarre train of events happened when Dennis's violent behaviour became too much. Harry and Gladys had moved with the two boys to the suburb of Ascot Vale.

I got sick and tired of him standing over me. I kept going crook at him and that, and he'd take to me. So we moved out, but we only went five houses down the same street, and he found us. One of his mates put him onto us.

Later, when the family was living in Richmond, Harry again found himself on the wrong side of Dennis's temper. He was brutally mistreating one of his guard dogs in his home in Chestnut Street, when Harry told him to leave the animal alone. But, says Harry, 'He took to me and give me a hiding—he said to mind me own business.'

Harry readily accepted Kathy and Dennis's way of life. Once

THE MATRIARCH

Dennis was in Beechworth Prison, deprived, he felt, of female company for too long. He had been granted a four-hour leave, and Kathy hatched a plot with Harry and Gladys. They drove up to Beechworth in separate cars. When Dennis drove out of the gaol for his leave, Harry and Gladys told him Kathy couldn't make it. But as they drove on, they saw a car parked by the side of the road. Perched on the roof were two prostitutes, and on the bonnet was a sign reading: 'Only twenty dollars.' Kathy was sitting by the roadside.

> *The car stopped that quick, he backed up and jumped out, he was that glad to see us. Then we had to sit in a room in the motel looking at one another like dills while he had his fun in the next room. And the fat girl went and robbed the motel as well. We got him a fat one and a skinny one. I didn't know what sort he liked.*

Harry's explanation of why Dennis's life went so seriously off the rails hinges on his early contact with the police.

I think it was the police down Carrum, meself. The Frankston police. They rode 'em into the ground, Dennis and Peter. They knocked 'em around. Dennis and Peter couldn't walk up the street without the police car going past and picking 'em up. They just had a set for them. Any trouble or that, they'd come down to my place, and my boys wouldn't be nowhere in the vicinity even. There was one time they took him down to the station, and I went down there, and I nearly got pinched meself. The police were supposed to have belted him up. Dennis told us over the counter, like. I nearly got pinched for having a go at the coppers. They give him a hiding in Frankston lock-up, and the wife and I are standing on the opposite side of the wall and we could hear Dennis screaming out. They was belting him around. We charged in, like.

By now Dennis's good looks were earning the attentions of the opposite sex. One of his first girlfriends was Kerry, and Dennis had one of his first tattoos done in her honour. It was on his chest and read 'The Brute', his pet name for her. 'He was really rapt in her,' Harry recalls. 'Fight like a man, she could. They went out a couple of years, he was pretty keen, and then he just brushed her aside, that was it.'

It was in October 1973, when Dennis was not quite twenty-two, that his potential for cruel and violent mayhem was first fully realised. He took young Peter, still only twenty, and two other men, Allan Rudd and Billy Webb, on a rampage that began in a flat in the bayside suburb of Sandringham and ended in a ten-year sentence for Dennis and a crushing fourteen-year term for Peter.

Born in January 1953, Peter was taken with Dennis while still a toddler to live with their grandmother Gladys and Harry Allen in Carrum. Harry believes that without Dennis's influence Peter could have carved himself out a career in law—an opinion not as biased as it might sound.

'Peter tried to keep up with Dennis,' Harry says. 'They were very close, and he started going off the rails as well. But he was a very clever boy. He would have made a good living as a lawyer. Frank Galbally [a prominent Melbourne laywer] said he was worth training as an articled clerk.' Kathy remembers purchasing $500 worth of law books for him to study in his cell in the 1980s. 'When he used to go into the Supreme Court his arms would be full of books, and he was handcuffed,' she says. 'All the screws would be carrying books for him as well. All the barristers used to go in and listen to him argue.'

It's true that on the many occasions Peter was to defend himself in court, prosecuting counsel who treated him as a pushover have had reason to rue their caution. He is generally considered to be the most intelligent of Kathy's children, but in the last twenty-three years has enjoyed less than twelve months of full liberty. Whether or not this appalling waste of a life is due to his older brother's influence is a moot point. It was not mere chance that he was dealt with much more severely than Dennis over the Sandringham episode in 1973.

According to prosecution evidence, they and their two accomplices, armed with knives and a gun, had gone to the flat, where three sisters were living, after having been offered $500 by an underworld contact to shoot the operator of a well-known massage parlour who was a friend of the girls. When the four men arrived, only two of the sisters were home, but they were joined shortly afterwards by the third and her boyfriend.

The plan was to use the three girls to lure the massage parlour operator to the flat, but for some reason he never showed up. Possibly because they were primed for and committed to an act of extreme violence the four men began to take out their frustrations on the three sisters and the boyfriend. Dennis raped the eldest girl and indecently assaulted one of the other two, while Peter joined in the sexual attacks, pistol-whipped the boyfriend and fired a shot which passed through a wall and narrowly missed a baby sleeping in the next room.

Dennis's display of violence was bad enough, but Peter's was worse. The attackers had only one gun between them and according to the four victims Dennis and Peter were arguing throughout for possession of it. Peter finally won. This might suggest that he was the stronger personality of the two, but Kathy's view is more realistic: 'Dennis was more pissed than Peter, that's all.'

The four men then split up. Dennis went to see Kathy at her Housing Commission flat in Northcote and then fled to Sydney with Billy Webb, only to be captured within a fortnight and brought back to Melbourne. Meanwhile, Peter teamed up with Allan Rudd to go on a rampage over the next two days through

Melbourne's eastern and southern suburbs, during which three people were wounded.

First they headed out to Springvale where, with Rudd at the wheel of the MG they were driving, they cut across another car and fired five shots at it, two of them hitting their target. Next they visited a pizza parlour in Glen Iris where Peter subsequently admitted firing a shot into the floor, wounding the proprietor in the foot. The same night the pair went to a flat in Port Melbourne, where witnesses claimed Peter shot a man named John Whittaker in the face.

Early the following morning Peter and Rudd attempted to gatecrash a party in Brighton. Among the guests were members of The Dingoes rock band, including Christopher Stockley and Broderick Smith. Stockley was shot in the back and spent several weeks in hospital. Finally Peter and Rudd, still in the MG, were chased by police into a dead-end street in the dormitory suburb of Dingley, where they were arrested after Rudd aimed two shots at the patrol car and was hit in the shoulder by return fire.

This was serious, big-time crime, much more significant and violent than anything Kathy had ever been involved in, and incurred suitable retribution from the courts. Dennis was given a ten-year sentence on the rape charge, with a minimum of five years, while Peter received what amounted to a total of fourteen years after being convicted of rape, shooting at police to prevent arrest and the wounding of two men. Webb and Rudd received similarly lengthy sentences for their roles in the events of October 1973.

The effect on Kathy was devastating. During the early stages of their trial she tried to deflect her fears with humour. As Peter was led up from the cells at the start of his case she shouted in open court: 'I thought there was a bounty on dingoes. It's two dollars an ear, isn't it?'

By the time the jury in Dennis's case was about to deliver its verdict Kathy suspected the worst and her mood had changed to black rage.

THE MATRIARCH

*Me and Dennis's girlfriend Kerry were going to bash these two
policewomen in the toilet at the court, but then this other one
arrived, built like a brick shithouse. That was the end of that.
I would have had a go, my bloody oath. Just revenge to let my
feelings out, because my temper used to get up shocking in
those days.*

In time, however, she channelled her grief into a determination to give the boys all the support she could muster by never
missing a prison visit.

Peter began serving his sentence at Pentridge before being transferred early in 1976 to the medium-security Beechworth prison
in northern Victoria. The reason for the transfer, which outraged
police, was that threats had been made against his life in Pentridge. Within days of his arrival at Beechworth he was planning
his escape with help from criminal connections on the outside.
By that March he had broken out, in the company of a twenty-
six-year-old armed robber, Donald Marshall.

While on the run, described by police as 'the most dangerous
man in Victoria', he telephoned *Truth* newspaper, where I was
working as news editor. During the twenty-five-minute conversation Peter spoke of his high life as a fugitive, including
meetings with women and drinking sessions.

On a more serious note he claimed police were out to kill him,
even though he had decided to 'end his career as a gunman'. He
was also at pains to absolve Gladys and Harry of any part in his
escape. 'My grandparents weren't involved,' he said emphatically.
'There was a heap of blokes involved, crims, they don't come from
Victoria. I planned it for a few weeks. When I was first transferred
up there I started planning it straightaway.'

He claimed, somewhat unconvincingly, that the main
purpose of his escape was to raise money to finance his appeal

against his conviction. He was incensed about the charge of firing at police to prevent arrest, maintaining that at the time he was alleged to have shot at the arresting officers he had already given himself up and was in custody. 'I am not a bad man,' he protested. 'These people [police] are just trying to paint a bad picture of me because I've just showed them too much contempt in my younger years.'

Peter's freedom was short-lived. He was recaptured in Sydney only days after his escape, but managed to cause more headaches for the police during his extradition to Victoria. Two Melbourne detectives had flown up to accompany him on a commercial flight from Sydney. As the plane prepared to take off Peter began shouting that a bomb had been placed on board. He so terrified the other passengers that he and his escorts were put off the plane and were flown down to Melbourne the following day on a specially chartered flight.

Apart from a quickly revoked period of parole, Peter served eleven years of his fourteen-year stretch, and was finally released in August 1985. He remained at large for only eight months before receiving a thirteen-year sentence on drug-related charges and conspiracy to commit armed robbery.

As for Dennis, the five years from his release in 1977 after serving four years of his ten-year sentence to 1982, when he moved to Richmond, were marked by a further decline into violence and lawlessness. In December 1978 he received three months for harbouring his fourteen-year-old brother Jamie, who had escaped from Turana boys' home, where he was awaiting trial for car theft. Later charges of possessing firearms were added to Dennis's growing list of court appearances. His reputation as a street and pub brawler full of what the underworld admiringly call 'dash' was keeping pace with his convictions.

Typical of this was a fight in which he became involved in 1978 in a pub in Collingwood. It all began as an ordinary fist fight between Dennis and two other men, but quickly escalated.

Starting with a broken billiard cue, Dennis went about his work with enthusiasm and vigour. Then he pulled a gun and fired a shot at one of his assailants, narrowly missing him. What the bullet failed to achieve the gun-butt did, as Dennis viciously pistol-whipped the man around the head, condemning him to a considerable period in hospital.

A second bar fight six months later saw Dennis for once on the receiving end. But the kudos he earned in underworld circles, both for his 'dash' and for his perceived victimisation, almost made the experience worthwhile.

He had been called to a hotel in Frankston, forty kilometres south of Melbourne, where a former girlfriend was reportedly in trouble. Armed with a length of lead piping, he strolled into the bar. Within minutes the place erupted and shots were fired in his direction, then he was clubbed around the head with a rifle. Further shots followed as he lurched outside, bleeding profusely from pellets embedded in his chest. The police arrived shortly afterwards and promptly arrested him for carrying an offensive weapon—the lead piping. No action was taken against whoever had shot and bashed him.

He was later gaoled for six months, but at his successful appeal before Judge Spence in Melbourne County Court he explained: 'I got to the hotel, and was only there for about two or three minutes when this man fired three shots at my table. I was then bashed over the head with the butt of the rifle, which caused me to have stitches later on.' For good measure, he said, he was also shot with a twelve-gauge shotgun outside the hotel.

Allowing the appeal, Judge Spence said: 'Mr Allen has a side to his nature that he takes the law into his own hands, which leads to problems ...'

One of Dennis's friends throughout the 1970s and '80s was John

Grant, chief crime reporter for *Truth* when I was working on the paper.* He had known Dennis since his teens and remembers him as a good mate and drinking partner.

> I first knew him through some friends down in St Kilda. A mate of mine, Billy, worked in the same panel shop Dennis was at when he was a little fellow down at Carrum. By the time he got to Richmond there were changes in him, but only on the outside. He'd become more wealthy, more cunning, more paranoid. The speed—he was addicted to amphetamines—made him spend more freely, I suppose. He promised me a diamond as big as his fingernail. But he died before he delivered.
>
> He bought one bloke a car, did heaps of things for people. He had a fleet of cars at one stage that he used to let everyone drive, mates and associates. He offered me the choice of the fleet one day, all I had to do was come to the police station at Richmond with him. He was going to introduce me as his publicity man. He used to put petrol in my car all the time if I drove him anywhere. That's when he was Mr D—short for his nickname, Mr Death—with all the gold chains, and Freddy Cook the football star in his pocket, one of his closest mates.

One thing John Grant and Dennis had in common was that

---

* It was John Grant who first introduced me to Kathy. At one stage photographs of both John and me were mounted on the wall in the visitors' reception area at Pentridge Prison. Under the two photographs were the words: 'Not to be admitted as visitors under any circumstances.' John and I had gained entry to Pentridge on numerous occasions posing as friends of the prisoners we needed to interview. The resulting stories inevitably embarrassed prison authorities and, further up the ladder, a succession of politicians with responsibility for the system—hence the photographs. Later John was to receive a letter from the office of the then Social Welfare Minister, Walter Jona, banning him from entry to all Victorian prisons. When John showed it to him, Dennis asked: 'Can you make it transferable?'

they'd both been bashed by police in their younger days. The pair would meet in a pub opposite Brunswick Courthouse, and it was not unusual for Dennis to reel across the street half-drunk to make an appearance before the bench. In the late 1970s Dennis joined the rest of the family in Ross Street, Northcote, where he and Grant would enjoy weekend-long drinking binges, consuming dozens of cans of beer.

There was a sheila there sometimes—Heather Hill, I think, the one he married—Sissy, they used to call her. He used to do silly things to her. He used to tell her, 'Clean up, you sloppy moll,' and all that. He'd cook the food. One weekend there was no food, just beer. So he said, 'Come on down the butcher's, we'll rob it.'

You'd get close on a weekend like that. He'd come across as quite fair, open, good company, quite intelligent in his own way. Always thinking of the easy way to get something, though. The simple way, usually the unlawful way. Early on he was quite macho the way he talked, but there was a warm side to him as well.

Even when, unknown to Grant, Dennis had begun his murderous spree, they remained good friends. According to Grant, Dennis never talked about killing people.

I can remember him referring to Victor Gouroff, one of his alleged murder victims, I think it was, as Vic the prick. It sounded like he disliked him from a long way back. He could be a hard man, to his enemies, to those that'd crossed him. He wasn't a big, awesome person, not at all, but he had a lot of heart. There was a time down in Frankston when there was a bit of a fracas. Someone called someone a moll and he took offence. There was a fight, and another fight. He went back to abuse them some more and the blokes pulled guns on him. He ended up getting shot, and he kept fighting on after he'd been shot.

Immediately after this incident Grant brought Dennis into the editorial offices of *Truth* to display the pellet wounds in his chest.

John believes that Dennis would have found a way to justify to himself the escalating violence, and finally the murders: 'He'd probably think he was looking after his friends who were now part of his criminal empire. He wasn't killing people, he was furthering his support from the fellow criminals that were with him. He was a proud man, the old school. I think the drugs got to him in the end.'

When Grant first got to know him, Dennis was opposed to drugs and wouldn't even have a marijuana joint. But in the end his drug abuse—especially his addiction to speed—was his undoing.

He got so distorted on his own power trip—Dennis the menace, that's what he was, a menace to himself. Comparing Dennis with people like Russell Cox, or 'Jockey' Smith ... Dennis wasn't in their league, but a terror among his own. That business of Mr D, that was Mr Drugs, not Mr Death. He wasn't Mr Death. He didn't look like a Mr Death. He didn't instil fear. He was a charmer with women. Shy at first but quite old-fashioned in his way. He did have a weird respect for them—chivalry. He aimed to please. I remember going to The Cherry Tree with him. They loved him in there.

When Dennis turned police informer Grant knew one of his first victims, a heroin dealer who had arranged to supply him with $45,000 worth of the drug.

This bloke brought all this shit back from Thailand. He organised to see Dennis down at the Riverside Hotel. Dennis had set it up with the coppers, and they arrived and took all the drugs and the money Dennis had with him to buy the smack. They had to make it look as if they were into Dennis as well. He was capable of that sort of thing, especially with someone he didn't know. It was an easy quid, but it wouldn't have gone down well with Kath.

Grant had a lot of time for Kathy. 'You can't blame her for what happened to the boys,' he says, 'She was a good Mum, did her best. Loved them.'

But given the opportunity people will be criminals—an easy buck. People don't even realise they're being criminals till they're caught, and then they're branded. Once they're branded they act like they're expected to. Without the speed Dennis would probably have chugged along, got into armed robberies and things.

As Dennis rose through the ranks of Melbourne's underworld he gradually lost a lot of his physical attractiveness. The baby Dennis of early photographs was a show stopper, but by early adolescence he had acquired that look of sullen defiance which characterised Kathy's early portraits. By the time he moved into Stephenson Street in Richmond in 1982 he still had enough of the good looks he had inherited from Kathy's side of the family to be presentable, even handsome. But there was a hardness around his mouth and eyes, born no doubt of his experiences both of the street and inside the 'bluestone college' of Pentridge Prison. There was also his voice—unusually gruff and gravelly. Dennis rarely raised his voice, but as with Kathy today, there was a quality of menace that had more to do with the way the words were delivered than with their volume. There is little doubt of the chilling effect he would convey. Like his mother, Dennis knew how to make himself understood and obeyed.

Completing the physical portrait were the tattoos, the clothes and the jewellery. Dennis acquired his first tattoo at the age of fourteen, more for bravado than aesthetic considerations. It was important to show his peers that the pain of the needle could be handled. By the time of his death he looked like the main character in Ray Bradbury's *The Illustrated Man*. Dragons, bulldogs, tigers, peacocks, swallows, sharks, panthers, scorpions and other representations of the animal kingdom competed for space on his body. Kathy remembers a time when Dennis was comatose with drink and a policeman was making notes of his various tattoos. 'You'll be there a week,' she told him.

If Dennis's body had become a lurid patchwork of human graffiti, the wardrobe he chose to hide the colourful parade of creatures in was in no way comparable. A sleeveless blue singlet underneath bib and brace overalls were his favoured mode of dress for most occasions, social or business. But what transformed this drab working man's uniform was the gold jewellery he habitually wore—diamond rings, bracelets, and neck chains, all of them in chunky 22-carat gold, much of it the soft, yellow variety from Thailand. Estimates of the value of his street jewellery have varied from $250,000 upwards. It says something for Dennis's reputation that he was able to mix in criminal circles with more than a quarter of a million dollars' worth of temptation dangling from his person without a thought for the risks involved. After his death much of this jewellery passed into the hands of various family members. It later became the subject of Federal Court warrants allowing seizure from a number of places, including pawn shops, to help pay off the massive tax debts Dennis's estate had accumulated on his undeclared income from the sale of drugs. Kathy took action to reclaim the jewellery.

After we got it the police seized it. So I went to court and got awarded it all back. At that time I was reporting at the Richmond Police Station three times a week. So after I got it back

*at the court I put everything on, every piece of his jewellery on
me. I had the mink coat on and all the jewellery. I mean the
rings were that big they were slipping off, the chains were
nearly killing me. And I go to sign the bail book and the duty
officer says: 'I see you got the jewellery back.' And as soon as
I got outside I had to take it off it was so heavy. Now when
Dennis worked hard, he did work hard renovating, he'd have
to wash his neck with Drive to get the black stains of the gold
off him. And of course gold in the heat makes you burn.*

The other distinguishing feature of Dennis's appearance during
his years in Richmond was his headgear. He and the entire
clan—soldiers, Kathy and the family, even the girls working in
Kathy's massage parlour—would go through a period when they
all wore Mexican sombreros. Next it would be headbands with
Japanese lettering on them; once black gangster hats were in
vogue, and so on. His women would wear T-shirts with the
words 'Dennis's Dirty Girls' printed on the front.

There was a distinct sense of camaraderie in these days,
before violence and murder replaced the laughs and the good
times. Dennis would take up to a dozen of the family, soldiers
and girls to his favourite restaurant, the Tai Ping at St Kilda
Junction, for crayfish and chilli lobster. Another haunt was the
Oyster Bar in the city, where his bill often came to more than
$100 a head.

*There was one time we were in the Tai Ping and this bloke had
a finch, a bird in a shoe box. He wanted to sell it, and he
happened to pass it across Dennis's plate. Dennis reached out
and bit its head off. It annoyed him, leaning across his plate.*

This cavalier attitude to the good manners and sanctity of the
dining table was typified during a visit to an upmarket Italian
restaurant in Carlton one evening. Dennis, his girlfriend Jenny

and The Enforcer and his wife were present. The Enforcer recalls:

> Dennis was wearing his overalls, and the only reason we got
> in was when he flashed this roll of notes. We were drinking
> $100 bottles of wine, and my wife and me ordered steaks, done
> medium. When they arrived and we cut into them, blood came
> out, so Dennis shouts 'Garçon!' and when the waiter comes
> over he says: 'We ordered medium steaks, these are rare.'
>
> Well the waiter takes a look and says: 'I'm terribly sorry,
> sir, they are medium.' So Dennis pulls out his .32, sticks it in
> the bloke's mouth and says: 'Are you calling me a fucking liar?'
> The bloke's shaking like a dog shitting razor blades.
>
> He says: 'I'll take them back.' But we said it was okay, and
> Dennis ordered a bottle of their best wine, you can imagine
> what that was worth. The bloke who was pouring it was
> shaking so hard he spilled it all over the table, and Dennis says:
> 'What's your fucking problem?' I said to him, 'Pull up, Dennis.'
> But he left them $120 tip to make sure we'd get back in next
> time. He liked their food.

No portrait of Dennis is complete without some reference to
his gross overindulgence in speed, which more than any other
factor helped create the dangerous and unstable monster he
became. Being so easily obtainable, speed has become increasingly popular in recent years, even though it's generally
regarded as even more harmful than heroin.

Falling asleep while under the influence of speed is virtually
a medical impossibility. The manic physical and mental energy
it stimulates does, however, wear off after a time. The user can
then choose to sleep it off or, much more dangerously, have
another snort or hit. The effect of a second hit is the equivalent
of sending a massive lie to the body's natural warning systems.
While everything is crying out for rest and recovery, the user

becomes convinced there is a bottomless reservoir of mental and physical energy still to be enjoyed. In extreme cases, users may go without sleep for days and nights on end, perhaps snorting or injecting the drug every two or three hours until total exhaustion sets in.

Most habitual users graduate from snorting speed—generally through a straw or rolled-up bank note—to injecting it. The most important difference between the two is the rate at which the drug takes effect—an injection is much more instant than when speed is ingested through the nose. The sudden jolt to the senses immediately after the injection, known as the 'rush', can in itself become addictive.

The extent of Dennis's overuse of speed at the height of his addiction would be difficult to believe if there were not so many witnesses to testify to the horrific behaviour it produced in him. According to The Enforcer, Dennis used seven grams of pure speed a day, 'enough to keep a herd of bull elephants on their feet until the middle of the next century'.

His usual method was to inject the drug into his arm, tying a dressing-gown sash around it, as often as every half-hour. Sometimes he didn't bother to remove the sash between hits. Occasionally when this enormous intake left him desperately in need of sleep, he would turn to tranquillisers. The Enforcer recalls:

> There was this time when he'd been up partying for days, and he said he wanted to sleep. Did anybody have any Serepax? Someone had a packet, and he took fifty. Fifty in one go. It would have killed a horse. He goes into his bedroom, and four or five hours later bounces out like an athlete. 'Come on, we're going to party on,' and he starts shooting up speed again. He must have had that much in his system the Serepax hardly had any effect.

Like Kathy, The Enforcer finally came to a theory that because of his addiction Dennis sometimes thought he was invisible and not responsible for his actions. 'Dennis was the only one in the regiment in step,' he says. 'Simple as that.'

Late one night he and Dennis were transporting a box containing six .38 revolvers down the lane at the back of Chestnut Street in Richmond, where Dennis owned a house, both were on tiptoe, trying to make as little noise as possible but Dennis's jewellery was 'rattling like two skeletons fucking in a 48-gallon drum on a tin roof'. Suddenly an Alsatian dog burst through a fence and bit The Enforcer, who promptly kicked it and sent it packing back through the fence. Dennis angrily told him to stop making a racket. After they had dropped off the guns and were on their way back, the dog leapt out again, this time biting Dennis. He pulled out a .357 Magnum, shot the animal three times in the head, and turned to The Enforcer and told him to cut out the noise.

The longest period Kathy can remember Dennis going without sleep as a result of speed was fourteen days, but a week was not uncommon. During these sessions, he insisted on playing music non-stop at pain threshold volume, generally reggae and preferably Bob Marley And The Wailers. (His passion for Marley was so great that one night he accosted a roadie in the toilet of the Riverside Hotel in Richmond. The unfortunate man's band had refused to play a Marley number Dennis had requested. Dennis was later charged with assault and illegal possession of a firearm.)

As he reached the final stages of exhaustion during one of his binges, he would be continually rocking backwards and forwards on his feet. The longer he had been without sleep the faster he rocked. In the final stages of exhaustion and intoxication Dennis was a grotesque, waking nightmare. Music roaring around him, a sash dangling from his arm, and a needle at the ready, he would rock backwards and forwards in the corridor or the doorway. He would forget who people were, people like his brothers and even Kathy. He would forget who he was, or where he was and became transformed into a jangling, incoherent exposed nerve, blindly probing for any physical sensation that could anchor him back to some semblance of reality. Sometimes that sensation would be a volley of gunfire, smashing and splintering wood and plaster. Sometimes the target was human, and it was bone and flesh that burst into fragments.

In this condition Dennis was every bit as volatile and dangerous as unstable gelignite—primed and ready to explode. You didn't cross Dennis at times like this. You didn't go near him if you could possibly avoid it.

If that was Dennis, what was his environment, those Richmond back streets where he sold his drugs and guns, and tortured and murdered his victims? Anybody living in Melbourne for any length of time will have passed within a couple of hundred yards of Dennis's territory, most without ever having seen it. The road taken is Swan Street, Richmond, heading from the affluent eastern suburbs into the city. Just before Hoddle Street, and within a kilometre of one of the world's greatest sporting stadiums, the Melbourne Cricket Ground, there is a railway bridge passing over Swan Street. At a set of traffic lights on the city side of the bridge is a pub/night club called The Depot. A little-noticed left turn can be made here into Cremorne Street. A few yards down Cremorne Street the visitor again turns left, this time into Stephenson Street, and the boundary of what was Dennis's domain. The first 200 metres of Stephenson are a curve, an unusual feature in itself for a city built almost exclusively on the American grid system of straight lines and right-angled intersections.

What makes this stretch of Stephenson Street even more

unusual is the ten-metre-high featureless concrete wall overshadowing one side of the street, hiding the railway line from view but never deadening the roar of passing trains, before it straightens out and narrows to almost single-car width.

Back in the 1980s one visitor to the area found out exactly who ran things in this tight little bottleneck. He parked a truck outside 37 Stephenson Street and was immediately told to 'fuck off' by a boy. The youngster, who looked about fourteen, was Jason Ryan, Dennis's nephew. This had no effect so the boy returned with a gun and began waving it about. Finally a man in bib and brace overalls strode out from the front of one of the little workers' cottages on the left hand side of the street, and began pointing to imaginary lines on the road.

'You can park here, and you can turn up to here,' he said. 'Anything past that and we'll blow your fuckin' van up.' The intruder must have wondered what he had walked into. Whatever went through his mind, there was something about the manner of the man giving the orders that ruled out any protest.

In the middle of this section of Stephenson are numbers 35 and 37. Kathy owned 37 and Dennis owned 35. Both have high, brick walls bordering on the pavement and today appear neat and well-kept. Ten years ago Kathy lived in 35 and Dennis committed his murders in 37. He also built the concealing walls.

A hundred metres down Stephenson Street on the other side of the road is number 102, owned by Dennis. Two doors up is number 106, which Kathy rented for a period. Next door to 106 is a vacant lot used as a car park. This was 108, where from 1982 Kathy owned and operated The Gaslight massage parlour after negotiating for the purchase in 1978.

Running parallel with the straight section of Stephenson Street, fifty metres westwards towards the city, is Cubitt Street. Here Dennis owned numbers 41, 43, 45, 47, and 49, adjoining

weatherboard cottages. Today numbers 41 to 47 are no more—
an untidy, grassed vacant lot is all that is left. Number 49, a
crumbling wreck, borders the vacant lot.

Back in the other direction, 100 yards east of Stephenson
Street, is Chestnut Street, where Dennis owned and lived in
number 86, before moving into 37 Stephenson. This completed
Dennis's real estate portfolio in Richmond. He owned a total of
eight houses, and Kathy two, within an area less than the size
of a city block. They paid a total of $280,000 for them. Today
their combined worth would be several million dollars.

On the corner of Stephenson Street is The Cherry Tree Hotel,
once the haunt of the legendary Melbourne criminal Squizzy
Taylor. When Dennis was a regular here, the pub was a typical
inner-suburban hole in the wall. Today it has enjoyed a facelift
with soft-toned timbers and chrome in evidence. The drinkers
are mainly locals with a sprinkling of yuppies.

(Since its metamorphosis The Cherry Tree has acquired a
fame independent of Dennis's legacy. In March 1991 it was the
scene of an attempted tryst between American singer Billy Joel
and Australian TV hostess Sophie Lee. The repercussions from
Billy's rejected advances echoed from the bar of The Cherry Tree
across the world to America, where his girlfriend, international
model Christie Brinkley, was said to be so unimpressed she
destroyed a hotel room.

In June 1994 the media spotlight again fell on someone associated with the hotel—a former employee, Kellie Wilkinson, was
murdered by Khmer Rouge guerillas after demands for a $50,000
ransom.)

The Cherry Tree borders Balmain Street and is directly across
the road from the disused Rosella food factory, which still towers
over most other buildings in the area. It was ideal for the police
as a vantage point from which they used to keep Stephenson
Street and Dennis's activities under almost constant surveillance.
When they knocked off at the end of a shift, Kathy says, Dennis

would occasionally pepper the building with gunshots, leaving them to worry when they returned about when the next volley was coming. Miraculously, Dennis was never charged or booked over any of these incidents.

What about the machine gun? The police come to me the next day because Dennis never got up till about two p.m. and I was an early riser. They said: 'You'll have to stop him taking pot shots.' I said: 'What at?' Little did I know they're in this factory straight over the road from The Cherry Tree. Dennis had driven past with my girlfriend, who is about six foot. We called her The Talking Bone—she was the topless, bottomless waitress. And I said to her: 'What about him machine gunning last night?' She said: 'Yeah, and I was the getaway driver.' Ooh God. And the police were all laying on the floor, and they come to me to complain.

The Enforcer tells the story of a similar occasion, when police installed one-way mirrors along the top floor of the factory.

They could see out, but you couldn't see in. One day it was just a shell of a building and the next day there were all these mirrors there, it didn't take long to work it out. I said to Dennis: 'They're up there fucking looking at us.' He said: 'At least we know where they're at.' But then paranoia got the better of him and he put twenty bullets through the windows, twelve from a .22 automatic and eight from a .45 Colt. Blew all the windows out, and they came and complained to Kathy again.

CHAPTER SIX

Bent Cops, Dogs _ and Soldiers _

IT'S THE EARLY HOURS OF THE MORNING ROUND AT DENNIS'S PLACE in Cubitt Street, Richmond. Bob Marley's 'Buffalo Soldier' is pounding from the stereo, and Dennis and The Enforcer sit in the half-light of the kitchen, talking, drinking and shooting up speed. Dennis has been without sleep for the best part of ten days, and things are becoming a little jagged. But The Enforcer is a close and trusted friend—outside the family, probably the closest of them all.

As Dennis reaches again for his bag of speed something wholly unexpected happens. At first both men wonder if the churning, vibrating sound they are hearing is coming from within their speed-raddled heads. But no, it's not—ornaments and crockery are visibly shaking. Something strange is going on. The two men lurch to their feet, the house trembling around them. A brilliant light sweeps suddenly over the building, lighting up the back yard as if it was daytime.

'Fuck,' says The Enforcer. 'They've finally done it, let off the big one.' 'What're you fucking talking about?' Dennis snarls. He grabs a Browning .25 automatic from its hiding place, taped under the table, and heads into the yard. The Enforcer prefers the front porch. If Melbourne has just been nuked, and the rumble and flash of the explosion is what they're experiencing, Cubitt Street and the front of the house will afford a better view. 'I'm going to kiss Melbourne goodbye,' he mutters as he stumbles out of the kitchen headed the opposite way from Dennis. As soon as he hits the porch The Enforcer grins sheepishly to himself. How fucking stupid, it's not the bomb, just the police helicopter hovering overhead, playing its new searchlight over the back streets of Richmond. He ducks back through the front door to find out if his boss has realised. But it's too late. Out in the back yard Dennis has been blazing up into the sky with the Browning. It's only his rage and ravaged state that prevent him from hitting the chopper. Even so he's fired six shots in its direction.

As he pushes past The Enforcer on his way back into the house he hands him the empty gun. 'Get rid of this!' He's gone, through the front door and down a few houses to number 45, another in the row of cottages he owns. The Enforcer stops to hide the Browning before following. But Dennis is already on his way back. Only this time, to The Enforcer's mounting panic, he's carrying a fully automatic SLR .308. As Dennis jams a twenty-round box magazine into the weapon and heads back out into the yard, The Enforcer's head suddenly clears. Jesus, he means it, he's really going to do it.

Out in the yard Dennis has lost it completely. Foam and spittle collect at the corner of his mouth as he screams at the chopper: 'You cunts are fucking gone, I'll blow you out of the sky!' The .308 is at his shoulder and although the chopper is drowning the sound of its retort, The Enforcer knows it's blazing away. He leaps for the gun and tries to wrestle it from Dennis, but he breaks free, spins around and points it upward again, firing off another burst, this time from the hip. The two men grapple again and go crashing to the ground, Dennis still holding the SLR. This is the only chance The Enforcer will get: his face a few inches from the raw madness of Dennis's range, he screams at him above the roar of the chopper. 'If you shoot the fuckers out the sky, the fucking chopper's going to come down right on top of us!'

Dennis stops struggling and looks momentarily pole-axed. Then a grin breaks across his face. 'You're fucking right. The cunts'd do that.'

Kathy provides her own vivid description of Dennis's life in Richmond at this time.

One day I went round around nine in the morning and he's rocking on his feet. He hadn't had any sleep for days, right? There's a little girl about two, right, and he told me to put a pea on her head. It was an imaginary pea. And he's weaving with the gun. And the mother of the child hid herself in the bedroom and didn't give a fuck what he did to her kid, right? And he's pointing this gun at the kid's head, a little girl. I said: 'Agh, put it away and stop acting like a fucking idiot,' and moved the child. Because I didn't want him to kill her. I don't know if he would have, I can't read his mind. But Leanne, the mother ... if that had been my child I would have picked her up and gone into the room, or got out somehow. That's how much I loved my children, and that's how much Leanne loved her heroin. She would have let him do it. Later on she was found dead in St Kilda. Dennis was on with her, right while he was still with Sissy, his wife. Well, he goes to bring Leanne into 86 Chestnut Street, thinking that Sissy's not home. And Sissy is. Sissy stabs her. Nearly kills her. Now Dennis had towels and stuff on her and races her to the hospital. She was only about twenty, twenty-one, I suppose. Nice-looking girl. And they saved her life, the doctors. I'd say two weeks bloody later, she's down trying to score again, and she had this massive *scar. But I don't think Sissy did any time over this because nobody gives anyone up.**

Now let me tell you one other thing. There was a lot of girls came there in the '80s. They'd just go and get in his bed, and this pair of sisters went and got in his bed, junkies. He said to me: Get 'em out of me bed.' He was outside and they were waiting for him to go in, right? So it was like taking a raffle ticket. And I said to the two girls: 'It's not your turn tonight, get out of bed.' To sleep with him they knew they'd get as much heroin as they wanted. But the minute they'd start to say, 'We'll get curtains for this window,' and that, he'd give 'em the arse.

Welcome to Dennis's world. A world where police helicopters and small children are used for target practice, where unlimited money, women, guns, booze and drugs are as easily attainable as a carton of milk, where torture and meat cleavers are a source of entertainment, where bent policemen can be paid off when things get a little hot. A world where barristers, priests, sportsmen and rock stars wander in and out. Anything goes. Absolutely anything. Just name it and it's yours. Even someone else's life.

But it wasn't always like that. Kathy remembers the first murder as the worst one. They say lying to your marital partner after the first infidelity is the hardest. The next time it gets a little easier, and by the fifth or sixth time, the words just trip off your tongue—there's nothing to it. That's how it was for Dennis with murder. No sweat, once he just got used to it.

At its height the Richmond era resembled a bizarre form of

---

* Dennis married Sissy (Heather Hill) while he was in Pentridge gaol in 1981 (see below). She was originally charged with attempted murder, but the offence was later reduced to one of grievous bodily harm. Despite alleged admissions she made, Sissy was found not guilty when the victim failed to testify against her.

medieval fiefdom, with the family holding absolute sway over the narrow back streets branching out from the railway line. Eventually Dennis's behaviour, and to a lesser extent that of the rest of the family, became so flagrant that the police were forced to mount a concentrated attack over the shootings, murders, bombings and open drug dealing. It was conducted, somewhat cruelly, under the name Operation Cyclops, after Kathy's one eye—possibly also an indication of the force's view of her dominating role.

Cyclops began in July 1984, and almost immediately roof-top surveillance was maintained over the area, sixteen hours a day. A hiccup in September saw the operation suspended for a week for reasons of internal policy, but it was up and running again by the middle of the month.

At its peak of activity raids on the various properties and The Cherry Tree Hotel, from where Dennis was openly dealing heroin, were coming as frequently as four times a week. The family responded by moving operations from one house to another and eventually dealing only late at night, in their efforts to avoid capture.

Over the seven months of the operation more than twenty raids were carried out and nine family members and close associates were charged with more than forty counts involving heroin and more than thirty involving firearms. Drugs with a street value of over $1 million were seized, together with more than twenty fire-arms of various descriptions. An additional twenty people not directly connected with the family were also charged with a series of offences.

It all began when Dennis was released from Pentridge early in July 1982, after serving a sentence for a breach of parole. Kathy was living in the rented house at 106 Stephenson Street and operated The Gaslight massage parlour next door at 108. By now her standing in the underworld was relatively assured. 'I knew the A to Z of crims, Dennis only knew the B to Y,' she says.

She had paid a deposit of just $20 on the parlour premises, partly because a high profile criminal had blown it up with a half stick of gelignite, and the front section was in ruins.

I borrowed the rest of the money from a loan place. I ran it and I used to be mistress of discipline. One detective told me recently: 'I can remember the time Jamie got arrested and we had him up at the Northcote jack shop. A customer came in to your parlour early in the morning and you gave him the best flogging for eighty bucks, then you came to the station and you were as calm as anything to Jamie.'

I didn't have to dress up in leather or anything like that— they didn't care about that. I could make them walk around with the dog's collars on. I had a bloke dress up in my high heels, he was a little bloke, brushed mo', wanted to be a French maid. I made him clean with the toothbrush, right? My girl-friend couldn't stop cracking up. She'd be sitting at the table watching. A stinking hot day. He said: 'Could I have a drink?' I said: 'Who told you to speak? Get on with your work.' I gave him a thimble in the end. She had to run out she was laughing that much. That was $80 a half-hour.

There was one man there was sick, sick. This girl came out of the room and her face was like this, white as your shirt, and she said to me: 'He wants me to cut his balls out.' She said: 'I don't mind doing it but I don't want to do the ten years for manslaughter.' He was a very sick man. You know what he used to do? The very worst things you could think of, the better he paid you. So I used to tie his thing to the door with a shoe lace, and I'd slam the door and go and have a cigarette. Then I'd go in and say: 'Are you all right?' and slam the door again. Well he'd want needles put up the eye of his thing and that, and then he got sicker and sicker and wanted young girls.

Blokes used to come in with their own pegs to put on their nipples and that.

And then another day there was a mother out the front, and the father, they were Turks. Now she's got the money in a hanky. So she sends her son in, pays at the door, and I give him to the girl, right, and the mother's out there crying. Must be their custom. Losing his virginity.

I went into the parlour one day and there was baby food on the kitchen table. I said: 'Who's brought a baby in?' The girl went: 'Sssshhh,' and I go in there, and here's a bloke with a bib on, and a nappy, and she's feeding him baby food. This is about ten o'clock in the morning.

Perversions apart, Kathy was also receiving a crash course in drug abuse.

It was at 106 Stephenson Street that I saw Dennis with a belt around his arm for the first time. I said: 'That doesn't want to be heroin, Dennis.' That was when he told me about speed.

Using heroin was something Kathy never wanted to see Dennis do. Selling it was another matter. The first time she realised how a bag of pure heroin could be 'stepped on' (diluted) was the first time she understood its financial potential. When Dennis started to realise that potential he was on the way to the incredible sums of money it later generated for him.

He was just out of gaol and we were in this hotel in Newmarket. I drove him. And he met a bloke. He handed Dennis a plastic bag and it was on the nod. Six grand it was, about an ounce. You can triple that. It was uncut. I was devastated. I said 'You're not going to take that, are you?' That was the first time.

When I saw him putting on this little belt . . . every junkie then wore them. They were a little slim belt with two little buckles, and they hooked on their jeans and the idea was you put it round and you made a tourniquet. The girls in the parlour did, or any junkie. It was the go, but I didn't know this. Later he had his dressing gown sash all the time. But that was for speed.

Police have estimated Dennis's income from heroin during the mid-1980s at anything between $30,000 and $70,000 a week. Kathy's estimate is much higher. On a good day up to a hundred addicts scored from Dennis, most of them spending between $50 and $100. Apart from that, he was selling to other dealers. This meant much larger amounts and much larger sums of money. It is not difficult to understand how the term 'drug lord' originated.

Kathy's attitude to the morality of heroin dealing changed drastically during this period. One of her most painful memories involves the addiction of Victor Gouroff, a prominent armed robber who became close to the family—with fatal results.

One day Victor came to the parlour door in Stephenson Street. And he used to be a grouse armed robber, before he became a heroin dealer. I think he did the Board of Works robbery in East Brunswick, I think it was. He was known as one of the real hard men. Well, I'd seen Victor a proud man, right? Well, he come to the parlour door and he was crying for heroin. And he took off his great big overcoat, and I think he got a cap of smack for it. I went home and I cried all night to see a man go so low. And I said to Jamie: 'What sort of world is it coming to when men like him have got to cry for it?' Jamie said: 'I don't give a fuck, I've got the coat.' 'Cos Jamie was young, and Victor had had his day.

None of the real crims ever touched the shit. My Peter was only on speed, but I don't think he ever injected it. And poor old Lex has only ever been on the smoke [marijuana]. *Trevor*

111

was a heroin addict. I didn't know, I'm always the last to know. But he did eight months at Odyssey [House, the drug rehabilitation centre], *for that.*

Rescue attempts after friends or customers had overdosed were another regular occurrence. Kathy thinks Dennis may have been responsible for the deaths from overdose of up to six addicts as a result of one incident alone. There had been a mix-up between Dennis and one of his soldiers, both believing the other had cut (diluted) a bag of heroin. In fact neither had, and when the pure heroin hit the streets the results were instant and, for a number of users, fatal.

Now this bloke, John, he nearly died on the floor. I rang Dennis, and if Dennis didn't want to save them, he'd say: 'I'm having a shit.' I worked on that man for three hours, 'cos my conscience wouldn't let him die. I worked and worked on him, I injected alcohol into his neck, I injected speed into his neck, which I'd seen Dennis do. At least he's alive. When I like somebody I go all out. But then he stole all the Christmas presents. I worked for five years to get people off heroin. I used to drive them to the Austin Hospital. I put them up, they robbed me, they shot up Vegemite under me bed, they did everything to me. And in the end I said: 'Well, fuck this.' And I've got the worst tolerance for addicts, I don't feel sorry for any of 'em any more.

Banking the takings was another occupational hazard.

You know how that Victor Gouroff was supposed to be afraid of Dennis? Him and Johnny ——? I've got a photo of the Jaguar that Dennis bought for Johnny. Well, this time I'm going up to the bank with Dennis's money to put it in the night safe. And something told me not to go under the railway tunnel. So I went the long way round. And, fuck me dead, I looked down the street to the tunnel, and there's the two of them waiting to rob me. And I kept that in me mind, and they were Dennis's friends. But when Dennis started with the heroin business, they were robbing him right, left and centre.

At a later court hearing evidence was heard that Dennis had bought heroin from a person called Alan Williams, allegedly a drug dealer. The pair had met in Pentridge where Dennis was serving his sentence for the Sandringham rape. Williams has become a significant figure in Australian criminal history because of his association with people like hit man Christopher Dale Flannery (known as 'Mr Rentokil' for his involvement in an estimated fourteen murders), Sydney crime boss Neddy Smith and disgraced New South Wales police officer Roger Rogerson. The ABC's excellent two-part TV series *Blue Murder*, first aired in September 1995 in all States except New South Wales, where it was principally set, deals with the story of these men and their relationship with undercover policeman Michael Drury. Dennis's close connections with Williams, and later his more distant dealings with Rogerson, made him a bit player in the saga.

Playing a much more important role in Rogerson's eventual downfall was a woman who, for legal reasons, will be referred to here as 'Miss X' (She is currently in a witness protection scheme). She claimed to be a girlfriend and close associate of Dennis, but Kathy emphatically denies this, saying the pair never met—'She saw him once through the peephole of a door and said he was a good sort, but they never even spoke.'

Miss X was a useful source of information to police, providing the evidence that produced the only conviction recorded against Rogerson. The same 'Miss X' testified that she saw Dennis commit a murder in the street in broad daylight ... and in the company of a detective.

The Williams–Rogerson–Flannery affair began with an

aborted drug bust in a Sydney hotel car park in March 1982. Michael Drury, working undercover, was set to pay Williams $110,000 for a package of heroin. But at the last moment Williams's instincts told him the deal was a set-up, and he took off in his car, though not before being recognised by Drury. Arrested later and charged with trafficking heroin, Williams was quick to realise that all chances of a conviction rested on Drury's identification of him in the car park. Williams had an almost pathological fear of returning to prison, and was prepared to go to any lengths to keep Drury from testifying against him. Initially he tried bribery, allegedly using Rogerson as go-between. (Williams later admitted attempting to bribe Drury, but Rogerson was acquitted on the same charge.)

Drury rejected all advances in this direction so murder became the inevitable option. At a meeting between Flannery and Williams, at which Rogerson was also allegedly present, Flannery agreed to murder him, reputedly for $100,000. A later court hearing was told that Rogerson received $50,000 of this fee. Unusually for him, Flannery botched the attempt. In June 1984 he shot Drury through the window of his Chatswood home in Sydney, critically wounding him.

Drury recovered, however, and alleged that Rogerson had offered him a bribe, sparking an internal inquiry which resulted in charges being laid against Rogerson of not only attempting to bribe Drury but conspiring to have him killed. Rogerson was acquitted but later convicted on a third count, involving none other than Dennis Allen and Miss X.

The story in this case alleged Dennis sent Miss X to Sydney Airport on 14 May 1985 with more than $100,000 in cash. As Kathy points out, there is one very good reason why this is unlikely— her son Jamie died of a drug overdose on that date and the whole family, including Dennis, were far too traumatised to be considering long-distance drug deals with rogue police officers.

According to Miss X, when she was thirty-one she was

deeply into drug and firearms dealing with Dennis. She was also supporting a heroin habit costing her between $100 and $200 a day. The sequence of events in 1985 surrounding her trip to Sydney, makes interesting reading:

9 May: Flannery leaves home at 8.15 a.m. with a false passport, a wig and binoculars, to keep an appointment with his boss, Sydney crime czar George Freeman. He is never seen again.

14 May: (Miss X's version) Dennis instructed her to meet Rogerson at Sydney Airport, giving her a black travel bag containing $100,000, and two airline tickets, to and from Sydney, under different names. She arrives in Sydney at 11.30 a.m. and finds Rogerson in the terminal close to the women's toilets. 'He sort of said: "G'day", threw the bag at me, and ripped the other one [containing the $100,000] off me and ran away,' she later tells a court in Sydney. The bag Rogerson threw at her contained clothing, books and 'plastic sandwich bags' of heroin weighing around a kilo. She flies back to Melbourne, where the heroin is collected from her, and the next evening an envelope containing $7,000 is placed in her letter box.

14 May: (Rogerson's version) After being phoned the previous day by Kath Flannery, Chris Flannery's wife, expressing concern over her fifteen-year-old son who is depressed at his father's disappearance, he takes the boy and his sister, together with his own two teenage daughters, on a boat trip on the Georges River, presumably at the same time as the airport exchange is alleged to have taken place.

21 May: Rogerson opens two accounts in false names at the York Street, Sydney, branch of the National Australia Bank, and in three visits deposits a total of $110,000 cash.

As a result of this chain of events Rogerson was initially convicted of conspiring with Dennis to supply heroin between March and May 1985, but the conviction was overturned on appeal. Later Rogerson was charged with conspiring to pervert the course of justice by allegedly misleading a policy inquiry into the source of the $110,000 deposited in the false accounts. Rogerson was initially convicted, but after serving nine months of his eight-year sentence was released in 1990, pending appeal. He lost the appeal and was returned to gaol in 1992 with a reduced sentence. He was released in December 1995.

Before his dismissal from the New South Wales police force in 1986 Rogerson was one of the most highly decorated officers in the force. He had also shot and killed two men. The jury sitting at the inquest into the death of one of them, heroin dealer Warren Lanfranchi, declined to find he was shot either in self-defence or in the course of duty.

(Rogerson's eventual imprisonment meant a special problem for New South Wales prison authorities. The first night he spent in gaol in 1988, after being charged with conspiring to murder Drury, a fellow inmate poured boiling water over him. After he received his eight-year sentence for conspiring to pervert the course of justice, his mother said in an interview he would cope with gaol 'because he has what it takes'. But within days of starting his sentence he was placed in protective custody along with child-molesters, sexual deviants, and particularly feminine-looking prisoners. Prison authorities used a computer to examine records of all the prisoners Rogerson had placed behind bars during his career, to find him a relatively safe cell.)

Rogerson's release pending appeal in 1990 didn't please Miss X, who claimed at the time, in an interview with Melbourne police reporter John Silvester, that her years as a protected witness had wrecked her life. Saying she would never have helped police if she had known the outcome in advance, Miss X spoke of living in five States under false names, costing her a settled relationship with her teenage daughter. She claimed to be in fear of her life from Rogerson who, she said, had mouthed death threats at her in court during his committal hearing. The

Left: Gladys with Dennis (left) and Peter.

Below: Dennis the teenager, with Gladys and Harry.

Kathy and John Farnham in Sentimental Bloke days.

Above: Kathy's sons (from left): Dennis, Victor, Trevor and Lex.

Below: Jamie, sleeping peacefully.

GASLIGHT
HEALTH STUDIO

108 STEPHENSON ST RICHMOND 3121

Above: A card for the Gaslight parlour—
unhealthy for some.

Below: Dennis and three of his favourite
things: his Mum, his gold and his gun.

Above and below: Dennis and two of his soldiers.

Above: Wendy and Katie amid the wreckage of Chestnut Street immediately after a raid by the police. *(Herald and Weekly Times)*

Below: Police demolishing Victor and Wendy's Chestnut Street home (previously owned by Dennis) in their search for Walsh Street evidence. *(Herald and Weekly Times)*

Above: Victor being carried into court: 'A circus for the media,' according to his counsel. (*Herald and Weekly Times*)

Left: Jason Ryan (second from right): 'wonderful with anyone's kids.'

Below: Kathy (front row, centre) and friends, Fairlea Prison, class of '93.

Kathy, her good eye blazing, confronts life without crime.
(*Mark Ruff Photography*)

restrictions of the witness protection scheme, she added, were barely preferable to the horrors of her alleged association with Dennis.

There was one genuine connection between Dennis and Rogerson—the New South Wales policeman was mentioned on numerous occasions in a court case involving the death of a man called Lindsay Simpson. Nine months before the alleged airport incident Dennis was said to have taken out a contract to have Alan Williams murdered, possibly over a drug debt rumoured to be in the region of $20,000. But the hit went horribly wrong and Lindsay Simpson was killed by mistake.

Until their dispute, although preoccupied with his battle to stay out of gaol, Williams managed throughout most of this period to continue supplying Dennis with heroin.

Kathy's views on the entire Rogerson–Williams–Miss X episode are typically to the point. She disputes the widely held view that Williams was Dennis's main source of heroin, conceding that the pair did do business, but not on the scale alleged. She also denies Dennis sent Miss X to Sydney to buy heroin from Rogerson.

Never happened. Never happened. I'll tell you why. It was the day Jamie died for a start, and Dennis never met Miss fucking X and he wasn't making as much as $110,000 at the time. The most he made at that time was much less. There was a connection between Dennis and Rogerson and Williams. They had their heads together. Williams was not his main dealer—that's a bloody fallacy. There were times he did buy heroin off him.

Dennis and Williams were talking about having Drury shot. I went up to Sydney for Rogerson's committal, but I didn't give evidence that time, it was later. It was at the trial involving the $110,000. I didn't have to say much, there weren't many questions. I was appearing on Rogerson's behalf to say the whole thing was bullshit. It was after Dennis died, *but I wanted to clear his name, to show he had nothing to do with it. There was no way of him getting $110,000. I spoke to Rogerson both times, I was filmed coming down the court steps with him. Rogerson said to me: 'You're a breath of fresh air.' He'd been speaking to me on the phone through another detective.**

You know who I'm talking about. He said to me: 'Would you talk to Rogerson?' I spoke to him on the phone and he told me what was going on, and I knew that was lies—there was no kilo of heroin come down from Sydney.

Kathy also denies Dennis took out a contract to have Williams killed. She believes he wanted to commit the murder himself, and attempted to do so.

When the Richmond era was getting under way, after his release from gaol in 1982, Dennis began living in a flat at Ascot Vale. Kathy wanted him to move to 106 Stephenson Street, where the rent was only $40 a week.

Having her own son in 106 would remove the risk of trouble from nosy neighbours about the parlour she owned at 108. Dennis agreed to the move, but he didn't stay long. He had married a woman called Heather Hill, amazingly enough inside Pentridge gaol shortly before his release.

Heather, or Sissy as she was always known, was the great love of Dennis's life and bore him two daughters, Lindy, in 1981, and Jade, in 1983. Tragically both girls were born addicted to heroin because of Sissy's long-term dependence on the drug, even during her two pregnancies. Lindy, Jade and his son by the girl over whom he was charged with unlawful carnal knowledge were the only three children he is known to have fathered.

---

* The name of this notorious Melbourne detective, gaoled on corruption charges, has been omitted for legal reasons.

Apart from her heroin addiction, Sissy was often before the courts. On one occasion in April 1982, Sissy then aged twenty-three, and her nineteen-year-old sister Tamara appeared with their mother Heather Bolden, forty-two, in Melbourne Magistrates Court. All three admitted shoplifting from a Myers store in Northland Shopping Centre. Tamara also pleaded guilty to kicking a security officer and a policeman who had arrested the two.

Kathy is unsure exactly when or where Dennis and Sissy met, but she knows where Dennis proposed—inside the cells at Brunswick Police Station. The couple had been out on the town together and were booked for being drunk and disorderly after a fight with a taxi driver. Being separated from his beloved by a cell wall did nothing to dampen Dennis's ardour, and his proposal was accepted.

Appropriately enough, their wedding took place in Pentridge where Dennis was serving one of his later sentences, with special dispensation from the prison governor. Sissy, eight months pregnant, had come straight from hospital where she was being treated for her addiction. The marriage did not last long, however, and they broke up soon after their second daughter, Jade, was born. This was when Kathy's daughter-in-law committed what was, in her eyes, an unforgivable sin.

In the hospital she had Jade all ready to be adopted, saying she wasn't married. And Dennis had gone into the hospital and brought the baby out to me. He took the baby from the cot by the side of her in the Royal Women's, because she was ready to adopt it out. And he brought Jade home to me and said: 'You've got a grand-daughter.'

He brought her about ten o'clock at night, pissed. He had her in a bassinet. At midnight there was a knock on the door, and it was Sissy. She'd discharged herself. Said she wanted to see the baby. She didn't want to see the baby. She wanted the smack underneath the mattress in the bassinet.

THE MATRIARCH

Today Sissy's mother, Heather Bolden, brings up the two girls.

According to Kathy, the marriage was a stormy, violent affair:

Round in Chestnut Street, where they were living, he used to chain her up on the washing machine of a night. She'd be standing on top of the washing machine with the chain round her neck, fixed to the ceiling. Mind you she loved that sort of thing, she loved being tied up.

And one day he told his sister-in-law Wendy to look in this soldier's car. He's bought an old car like mine. He'd paid $300 for it. Dennis said to Wendy: 'Go and get something out of the boot.' So she opens the boot and there's Sissy gurgling in her own blood. And Wendy slammed the boot down, right, and Sissy had to go and have all these stitches in her head 'cos he'd bashed her something shocking. And I said to the bloke: 'Why didn't you fucking drive it into the Yarra? I would have given you the three hundred you paid for your rotten fucking car.'

One time I went back into Pentridge, and I got called to classo [classification]. They said to me: 'What would you do if you got to Fairlea Women's Prison and Sissy's there?' I said: 'I'd murder her.' Just like that. So I stayed at Pentridge for five and a half months. Soon as she left Fairlea I was taken over there. I had no love for her. Her kids were born junkies and she tried to adopt one out.

One day Sissy's mum was round at Cubitt Street, where Dennis used to fly the Jolly Roger* outside, and she's been saying things about Dennis's little son. So Dennis rang me and said: 'Get round here.' Because she mouths off when she's drunk. I said: 'If I hear another fucking word about you saying

---

* Dennis painted a black satin sheet with a white skull and cross bones, and flew it outside 49 Cubitt Street.

anything about Dennis I'll put a bullet right through your
fucking brain. Right here and now.' We never got on.

Sissy's end, like her wedding, took place in Pentridge. On 27
August 1986 at the age of twenty-seven, she was admitted to the
prison and later the same day took her own life. Kathy believes
Sissy didn't intend going the whole way.

She thought she'd be discovered. She didn't hang herself—she
choked to death. It was eight months before Dennis died. He
was upset, but none of the rest of us were. We boycotted the
funeral. I reckon he really loved her.

He may well have done, but by the time of her suicide, Sissy
didn't reciprocate—none of the notes she left behind in her cell
mentioned Dennis. This didn't stop him placing a death notice
in the *Sun*—'Sissy. Gone but not forgotten. Forever in our hearts.
Loved forever. Your husband Dennis, daughters Lindy and Jade.'
Of the other sixteen notices only one, from Vicki, was placed by
a member of Dennis's family.

In one of those unthinkable strokes of coincidence the inquest
into Sissy's death took place on 13 April 1987, the day Dennis
died, only a kilometre or two across town in St Vincent's Hospital. The coroner found that she had died ... by hanging in
circumstances of being locked within her cell, writing notes indicating an intent to take her own life, standing on furniture to
secure a bed sheet to pipes near the ceiling, then proceeding
down from the furniture with the sheet around her neck, and all
without prior indication or warning to anyone. I find the
deceased herself contributed to the cause of death. I am
satisfied ... that Heather Allen, for whatever reasons, intended
to take her own life, and did so.

A letter and three notes were discovered on a table beside
her body. One of the notes was to her sister Kerry, and read:

121

'Kezza, I love you. Sorry this has happin [sic]. XXX and you will always be my best sister. Love ya. Sissy.' The second note was to her mother, Lindy and Jade: 'Well, my time has now gone, but I love you all so much, and I couldn't handle any more hurt. Love Sissy.' The third note, and the letter, were expressions of love to a man named Peter Gaidan.

The only other exhibit tendered to the inquest was Dennis's handwritten identification of Sissy's remains, made the day after her death.

Evidence was put to the coroner by Pentridge governor Peter Hannay that Sissy had previously 'made a number of what appears to be attention-seeking self-inflicted wounds to her person'. These included an incident in November 1984 when she swallowed a razor blade and vomited blood.

By the end of 1982 Dennis had amassed enough capital from his drug dealing to purchase the house at 86 Chestnut Street for $35,000 cash. He, Sissy and Lindy moved in immediately, but before the purchase Dennis accepted some advice from Kathy.

We went and looked at the house in White Street, Richmond. It was a shack of a place, right? Well, the bloke who owned it had died eating his dinner. And there was the bloody rancid butter, and there was the plate with the maggots and the knife and fork. And it had no bathroom inside. But Dennis said: 'I'm going to buy this place.' I said: 'No you're not. No, you're not. It'll cost you a fortune to redo.' So we walked round the street and he bought 86 Chestnut Street instead.

This is the part where it gets funny, right? We lived in the Shire of Jika Jika, same as the maximum security unit in Pentridge. We get the deed of the house—the man's name that Dennis bought it off was Crook. And I said: 'How poetic is that, Dennis? A Crook owned it. You're a crook, and we live

122

in the Shire of fucking Jika Jika.' I couldn't believe it.

Dennis's next purchase, late in 1983, was the little weatherboard worker's cottage at 102 Stephenson, a few doors down from Kathy's parlour at 108 and a stone's throw from the pub that was becoming his local—The Cherry Tree. He paid the $37,000 asking fee with cash, and got $4,000 knocked off the price simply by standing on a floor board that broke under his weight. Within a matter of weeks before the end of the year, he and Kathy had bought two more houses in Stephenson Street, number 35 for $38,000 and a few days before Christmas, number 37, for $20,000. This was badly in need of repair, but Dennis earmarked the property as his future home. When he first saw it there was little more than the front door and wall intact. He opened the door and, surveying the wreckage, commented: 'Jesus, I love the air conditioning.'

Dennis had only been there for a while when he acquired a neighbour.

At 39 Stephenson Street a little Vietnamese moved in. Dennis was in gaol before I got him out on bail, right? So this Vietnamese must have dumped rubbish in the lane out the back. So Dennis goes to his front door with the meat cleaver, and told him he was going to chop him up, right? But after that the two of them became friends, how I don't know 'cos neither of them could speak the same language. And Dennis had gold numbers, 35 and 37 on Stephenson Street, and he got gold numbers put on 39. A present, 'cos he liked him. And the slope'd make him meals and stuff. Well, the police thought, seeing the 39, he was part of our stuff, and they used to raid the poor bloke.

When Dennis died the slope said: 'Where's Den?' and I couldn't explain it to him. I tried all sorts of languages—I said 'Morte' and 'finito', and things like that. I didn't know the slope word for dead.

By the time he moved into number 37 Dennis had developed a taste for fine furnishings, particularly eastern antiques, and having a place to showcase his growing collection of statues, wall hangings, sculptures and $15,000 worth of gold-plated lighting was his way of rewarding himself for the growing success of his heroin business. Within six months he had moved in. This was due largely to the hard work of a builder named Wayne whom Dennis paid $500 a week and allowed to stay rent-free at 102 Stephenson Street while he refurbished a number of the properties. Not long after Wayne had made 37 habitable for Dennis, Kathy moved in next door at number 35.

Dennis's pride and joy at number 37 was the four-by-two-metre fish tank, taking up an entire wall in the loungeroom. Significantly none of Dennis's random bullets ever found a target near the fish tank, and on one occasion when he was firing shots in the room a visitor took refuge by standing beside it. Dennis insisted he was the only one who could feed the fish, a number of which were worth $800 each. 'There was no TV round there,' Kathy laughs. 'You had to watch the fucking fish all the time.'

Within ten months Dennis doubled his Richmond real estate portfolio, buying the five run-down weatherboard cottages in Cubitt Street for a total of $125,000. This purchase was made through a registered company called Mr D Investments, named after Dennis's nickname—the 'D' standing for Death, not Dennis. The company, which listed among its directors one of Dennis's girlfriends and a builder friend, lasted four years before a series of resignations led to its deregistration in 1988.

A few weeks after buying Cubitt Street, early in December 1984, Kathy sent Dennis to buy dog meat. On his return he said: 'Give me a cheque for $7,000, I've just bought another house.' 'Yeah, but did you get the meat?' Kathy responded. This property, in nearby Dunn Street, would have been Dennis's ninth, but for some reason negotiations for the $74,000 deal fell through. Dennis made his displeasure known with a display of macabre humour and his growing awareness of his power to intimidate others.

He had been on the telephone to the local representative of the finance company involved when he realised he was getting nowhere. Calling on The Enforcer to accompany him, he picked up a garden spade and walked to the company's premises. Ignoring the protests of the receptionist, they strode past her into the manager's office, where he was interviewing a client. Without saying a word Dennis walked in and stood with his back to the wall, leaning on the spade. The Enforcer, equally silent, beside him. The manager looked up uneasily: 'What do you want?'

Dennis glanced down at the spade. 'We've come to bury you,' was all he said.

Needless to say, the manager proved more cooperative, though the deal was never actually completed.

Another incident illustrating the same cruelly extravagant streak of humour came during Dennis's much publicised relationship with champion footballer Fred Cook. One night, with a girlfriend in tow, he visited the Station Hotel in Port Melbourne, run by Cook.

Dennis had invested several thousand dollars in the hotel, and no doubt felt entitled to enjoy its more private amenities. In need of somewhere quiet for him and his girlfriend to express their affection, he decided to borrow the Cooks' marital bed for a while. His nephew Jason Ryan walked into the room in the middle of things and switched on the light. Dennis immediately pulled a gun out from under the pillow and shot out the bulb.

Nor did he hesitate to interfere in his family's personal lives. On one occasion when Dennis was rapidly tiring of a 'squarehead' (someone with no criminal record) named Ron, who was having an affair with Kathy, he let his feelings be known in a particularly unsavoury manner.

Well something happened to this fucking dog, and it died and

Dennis put it in Ron's car. In the back seat. And Ron's driven to work down at Port Melbourne, right, and he's with Telecom at the time. And he goes up the bush, and his car was left in the yard, with the dog still in the back, and it was 100 degrees, and a week later he comes back. I never saw him again. Dennis and the soldiers wanted to get rid of him. I wasn't allowed to have a boyfriend. Dennis was always worried they'd get me money.

Apart from refurbishing the homes he bought, Dennis also spent considerable attention and money on making them more secure. He had little choice—growing police interest in his burgeoning empire made it essential for him to control access to the properties he used for dealing drugs, and later, firearms. Some of the precautions he took were deceptively simple—like using the window already present in the wall between the massage parlour at 108 Stephenson Street, and the house at 106. On one occasion Kathy found Dennis smashing into the wall with a sledgehammer.

I said: 'What have you done?' He said: 'I've dropped me bag of speed in the gap between the walls. About three or four thousand dollars. And I'm sledgehammering it to get it out.' I said: 'Have you ever heard of a stick with a bit of chewy on it?' So I got the chewy and the stick and got it out for him. Another time seven grams of smack went through the washing machine in someone's clothes. They forgot to take it out.

Most of the drug-dealing at this time was done from the parlour, but the heroin was kept next door. When the buyer gave his order the required deal would be handed through the window in the wall. This meant that large quantities of drugs were never kept on the premises from which business was conducted—an essential precaution for trouble-free dealing. Another measure was to keep a fire burning in the grate whenever drugs were around in quantity. However uncomfortable this may have been on hot summer days, it guaranteed a ready means of destruction if an unexpected raid took place.

Metal security doors, spotlights, high brick walls and barbed-wire fences were erected around various of the properties, and at 106 wide steel cages were built around the back door, with metal meshing forming a roof over the entire concrete back yard. Dennis also had his dogs and soldiers. Kathy was not impressed with either.

He'd have up to half a dozen soldiers at one time, not all paid. The ones that bodyguarded me were paid $300 a day. I only had one soldier at a time. He had more, real hangers-on. He paid them money, but mostly drink and whatever. There was no bodyguard for Jason, my grandson, like they said. Jason just ran in the streets. There were about fifteen soldiers altogether at different times. All crooks.

They weren't my sort of men, not what I'd call hard men. They were about Dennis's age. There was a toilet in the yard next door to 86 Chestnut Street. So one day this particular soldier who thought he was tough goes into the back yard, and all the guns come to his head, they're going to shoot him, and a voice said: 'The wrong one.' So he walked back inside, crying, and said: 'I resign.' He was frightened. It was the jacks. They thought it was Dennis walking out there. Dennis would have been off [dead]. There was another time when two of them took him for a ride in their car, and he came back white-faced, and the hair's sticking up on him. I was there. The police were blind drunk. There were times when they got like that, they would have killed him.

An event that Kathy still finds difficult to discuss took place when two ex-soldiers kidnapped her, holding her against her will for ten days. Initially three soldiers lured her to the South Yarra Arms Hotel near Richmond for a lengthy drinking session which carried on to a motel, where Kathy eventually passed out. While she was unconscious one of the three men got cold feet about the scheme they had in mind and cleared out.

Over the next week-and-a-half the two remaining soldiers forced Kathy to drive them around the state and even into New South Wales, keeping on the move and never letting her out of their sight. At a hotel in Lakes Entrance, in Gippsland, Kathy recognised a police inspector from Melbourne having lunch, but failed to catch his eye. She had around $10,000 in a bank account which the men forced her to withdraw and hand over to them. They then sent a note to Dennis saying: 'Have kidnapped Hell City Kate.'

Surprisingly, Dennis did nothing and it was left to Victor to deal with the matter. Not content with their note, the two men threatened to kill her or take her to a tattooist and get the letters 'DRUG DEALER' inscribed on her forehead in large letters. While Kathy did not really believe the death threat, she had no doubt they would have gone ahead with the tattooing.

By this stage the $10,000 was running out, and the two men decided to return to Melbourne, where Kathy was finally able to make her escape, just as Victor was about to inform the police. She persuaded them to stop on St Kilda Road so that she could go to the toilet and ran across the parkland near the Shrine of Remembrance, leaving her purse in the car. Her two abductors were never seen again. But the other man who had dropped out of the project later had half his nose sliced off by her grandson Jason, in an entirely unrelated incident.

When Kathy returned home she decided against telling Dennis exactly what had happened, and the episode was eventually forgotten. But later, she was able to turn her ordeal to advantage. Some time previously Dennis had given her a $10,000 magnum revolver bearing the American Presidential seal for her protection. Only the day after her return police carried out one of their regular raids on her home and seized the magnum. When she appeared at Melbourne Magistrates' Court to answer the subsequent charge of unlawful possession of a firearm, her lawyer submitted the kidnap note as evidence of her need to have a gun for self-protection, thus securing her acquittal.

To this day Kathy is unsure of the real motive behind the kidnapping. Until now she has spoken only to her son Peter Allen about the incident.

He said: 'I think you should tell me their names, because one day one of them is going to come up and say: "What have you got to say about your mother's kidnapping?"' And I told him the names. So he knows who they are, but I've never told anyone else. I didn't tell Dennis ... I don't know if he'd have killed them, but I know someone else would have.

Dennis's dogs were only slightly more friendly than his soldiers. One was a Doberman, Julie, and the other a Rottweiler, nicknamed Fatso, but with a pedigree name half a block long. Anybody touching Dennis while they were around risked an unpleasant bite, despite their treatment at his hands. His favourite punishment for any wrongdoing, real or imagined, was to pistol-whip them close to death. But their diet consisted of highest quality beef.

Other security measures were more sophisticated, in some cases too much so. Dennis was probably one of the first criminals in Australia to own either a car phone or a phone scrambler, both wildly expensive items in those days. He had difficulty working out the intricacies of such forms of communication, and when it came to an intercom system for one of the houses, he did little more than provide Kathy with something to chuckle over for weeks to come.

You would have laughed. He's put this intercom on back to front at 106 Stephenson. I'm outside and I can hear what he's saying inside. So I've knocked on the door, and he says, 'Why didn't you speak into the thing?' and I said: 'Because I'm listening to everything you're saying, I can hear it out here. You've put it on back to front.'

Oh God he was a dill at times. How'd it've been if I'm a policeman? We had walkie-talkies, we had scramblers, we had a scanner, and we had them come in and sweep for bugs. But Dennis got them that pissed that they left their equipment behind. And the walkie-talkies, well listen to this. He's paid about three grand for them, right? So he's in his bed and I'm round in Stephenson Street, but the buildings were in the way. So I keep walking and I get to his front door, and I go in, and I'm standing right outside his bedroom door, and talking real quiet. He says: 'That sounds real good.' I said: 'Yeah, it should be, I'm right beside you.'

He used to pay this old bloke, an alcoholic, four dollars a day to clean up the dog shit at 86 Chestnut Street. That's all he was allowed to have by his wife Jeanie. So the old man sees this thing on the table, wraps it up, puts it in the burner, and sets fire to it. It was the walkie talkie. He was drunk. What do you reckon Dennis did? Flogged him.

And the fucking scrambler. We had the biggest giggle. I had to go and see that James Bond movie Goldfinger *to see how it works. We're ringing the house where the scrambler was, and it sounds like Chinese. Little did we know you had to have two phones, and put the scrambler on one and use the other. It was funny.*

Before the slope moved in next door there was a young girl living there who worked at a travel agent. And she knocked on Dennis's door one night, and she said: 'Look, I don't want to interfere with you, but your telephone conversations are coming through my television, and I can hear everything you're saying.' She was warning him.

*But what about when the jacks used to keep watch? I see
this plainclothes copper poking his head in and out. So I go
over to this bloke we knew who owned the factory, and I said:
'What's this bloke doing poking his head in and out like a
fucking chook?' Well I'd blown his cover. So I'd bought Jason
one of those unicycles, one wheel, and I said to Jason: 'Go round
the street and tell him he can fuck me if he ain't a jack.' So
Jason pedals round the back and says it. And there's another
jack there, and he cracks up laughing.*

*And then they perfected Dennis's whistle, the all-clear
whistle at ten o'clock, to tell me if I was in bed that everything
was sweet. Well they did it, didn't they?*

By now Dennis had acquired a growing arsenal of guns and
explosives. Many of the firearms were for his own use, but others
were purchased, as Dennis put it, 'so they can never be used
against us'. They were concealed in a pile of rocks bordering the
nearby railway line. 'It was Crown land, and they weren't going
to arrest the fucking Queen of England, were they?' Kathy says
laconically.

Before police from Operation Cyclops began raiding on a
regular basis, 86 Chestnut Street received a visit from the drug
squad early in 1983 when a small marijuana plantation was
uncovered, resulting in possession and cultivation charges
against Dennis. By the time Cyclops was in full swing heroin,
speed, firearms and explosives were being found both inside the
houses and underground in the gardens. Once Federal Police
'lost' a significant sum of money seized from one of Dennis's
properties. This money was presumed to have been the proceeds
of drug sales, and its disappearance resulted in an internal
inquiry.

During one major 'dig' on a blazing hot day in the back
garden of one of the Stephenson Street houses Kathy actually felt
sorry for the policemen wielding the spades and took them each

out a glass of lemonade. All except one. This officer had called her a 'fucking slut' a few days earlier, and she told him he could die of thirst before she helped him. Later the same afternoon another officer suggested they had gone deep enough and it was time to finish for the day. 'No, keep 'em at it,' Kathy told the officer in charge.

'I wanted a swimming pool or at least a jacuzzi, and they'd nearly gone far enough,' she explains.

Many tall tales have been told about the methods used to bring drugs to the various houses in Richmond. One popular theory had couriers catching trains from nearby Richmond Station and throwing the packaged heroin from the train directly into the back garden of one of the Stephenson Street houses. Kathy won't detail the actual means of delivery, but she laughs at the railway line story.

> *Never. Never. How can you open those bloody train doors or windows? And what about the other passengers? That's a load of shit. I suppose it'd get thrown right into the very holes we used to dig for it in the back yard. They must have been Deadeye Dick to chuck it so straight.*

Dennis's journalist friend John Grant pours similar scorn on this myth: 'He used to joke about it. He was paranoid about the police watching him and he'd insist that we talked out in the yard near the clothes dryer, because the electric motor gave off frequencies that interfered with the police listening devices. He'd say: "Watch out for the bags of heroin, you might get hit by one from the train." He reckoned the police had tried throwing things out of the trains themselves to see if it could be done. He said the police were just making it all up, it was stupid.'

Somehow Dennis always managed to have the money for bail—

or property as surety—on the mounting list of charges he was facing, even when the total amount was around $250,000.

In November 1984 he raised $70,000 to bail Kathy and her youngest son Trevor out, after police dug up heroin in the back garden of number 35. Trevor had been living with Kathy at 35 Stephenson Street since early that year and Jamie arrived some months later on his release from gaol. They were both playing an increasingly important role in Dennis's growing empire, particularly Jamie, who acted as an enforcer over bad debts. Another brother, Victor, was involved to a lesser degree, and had moved into 86 Chestnut Street during 1984.

At the time of his death in April 1987 Dennis faced a total of more than sixty charges, ranging from murder to possession and trafficking in drugs, possession of firearms and explosives, and serious assaults. The vast majority of these charges were brought against him during the five years between the time he moved to Richmond in 1982 and his death. Yet he spent less than two months of the entire period behind bars. Most of the charges Dennis faced would have meant a remand in custody for a first offender, let alone a career criminal coming before the courts for fresh offences while on bail for others still unheard.

So how did he convince the courts to allow him bail? The answer that he enjoyed good legal representation does not tell the whole story. The simple fact was that on many occasions police officers spoke on Dennis's behalf, supporting his applications for bail. And why did they do this?

The complete answer will probably never be known, but it is beyond doubt that Dennis had certain officers in his pocket. A number of internal inquiries were held by the police into this aspect of his operation. Witnesses have testified at various hearings to having been at one or other of Dennis's properties when phone calls were received warning of imminent police raids. There was little doubt these tip-offs came from corrupt policemen.

Jason Ryan and Peter Allen told different court hearings of being present when officers arrived at Dennis's home so he could comply with the reporting conditions of his bail. Normal practice, obviously, is for the person on remand to report at the local police station. Kathy is quite frank about the situation:

> *I knew for certain Dennis used to be in the lock-up. He'd be brought home by the cops to 102 Stephenson Street, and they'd all have a drink and everything, take him back a couple of hours later, and make out they were taking him for questioning. Certain members, that is.*

Dennis undoubtedly paid bribes to corrupt policemen, and boasted of forking out $25,000 for copies of documents detailing the Cyclops inquiry. He claimed the documents influenced him to reinforce areas of his operation the police saw as vulnerable.

One legitimate reason for Dennis's good relationship with certain officers was that he had turned informer, and was more valuable to the force on the outside supplying information about other criminals, many of them armed robbers, than languishing in gaol. This was unthinkable to Kathy, and totally opposed to the code on which she based her life.

> *I never believed it at first. A bloke flew in from Asia with condoms full of smack down his stomach. Dennis arranged to meet him outside the Riverside Hotel but gave him up. When he got there with the smack to meet Dennis the cops jumped out and arrested both of them. They pissed the bloke off and then gave Dennis the smack. They kept the money. Dennis an informer—that shocked me. When he gave up people that he liked, it was the paranoia from the drugs.*

An example of the extent to which police were prepared to keep Dennis out of harm's way involved the armed robber Jimmy

Loughnan, who had attacked Dennis in gaol (see Chapter Four) and was to die in the Jika Jika prison fire at Pentridge in 1987.

Three years before that, in 1984, Dennis informed on Loughnan and his role in a suburban bank robbery. According to Kathy, he probably even supplied Loughnan with the guns that were used in the robbery. As a result police were able to make a successful arrest, but Loughnan escaped from custody not long afterwards. So concerned were police that Loughnan had found out who gave him up and would go looking for Dennis that they supplied their prized informant with an official-issue bullet-proof vest, which later turned up in the possession of Peter Allen.

> *I know that's right about Loughnan. Because I saw him myself. I went to walk in The Cherry Tree, and all the doors except one were shut. And as I walked in Loughnan pushed me out of the way, not knowing who I was. He was going in there to see if Dennis was in there, looking for him. I told that dog, that journalist I hate, Derryn Hinch, that he didn't have a bullet-proof vest, and I had it in the bed one raid, pushing it down with me foot.*

It is impossible to make even an informed guess about how many criminals Dennis put behind bars with his information. For obvious reasons no records are kept of such matters. But the frequency with which the police supported his bail applications indicates the number was significant.

When he didn't have a police officer to stand up for him if the going was getting tough in court, Dennis was prepared to take extreme measures of his own. During one particularly difficult trial in mid-1985, facing charges of possession of drugs and firearms, he shot himself in the leg. Kathy remembers this incident well, having hidden the incriminating blood-stained jeans, though she denies another story at the time that he took rat poison to gain vital adjournments.

I took the jeans because I knew the police were coming. I ran down and put them in cold water and salt in the parlour. What amazed me, I couldn't find a fucking hole in the jeans. He must have pulled the jeans down to shoot himself.

Relations between Dennis and the police plummeted, however, on 4 September 1985, when a shot was fired through a window at Prahran Police Station, missing by inches an officer on the Cyclops task force. But police were unable to prove that either Dennis or one of his brothers was involved.

I don't know anything about the shooting at Prahran, but I know about when Dennis got the Prahran jack shop raided. Because he got sick of being raided. So he got them raided by their own mob, and when they opened the Prahran cops' lockers they found jemmies, and a sergeant was charged.

The Enforcer was the longest-serving of the soldiers, a man whom Kathy had known for years, and whom she drafted into the ranks. He also doubled as bombmaker. Not a particularly large man, he had, as Kathy puts it, a mean look, which instantly discouraged all thought of aggression except from the very brave or the very stupid.

There's not much known about him because he keeps to himself. He was a shifty man, used to drink a bottle of Scotch a day, so he couldn't do nothing, no work. One day one of those five houses Dennis bought in Cubitt Street needed renovating, and he needed a tiler. Well, The Enforcer comes out with: 'I used to be a tiler.' Well, was it on, with Dennis and him! 'You shifty fucking cunt, you've let me do all this work for years, and you've sat there, and drank me grog, and you've fucking done nothing.' The Enforcer just laughed.

In January 1996, I was present during a reunion between Kathy and The Enforcer and the Talking Bone at Kathy's home at Venus Bay. The three had not been together for seven years, and conversation soon settled on Dennis and the Richmond years.

Once again the extent of Dennis's depravity became chillingly apparent, but so did the obvious loyalty and even affection which he inspired. The Enforcer was probably as close to him as anyone, apart from Kathy, during this period. He was paid an average of $2000 a week for four years to act as number one bodyguard.

As I stood in Kathy's sun-filled garden, watching him climb from the car which had brought him down to Venus Bay, I was subconsciously bracing myself for the physically daunting nature of his appearance. I was pleasantly surprised. The man who emerged to shake my hand was dressed in Dennis's old uniform of singlet and overalls, had his steel grey hair tied in a pony tail, and wore 'granny' spectacles which, with his high, domed forehead, gave him a slightly professorial look. The tattoos on his forearms were a more accurate pointer to The Enforcer's real nature, however, as was his conversation once we settled down inside the house. Pleasant and amiable as he was throughout, there was no escaping the air of menace that emanated from the man. It was expressed in the manner in which he discussed the taking of human life and the extent to which he clearly accepted Dennis's worst atrocities.

The Talking Bone was a different prospect. The ravages of her heroin addiction and life as a prostitute were evident in her face. But, as Kathy proudly explained, Dee (Kathy's pet name for her) had been on a methadone program for some time, and seemed to have her addiction beaten. She had also been off the game for a considerable period. So, as she began to relax, something softer and more intelligent began to emerge from behind the gaunt and wary mask. Even so it was The Talking Bone who uttered the days only threat, albeit humorously: 'We might not be able to let you go home after what you hear today,' she told me early in the conversation.

We had barely settled into our chairs in Kathy's living room when The Enforcer spotted a photograph of himself on the wall, wearing a green shirt.

That's the shirt Dennis gave me $200 for. He couldn't handle anybody wearing green, it reminded him of what they made you wear inside *[in prison]*. It was 1985, my thirty-ninth birthday. My wife bought the shirt, paid $20 for it. Soon as I walked in he said: 'What the fuck are you wearing that shirt for?' He told me to get rid of it, and went to hand me $200 to buy another one. I told him I couldn't, because it was a birthday present from my wife. He said he didn't know it was my birthday, and gave me the $200, and another $1000 to take my wife out. He said to go and enjoy ourselves, and I needn't come back till tomorrow, but make sure I got rid of the shirt. That was the start of giving all the soldiers $1000 for their birthdays.

It was also the start of an escalation involving Dennis's aversion to the colour green. Soldiers and the family began deliberately wearing green to see how much Dennis would pay to watch them burn the offending garments. His youngest brother, Trevor, turned up one day in an apple green number he swore he had paid $300 for. Dennis coughed up without argument.

'He was generous,' The Enforcer remembered.

I was in the Cherry Tree with him one day when he gave a paper boy two $50 notes for a paper and told him to keep it. Then he gave him the paper back and told him to sell it again, because Dennis didn't read papers, said they were full of shit. Even when there was an article about him and I'd tell him, he'd say: 'Don't bother reading it to me, it'll be shit.'

But he was strange with money. He'd lend you $100, and

if he thought you were trying to get away without paying it back, he was capable of killing over it. But if you went to him and told him you were having trouble, he could say, 'Forget it,' wipe the debt, and give you $200 to get you by. That was Dennis—if he liked you he'd kill for you, but if he didn't like you, you might as well start digging your own hole yourself.

Even stranger was the way he practised his shoplifting skills. On more than one occasion Kathy has been known to say, 'I stole everything I'm wearing.' Dennis inherited the same cavalier attitude to the tiresome business of paying for one's shopping as The Enforcer was able to testify. Together they made many trips to the local hardware stores to buy supplies for the latest refurbishment project on one of the properties.

We'd be buying timber, paint, the works, and often the bill would be around $2,000. We'd go up to the counter and Dennis would pull out this wad and tell me to settle it. While the bloke was doing up the invoice Dennis would take this packet off the counter with drill bits or something in it. He'd slip one of the bits into his pocket and put the packet back. Half the time the bloke would know what was going on and he'd look at me, and raise his eyebrows and I'd just nod to put it on the bill. We'd get outside and Dennis would say: 'Got away with it again.' He thought he was keeping his hand in.

When he found out his Vietnamese neighbour didn't own, or as it turned out, particularly want a TV set, Dennis went out and bought him one—'Poor bloke hasn't got a TV,' he kept mumbling to himself.

It was from the Vietnamese neighbour that Dennis acquired much of his legendary cooking ability. 'He used to call it Dennis's triple chilli,' The Enforcer said, 'and none of us could handle it, used to make your mouth numb. I'd tell him I wasn't hungry and go and buy six dim sims and eat 'em outside.'

The Enforcer was paid his $2000 a week to protect Dennis from his enemies, but actually earned the money by protecting Dennis from himself—the single, biggest ongoing threat to his existence. This included taking a gun from him—something he doubts anybody else ever did—on three separate occasions, including the incident with the police helicopter.

'There's no doubt he would have blown the chopper away if he'd hit it,' he says. Kathy and The Enforcer share a theory that the absence of any comeback over the helicopter shooting was because the noise of the engine drowned the sound of gunfire; and the chopper's position, over Dennis's Cubitt Street back yard, made it impossible for the occupants to see what was happening directly beneath them. The possibility that one of Dennis's influential police contacts got him off the hook for such an act cannot be entirely discounted. The Enforcer recounts another shooting incident.

Then there was New Year's at the Bryant and May factory, I think it was 1983-84. There was a tower with a clock on it, and Dennis had two guns, one a .357 Magnum with a thirty-centimetre barrel. He was about 150 metres away and he shot the minute hand, it hung down swinging like a pendulum. Five minutes later the cops came and knocked on the door: 'Dennis, we know this is New Year, but can you pull up on the gunfire?' Dennis says: 'What are you fucking talking about?' 'Someone's shot the clock tower.'

He comes back: 'Every time something gets shot in Richmond I get blamed.' So they said: 'We've got to be right 90 per cent of the time. Happy New Year.' And Dennis says: 'Happy New Year you dogs, go and get fucked.'

And when Dennis tripped over a pile of rubbish in the back lane at Stephenson Street, lost his temper and started a blaze big enough to bring several fire engines racing to the scene, it was again The Enforcer who had to smooth things over—with near fatal results.

> I heard all these sirens going from Stephenson Street, and to get there in a hurry I ran across the railway line and nearly got my head knocked off by a train. I was on $10,000 bail at the time, and Kathy said: 'Never mind, as long as your head would have rolled down here I could have taken it to court and got the ten thousand back.'

Dennis's rage when crossed was legendary, and The Enforcer was one of the few people prepared to attempt to calm him down. The two men made a bet with one another during the height of the heroin dealing, mainly because they were often paid by small-time users in small change, including one-dollar coins. Each bought a giant-sized beer can money box and began keeping the one-dollar coins in them. The one who filled his can first took the lot. Some months into the bet The Enforcer was short of cash and told Dennis he was going to open his can—and together they counted out $3,000 in coins.

> We were both on speed so Dennis decided it would be a good idea to count his. It weighed about three times as much as mine, so we figured it should be around $10,000. He got the top off and poured it on the floor, and out came ten kilos of half-inch washers. We worked out straightaway what had happened.
>
> Cossie, the house guard at one of the properties, had just shot through, we knew he'd gone to Adelaide where his family was. He must have gone and bought the washers, and another beer can money box, and put the washers in until they weighed the same as Dennis's can and then swapped them over. Dennis was frothing at the mouth and his eyes were popping out of

his head. It was two o'clock in the morning, but he didn't care.

He told me to get straight out to Tullamarine and get a plane to Adelaide. I told him: 'Dennis, there's no planes flying at this time.' So he pulled this roll of notes out, about $50,000, and said: 'Get down to Mordialloc *[light aircraft airport]* and charter a plane and get over there.' Then he gave me a .357 Magnum to shoot him with. But we didn't know where Cossie lived in Adelaide, and when I reminded Dennis of this he said: 'Just ask people.' 'Sure Dennis,' I said. 'Wander around Adelaide with a .357 Magnum in me hand and say, "Excuse me, I'm looking for a bloke called Cossie, do you know where he lives?"' We found out later he'd gone to Perth, anyway.

Another acquaintance, Scotty, also ended on the wrong side of Dennis, but was less fortunate than Cossie. The Enforcer remembers Scotty as a street dealer who informed on Dennis when police put him under pressure.

What I liked about Scotty was he declared himself, he said as soon as the cops threatened him, he told them anything they wanted to know. This time he'd said something about us, and Dennis was waiting for him to come round. He had put a poker in the fire, getting the end white hot. I got fed up with waiting and went down The Cherry Tree. I was sitting there and Scotty comes running past at 100 miles an hour with an ice pick hanging out his back. Dennis had changed his mind about the poker, but when we saw him later Scotty was more worried what the ice pick did to his leather jacket than the hole in his back.

Every now and then the pace became too hot, even for The Enforcer, and he needed to get away. 'There was one time I had to have a break from Dennis and everything, so I went into hiding for a week,' he said. 'Dennis shit himself, because he thought I was dead, and he was next. We always said if the police or his enemies were going to kill him, they'd get rid of me first, so I wasn't running around after he'd gone.'

The Enforcer knew things were starting to get out of hand, even for Richmond, when he noticed how children involved in the extended family of Dennis's evil umpire were being affected.

One time I was at 102, the drug house, and we'd closed the doors for the night. There was this woman junkie banging at the door, shouting: 'Kathy, open up! Sell me some smack or I'll call the police.' I ran out with a .38 in me jocks, and there's this woman, about twenty-one. She says: 'Where's Kathy?' I told her to fuck off and she kept on, so I pulled the gun out. She had a baby and she held it up in front of her face and said: 'If you shoot me, you'll have to shoot the baby first.' I said: 'Christ, lady, just go home.' There was another junkie wanted to swap her ten-day-old baby for a cap of heroin.

Children within the inner circle were faring little better. One six-year-old was well known for her impersonations of her own mother. On request or to impress strangers, she would jab an imaginary needle in her arm, stick out her tongue and keel over, lying motionless. 'That's Mum OD-ing [over-dosing],' she'd explain.

Equally shocking was an exchange The Enforcer overheard one morning. He and Dennis had been discussing the need to cut a shipment of heroin, otherwise it would be too strong for the street and cost people their lives. Throughout the conversation a five-year-old had been watching a children's program on TV in the same room, apparently riveted to the screen. Later her mother arrived and asked what she'd been up to. 'Just watching TV.' And what had Dennis and The Enforcer been doing? Without turning from the television the five-year-old said matter-of-factly: 'They've got to cut the smack again so nobody OD's.'

THE MATRIARCH

About a year later the same child accompanied her father and
The Enforcer to a Richmond hotel for a drink in the beer garden.
When the barmaid left the till unattended to go inside the hotel,
The Enforcer's companion turned to the girl and said: 'What does
Daddy do when the barmaid's back's turned?' Wordlessly the
six-year-old walked behind the bar, expertly opened the till
without registering a sale, and returned to the table clutching a
wad of notes.

One youngster The Enforcer took particular notice of was
Jason Ryan, Dennis's nephew, who arrived in Richmond at the
age of thirteen. 'I picked him as a coward straight away, and I
told Dennis to get rid of him, but he wouldn't listen. He'd done
something and I went to belt him and he pulled a knife on me.
At thirteen. I was going to break his arm, and I should have
done. He went off crying to his uncle.'

Champion footballer Fred Cook, who has blamed Dennis for
introducing him to the drugs which led to several court appearances over the years, was someone The Enforcer remembers with
little affection—'He was good with words, but he was a user.'

The night before his wedding Cook arrived at Richmond to
explain to Dennis and The Enforcer that, despite their friendship,
he couldn't invite them to the ceremony because the media
would be there, and he couldn't afford to be seen associating
with them. 'It didn't stop him asking for some speed though,'
recalls The Enforcer.

> He wanted two grams for $100, so I went and got it and gave
> it to him and said: 'This is a wedding present from Dennis and
> me.' Dennis's eyes popped out of his head, because we were
> both flat broke at this time. But he didn't know what speed it
> was. About three months earlier we'd got this stuff and it was
> mostly Epsom Salts—we spent the entire night fighting each
> other for the shithouse. I gave Fred four grams of this stuff. He
> told us later it ruined his wedding and his honeymoon.

144

There was another time when Dennis OD'd and the intensive care ambulance came. Fred was there and I gave him $1000 to pay them not to say anything about what had happened. When he came back in from seeing them off I asked if he'd given them the money. He said: 'No, I gave them something more valuable, I gave them my autograph.' But he did do the right thing and give us back the $1000. That was Fred Cook.

CHAPTER SEVEN

Charnel
▪ House ▪

'GET OUT OF THAT FUCKING BED, CUNT. I'VE JUST BLOWN THAT fucking arsehole's head off. Get in there and clean up.'

The voice coming from Kathy's bedroom door at 35 Stephenson Street is unmistakable. It's Dennis. He's been days without sleep and, as always, he's rocking backwards and forwards on his heels, his form silhouetted in the doorway by the hall light. He wears a jacket over his bib and brace overalls.

It's two o'clock on a Sunday morning in mid-August 1984. Kathy has gone to bed about three hours earlier. A party of sorts has been going on at Dennis's place next door since the previous afternoon. Besides Dennis, those present are his girl-friend, known as 'Miss Jones' for legal reasons, his thirteen-year-old nephew Jason, Wayne, the builder Dennis has employed for the last eighteen months to renovate his various properties, Wayne's wife Sandy and the couple's son, Dale, still in his early teens.

The final member of the party is Wayne Stanhope, twenty-nine, an open-faced, relatively recent acquaintance of Dennis. Kathy met him for the first time a few weeks earlier when Dennis brought him to the Gaslight massage parlour. Unknown to Stanhope, some days ago Dennis has been shown a photograph* which will come to assume considerable influence over the events about to unfold. In the photograph Stanhope wears a policeman's hat with his arms fraternally around the shoulders of two uniformed officers.

During the afternoon the party proceeds uneventfully enough—Dennis and Stanhope go down to The Cherry Tree a couple of times, a few phone bets are made on the race meeting at Sandown, and everybody gradually loosens up. By early evening Dennis is acting the generous host, pouring drinks and injecting himself and Stanhope with free hits of speed. The tasteful and expensive furnishings of his new home provide a bizarre setting for a social gathering that is about to go hideously off the rails.

It's around 11 p.m. when Dennis changes from congenial host to maniacal killer. Jason is in his room by now—even criminals' nephews get sent to bed before the grown-ups. Dale has gone with him, but the rest are in the lounge room. Stanhope is standing near the record player when without warning Dennis pulls a silver .38 pistol from the front of his trousers and fires across the room. As the first shot rips into his shoulder Stanhope spins around and says just three words: 'Oh, no, Dennis.'

A second shot explodes into his forehead and a third into his chest. He slides down the wall and slumps face down onto the carpet, a couple of metres from where Sandy is sitting in mute horror. Dennis walks deliberately across the room, holds the silver pistol a few centimetres from Stanhope's head and empties the remaining bullets into him. At each impact his head jerks and convulses, blood starting to seep onto the carpet. Nobody

---

* There have been many theories put forward to explain what happened next. One is that Stanhope changed a record at the wrong time. Kathy scoffs at this: 'Nobody but Dennis was ever allowed near the record player.' Jason Ryan suggested that Stanhope planned to steal Dennis's jewellery. Kathy firmly believes the photograph described above was sufficient reason to convince Dennis that Stanhope was a police informer, there to collect information.

speaks as Dennis walks over and, incredibly, knocks on the door of the bedroom where Jason and Dale are sleeping.

Jason opens the door almost immediately and Dennis mutters something inaudible to him. Jason ducks back inside the room and returns with a firearm which he hands to Dennis. Dennis walks back to where Stanhope is lying. Jason follows him as if hypnotised. Again Dennis places the weapon inches from Stanhope and empties its contents into his head.

By now Dennis is beyond reason, beyond control, screaming his rage at his horrified guests. 'That'll happen to all of you if you don't keep your mouths shut.' For some reason he won't believe Stanhope is dead, and orders Miss Jones to pass him a knife. She hands it to him and he pulls his victim's head off the floor by the hair and cuts his throat, the sudden welling of blood adding to the gore which already stains the carpet.

Someone is vomiting. Someone else is screaming their terror. The deed is finally done, and now it's clean-up time. Where's Kathy?

I'm not sure what time it was he came next door to my place, about two or three in the morning I suppose. And he's standing at my bedroom door. I sensed someone was there, I wasn't in a deep sleep. He says: 'Get out of that fuckin' bed, cunt. I've just blown that fuckin' arsehole's head off.'

I said: 'What arsehole?' He said: 'That fuckin' Wayne.' I wasn't sure which one he meant. I said: 'Well, who else is in there, Dennis?' and he mentioned all those names. And I said: 'Well, I'm not getting out of this fucking bed 'til you go in there and you knock 'em all.' Because I knew they'd give people up. I knew it. I'd already sensed it. Not Jason, I wasn't worried about Jason.

He was going to kill Stanhope right from the start. But I didn't think he'd shoot him in the house in front of all those

*people. But that's Dennis. He shot everybody in front of people.
He always wanted an audience. Anyway there was a load of
shit written about the clean-up, about dragging the body onto
the tile floor. He died in one small square of carpet which the
police took up later for forensic reasons. But he'd had my
vacuum cleaner which had a tin base. And that's what he used
to vacuum up his brains and that. And then he burnt my
bloody vacuum cleaner, which he didn't have to do because it
was tin.*

How has Kathy come to this, more disturbed by the waste of a
vacuum cleaner than the waste of a human being cold-bloodedly
murdered by her own son? And how could she have considered
using the appliance again after it had been employed to suck up
'brains and that'? The same way, presumably, that she could
consider giving Jamie the tracksuit trousers removed from the
battered frame of another of Dennis's victims.

How could she have allowed things to reach such a stage?
When she learned of Dennis's first murder, or the first time he
informed on a friend, why didn't she read him the riot act,
disown him, or segregate him from the rest of her boys?

Logical as this may sound today, there was too much in the
way. Only sixteen years separated the two of them, and Dennis
spent half of his life under the impression Kathy was his sister,
not his mother. By the time he became blasé, even about murder,
it was too late, and his addiction to speed made communication
virtually impossible. Kathy rejects any suggestion that she had
the opportunity of influencing, let alone disciplining her murderous son in his last few years.

*You couldn't do it. He was mad by then. You would have had
to find the time to say it, and then it would have preyed on his
mind, and the next time he was rocking on his heels and gone
thirteen or fourteen days without sleep, I would've got a bullet.*

I wasn't frightened of him, but at times he forgot who I was. Like when he chased me into my house, and I slammed the door, and he kicked it open. He didn't know who I was that night. He confused me with one of his girlfriends. He followed me in and I said: 'Listen, Dennis, put the gun down, I'm your mother.' And he turned around and left. Even before Richmond when we were at Northcote, Dennis and I had a fight. He chases me round my place, handcuffs me and steals me money. I was there for hours. What could you do?

If there is any blame to be attached to Kathy for Dennis's life, maybe the roots lie somewhere among her childhood memories of decapitated corpses and dead men's teeth. Or perhaps they can be found in her later experiences after Dennis joined her in Richmond in July 1982, some two years before the murder of Wayne Stanhope. As the death toll mounted in the charnel house of 37 Stephenson Street and elsewhere, perhaps Kathy, like Dennis, was becoming oblivious to human suffering and pain.

I think I got blasé about murder in the end. The first murder of Greg was the worst. I'll tell you about Greg's death.

The very first murder, in May 1983, of Greg Pasche, a twenty-two-year-old whom Kathy regarded in many ways as her own son, is something she still remembers with horror and remorse. Kathy had first met him in his early teens when he was an inmate of Turana Boys' Home at the same time as her fifth son, Lex. From then on, typically, she regularly had him to stay, and unofficially adopted him.

Greg's death came not long after Kathy had been involved in a punishing binge at Dennis's place at Chestnut Street. Finally she told him: 'Dennis, I'm not drinking no more after the next one.' So he gave her a 'half a yard' (a long glass tube holding more than a litre of liquid) containing half a dozen different varieties of spirits mixed together. Kathy eventually knocked it back and lurched off home to Stephenson Street. Her head hit the pillow around four o'clock in the morning, but two hours later she woke to a banging on the front door.

It was Dennis. 'You've got to go to Sydney.' Kathy, still drunk, asked: 'What for?' Dennis told her her son Peter, then on the list of the ten most wanted criminals in Victoria, had just been arrested on the run in Sydney, where he had been operating a drug ring.

Dennis told Kathy to follow him round to Chestnut Street, where he would give her the money for the next flight to Sydney. Then three or four of Dennis's soldiers, who had accompanied him to Kathy's house, jumped her. A week earlier, at Dennis's insistence, the same soldiers had taken Kathy through a bizarre form of dress rehearsal to gauge her reaction if police sprang a surprise raid. On that occasion Kathy was prepared, and kicked and punched her way free. This time the element of surprise, and the alcohol still befuddling her brain gave her little chance. The soldiers had her securely held.

I'm thinking: 'What the fuck's going on here?' Next thing Dennis whacks a needle in me arm. It was speed. Because I got the worst hangover, right? By the time I got to Sydney, the minute my foot touched the ground I was buzzing. It's the answer to all hangovers.

Kathy visited her son Peter where he was being held in Long Bay Gaol after his arrest, and then returned immediately to Melbourne. Dennis ordered her to go straight back to Sydney, this time by road in the company of three soldiers. The plan was to bring Peter's car and machine guns back—a little difficult on Ansett Airlines. The other job for the soldiers was to stand over the people who owed drug money to Peter and collect it where possible. Kathy, meanwhile, was in the Sydney flat where Peter had been staying while on the run.

Kathy managed another visit to Long Bay to see Peter again on this second trip. He told her he had found out Greg Pasche was also in the prison. She immediately paid the $500 bail to secure his release and took him back to Melbourne with her and the soldiers when their debt collection duties were finished three or four days later. Then on the Friday following his return, Greg suddenly disappeared. Kathy assumed he had gone back to Sydney to collect his valuable Harley Davidson motor cycle he'd left there.

The next day Kathy called around to Chestnut Street to get money off Dennis for her weekly trip to play bingo. He had just lost $10,000 on the races and was sulking. He wouldn't let Kathy in, but gave her the money anyway. When she got home later in the day Dennis sent a message that he needed to borrow her electric heaters. Kathy couldn't work out why he wanted them, but took them over to Chestnut Street where, for some reason, the carpets had been stripped from the floor, which was noticeably wet. Then to her amazement Dennis suddenly threw some bizarre form of fit, cowering in a foetal position in a corner of the room and moaning. Kathy had never seen him behave like this before and was genuinely shaken by the experience, particularly because she had no idea what might have caused it.

Two months later Kathy and Dennis were drinking together in The Cherry Tree Hotel when Dennis dropped the bombshell. 'Greg's dead,' he said. Kathy simply refused to believe him. But a few days later a detective from Greensborough called in to see her at 106 Stephenson Street and said: 'There's no nice way to tell you that Greg's dead.' Greg's body with its badly battered skull and multiple stab wounds had been found near Mount Dandenong not far from Dennis's boyhood home at Monbulk.

Well, I went to pieces. I've never gone to pieces like that since. Never. It was killing me. I was guilty. I brought him down to be murdered. I didn't even ask the copper how or what or why. I just went berserk. That's the only word. I was like a wild animal. I finally worked it all out. That the wet floor is where he died. His body was found at Ullnulu, he's been stabbed to death. Greg is the sort of person, if he didn't like you he wouldn't speak. Don't forget he was only twenty-three. And they took it for arrogance. So this Victor Gouroff I believe he murdered him, maybe Dennis couldn't stop it. He had the fit later on for remorse, fear, whatever, I couldn't say.

Kathy is still unsure of the role Dennis played after Greg's murder. She is certain, however, that Dennis took no part in the act itself.

I'll tell you why. I was living with this bloke at the time. He was coming down the back lane, and Dennis was paranoid, and he heard footsteps, and got up on the back fence and went to shoot him. And he saw it was my bloke. And his first thought was: 'What would me mother do if I shot him?' So, he knew how much I loved Greg. He would have thought, 'No.' So he either wasn't there, or he'd gone to The Cherry Tree, or he'd gone, maybe out to tea or something. I don't think he was in the house even.

So if Gouroff was the killer, whether Dennis actually assisted him in the murder, or whether he simply didn't do enough to stop him is unknown. Either way, Pasche's body was found three months after his disappearance. Kathy hadn't seen anything sinister in his absence—he had always drifted in and out of her life, and three months between visits was nothing out of the ordinary.

The search for Pasche's killers was hampered by two red

herrings—the first being a theory that he was murdered by someone employing him as a male prostitute. Police made special appeals in the red light district of St Kilda for information from street kids who sold themselves for drugs, or even food. Pasche was believed to have been a part-time male prostitute working the notorious Fitzroy Street beat. The second theory was very much a sign of the times. His death was linked with that of two drug-related slayings around that period. This was the mid-1980s and Melbourne was only just getting used to the idea that heroin dealers would murder one another to protect their territory. Much more realistic was the anonymous detective who told the *Sun* he believed Pasche had got out of his depth in his dealings with 'a group of notorious Melbourne criminals'.

Kathy's theory today is that Pasche had taken a dislike to Gouroff on that Saturday in May and had reacted in his normal way, by refusing conversation. In the resultant conflict, he was stabbed and beaten to death. Six years later, at an unrelated trial, Kathy's daughter-in-law, Wendy Peirce, gave evidence that she was present when a man called Peterson cut Greg's throat. He was carried out into the back yard where Dennis 'did something to his head' and his body was then disposed of.

The inquest into Pasche's death was held on 29 June 1984, and found that he died from multiple stab wounds and a fractured skull, having been murdered by persons unknown. Giving her occupation as 'housewife', Kathy said in evidence that she had last seen him alive on 27 May 1983. Today the one point about which she has no doubt is that the murder took place in Dennis's house in Chestnut Street, where the heaters were used to dry the floor. Whether or not Gouroff murdered Pasche, he did not live long to tell the tale. But before he died there was a second murder for Kathy to grieve over—although this one had nothing to do with Dennis. The victim this time was Tom Wraith, thirty-three, a close friend.

He was God to us. We all loved him. I've got a photo of Tom with Dennis and my daughter Vicki, because she lived with Tom, but she wasn't the one that murdered him. He was murdered with my tomahawk.

The woman who was eventually charged and convicted of Wraith's manslaughter was Rae Elizabeth Collingburn—wife of Neil Collingburn, whose death two days after an incident at Russell Street police station in March 1971 resulted in manslaughter charges against Detective Senior-Sergeant Brian Murphy and another officer. Both were acquitted.

Wraith, a heroin addict, had been at the drug shop in Stephenson Street with Kathy on the night of 14 September 1983 until about 11.30 p.m. By two o'clock in the morning he was dead, killed with Kathy's tomahawk, which he had borrowed to chop firewood. Kathy was not called as a witness at Rae Collingburn's trial, although evidence concerning the tomahawk could have played an important part.

In her defence Rae Collingburn claimed Wraith kept the tomahawk by his bed, but made no mention of his having borrowed it from Kathy. Collingburn had said on the night of Tom's death he was telling her about a woman called Grace O'Connor whom he had killed in England. 'He was cleaning his gun and clicking it and pointing it at me,' she claimed. Wraith finally put the gun to her head, so she grabbed the tomahawk and hit him in the head. Wraith fell back but then started to get to his feet. So Collingburn hit him again.

She denied having murdered him but was convicted of the lesser charge of manslaughter, being sentenced to four years' gaol. Mr Justice Southwell, sitting in the Criminal Court, told her that with remissions for good behaviour she would probably serve only one year. She did, but died not long after her release, leaving Kathy outraged that she could not take the revenge she had planned when told in prison of Collingburn's death.

> I said: 'What? She's dead? I've been looking for her for three
> fucking years. And I haven't had any justice.' Tom used to
> come to me every morning, because I was in bed with the grief
> with Greg. He'd bring me a flower and wipe me dressing table
> over. He was a very good gentleman, right. And three weeks
> after Greg's body's found he's dead too. So I had two tragedies.
> He was my best friend.

Today most police who were involved with Dennis believe he
murdered both Greg Pasche and Victor Gouroff. Kathy disagrees.
She believes Gouroff was responsible for Greg's murder.
Gouroff's body has never been found, but nobody police or
underworld, doubts that he is dead. For a long time Dennis was
rumoured to be Gouroff's killer, as a payback for Greg Pasche's
death.

In many ways it suited Dennis to be known in underworld
circles as Gouroff's murderer. The dead man had once enjoyed
a reputation as one of Melbourne's heaviest armed robbers, and
the rumours sent out a clear message that anybody who messed
with Mr Death, as he was starting to be known, was in deep
trouble. Wendy Peirce told the same unrelated trial mentioned
above that she saw Gouroff sitting dead in a chair. A drug addict
with a long and varied record for crimes of violence and dishonesty, the German-born Gouroff was known to police to have
been an associate of Dennis, adding further credence to the
rumours. However, Kathy has a different theory:

> Victor Gouroff did kill Greg, but Dennis didn't kill him. I know
> that because I know who did. It was his friend that killed him.
> He injected him in the neck.

Despite what Kathy says, a protected witness in a Sydney court case, the previously mentioned 'Miss X', later gave evidence that Dennis was responsible. Miss X told the Glebe Court in 1988, a year after Dennis's death, that she had been taken by him to meet an unnamed Melbourne detective in the outer suburb of Nunawadling. Dennis and the detective told her they were to meet a man, who she later learnt was Gouroff. Miss X told the court she watched from Dennis's car, parked in a deserted side street, as Gouroff approached. Dennis and the detective spoke with Gouroff for a few minutes before Dennis pulled a gun and shot Gouroff four or five times, she said. Again, Kathy denies that Dennis ever met Miss X.

Whoever killed him, it was in November 1983 that Gouroff went missing, two months after Tom Wraith's death. Wayne Stanhope was next, nine months later in August 1984.

Stanhope's was the only murder with which Dennis was ever charged—albeit nearly three years after the event. The breakthrough came as a combination of thorough police work early on, and the decline of Dennis's power towards the end of his life. Much of the credit was due to Detective Irene Moir, who was travelling in a patrol car down Stephenson Street on the night Stanhope was murdered. Because of the unsavoury reputation of the area she noted the numbers of several parked cars. One of these was a green Ford van owned by relatives of Stanhope, and lent to him earlier on the day of his death.

This same van was found the following day by a farm manager, deep in bushland nearly 100 kilometres from Melbourne, having been deliberately set on fire. The manager also reported seeing a car containing two males in the vicinity at the time. Within days police had linked Irene Moir's routine noting of the van in Stephenson Street with the burned out shell found in the bush. But there was no indication that anything untoward had happened to Stanhope or that there was anything suspicious about his sudden disappearance.

Nonetheless Dennis was interviewed, but naturally denied any knowledge of having seen Stanhope on the night he disappeared. It is easy to reflect on how many lives might have been spared over the next three years if some form of admission had been obtained from him.

Although Stanhope's body was never found, the reason police were eventually able to charge Dennis with murdering him was due to Dennis's declining power. However loyal Wayne the builder remained after the event, he and his wife Sandy had been profoundly disturbed by the horror of that night. And so had Dennis's girlfriend, Miss Jones. Eventually, as Dennis's health confined him to a hospital bed, the three of them decided to make statements detailing what they had seen. They were then placed under the care of the witness protection scheme—hence the need, even today, to conceal their identities.

In his statement on Stanhope's death, Wayne implicated Victor, 'and either Jamie or Trevor', in the removal of the body from the sitting room. He also described Dennis burning clothing and towels in an incinerator. At the inquest he described the attitude of those present as 'quite shocked and hysterical'. The following day, Wayne continued, Dennis ordered him to buy caustic soda and clean the back of a truck parked in the laneway behind 37 Stephenson Street.

It was not until 11 April 1988 that an inquest was held into Stanhope's death. Sandy's evidence included an account of a strange episode in which Dennis carefully wrapped up two tins of dog food as a birthday present for his sister Vicki. 'Dog' means an informer in the underworld argot and Dennis, despite his own similar failings, had long suspected Vicki of passing on information to police. He constantly taunted her with gestures like the cans of dog food. At the same time he was still capable of demonstrating a brother's love for her. When, on one occasion,

Vicki arrived in Richmond barefoot and destitute, Dennis immediately walked her up the street and bought her an entire wardrobe of clothes.

Sandy testified that Dennis had emptied two guns into Stanhope and then waved the second of them at everyone present, telling them, 'Keep your mouths shut.' Then he added: 'This bastard is still alive ... pass me a fucking knife and I'll cut his throat.'

Under cross-examination she described how her son Dale, who was asleep at the time of the murder, had been kept by Dennis overnight at the house. When she told her husband as they were departing to go and get the boy, Dennis had said: 'No, leave him where he is, he'll be all right. Just leave him where he is. You can get him tomorrow.'

Sandy also spoke of threats from Dennis to the lives of her family. But despite this she admitted that she and her husband moved into 102 Stephenson Street four months after the murder and stayed there for twelve months. According to Kathy, however, it was only one week later that they moved in. Once they left, Sandy said, they had no further contact with Dennis and went to great pains to hide their address from him, moving on one occasion when they learnt he had been told of their whereabouts.

Miss Jones did not appear at the inquest, but a statement by her describing the murder was read to the court. In it she said:

Dennis then walked over and emptied every bullet he had left into Wayne's head. The gun would have been about a foot to eighteen inches away from Wayne's head when Dennis fired the shots. I can remember the jerking movements of Wayne's head as the bullets struck him. [Sandy] did not move. I remember one bullet seemed to go just past her face. She just froze. I was in shock, and just couldn't believe what I was seeing.

159

On 19 May 1990, Miss Jones gave evidence in an unrelated Supreme Court trial which provided a chilling insight into her life as Dennis's partner. She told the court she was suffering from heroin addiction during this period, costing her $200 a day, and was occasionally kept in chains as a prisoner by Dennis at both 35 and 37 Stephenson Street. Although she 'handled' her heroin addiction, speed was different. 'I was getting it shoved into my veins by Dennis,' she said. 'It would make me crazy in the head, just very uptight and stupid and confused.'

Miss Jones also explained how she had escaped her captivity in Stephenson Street by grabbing a key, letting herself out and 'running for my life' while Dennis was absent. Nowhere in her statements or evidence dealing with Stanhope's murder did Miss Jones mention Kathy, although she implicated Trevor and Jamie Pettingill in the clean-up afterwards, describing the burning of clothes and the removal of the body.

Kathy in fact stayed in bed next door, well out of the way.

I didn't go next door. You see, at times later on when he said he had killed people, half the time you didn't know whether it was the truth or not. Because he wasn't coherent. I stayed in bed. That's when he took the vacuum cleaner in. Why would I go in there with all those witnesses? No way. If he wanted me in there ... but why do it in front of an audience, big-noting himself.

We all went to the inquest, right? And by this time Sandy and Wayne are in the witness protection scheme. We had a barrister, and I asked him: 'If they were so terrified for their lives, why then did they move into Stephenson Street after the murder?' But the Coroner did find that members of my family removed the body and did whatever.

Despite the absence of a body, Coroner Hal Hallenstein found Stanhope died from cardio-respiratory failure following multiple gunshot wounds to the head. He also decided:

The deceased's body was removed from the premises by Allen and members of his family, and then disposed of at a place, in circumstances and by a person or persons unknown ... And I further find that Dennis James Ryan (also known as Dennis Bruce Allen) caused the death of Wayne Patrick Stanhope by shooting.

Then, in a dramatic afterword, the Coroner passed final judgment on Dennis—exactly a year, less two days, after his death.

In this matter the actions of Dennis Bruce Allen indicate him to have been a vicious, dangerous and unstable person surrounded by people who both supported and assisted him. In this matter a number of relevant people are still alive, and three key witnesses in these proceedings fear for their lives, and live in hiding from those they believe continue to cherish Allen's way of life and memory.

The Coroner then explained why the identities of the three witnesses, Miss Jones, Wayne and Sandy, had been suppressed: 'It would be unreasonable to risk life for the purposes of this inquest.'

Although Stanhope's body has never been found, Victor's wife, Wendy Peirce, probably led police to his final resting place in 1989 when she was under the witness protection scheme during the period leading up to the committal of her husband and two other men for the Walsh Street killings. After hours of digging in bushland in a national park, police uncovered items of clothing identified as belonging to Stanhope. The theory at the time was that wild pigs may have consumed the body.

Kathy will not comment about rumours circulating among police that when the body was being buried Dennis had jumped on Stanhope's head to force it into the ground, causing it to break apart and making Jamie throw up by the makeshift graveside.

THE MATRIARCH

One month after Stanhope died a man called Lindsay Simpson was murdered in what was possibly the most tragic and senseless of all the killings involving Dennis. Simpson, a thirty-two-year-old council worker, was slain on 18 September 1984 in front of his wife and baby daughter, because his killer, Ray 'Red Rat' Pollitt, thought he was someone else—Dennis's heroin dealer, Alan Williams. Simpson was, in fact, an entirely innocent man, unconnected with the underworld. His only mistake was to be married to Williams's sister, Leonie.

The link between Dennis and Alan Williams has been explained, but what is unsure is why Dennis wanted Williams killed, something which led to much confusion in media coverage of Pollitt's various trials. One paper had 'drug deals and counterfeit money' behind the dispute, but the sums mentioned varied up to $20,000. Whatever the figure, it is unlikely that Dennis, who was regularly paying Williams larger amounts than this, would have paid Pollitt to kill a reliable dealer simply because he owed him money.

Kathy says simply: 'I don't know what it was for sure, but they fell out over something.' When Alan Williams gave evidence in Pollitt's trial he was serving a fourteen-year sentence for conspiring to murder New South Wales policeman Michael Drury (see Chapter Five). Williams told the jury Dennis had owed him between $15,000 and $20,000 for heroin. He also said he carried a gun when he went to see Dennis because he was 'always on speed, souped-up and crazy'.

So perhaps there was sufficient bad blood between the two men for Dennis to want Williams out of the way. Either way, the circumstances of Lindsay Simpson's murder were tragically simple. On that September evening he and his wife drove with their eight-month-old daughter to spend an evening with Williams and his wife Linda in their home in affluent Cheverton Road, Lower Plenty. They arrived about 8 p.m. on a cold, wet night.

Simpson climbed out of the car and walked around to the back to remove the baby's stroller as Leonie reached over into the back seat. Suddenly she heard voices, and her husband saying something like, 'You've got the wrong man.' Then came the words, 'Get down, sucker,' and the sound of a click, followed by a shot. (Evidence was given that the first weapon used in the slaying, a sawn-off shotgun, had jammed, and a revolver was used to fire the fatal shot.) Leonie Simpson froze. She is not sure how long passed before she went around to the back of the car to find her husband dying in a pool of blood.

Police immediately realised that the intended victim was Alan Williams. Early newspaper stories linked the killing to a 'three-state heroin ring' and mentioned the previous attempt on Michael Drury's life. It was still several years before Pollitt came before a court, however. In August 1989 he and an accomplice on a previous bank raid, Gary Jones, were charged at a Melbourne Magistrates Court with conspiring with Dennis, who had been dead for two years, to murder Allan Williams. Pollitt was also charged with murdering Simpson, a count on which Jones had first been remanded two years earlier. A minor furore was created by Pollitt's counsel, Chris Dane, alleging his client had been bashed by police while in custody, and was being kept in conditions which breached the United Nations Charter.

The subsequent Supreme Court trial before Mr Justice Beach also had its sensational aspects. Names like Rogerson, Flannery, Williams and Drury kept cropping up, and much was heard of Dennis's evil empire. It was even said that many police regarded Dennis as an untouchable—impossible to prosecute because witnesses were unlikely to live long enough to testify.

Once again the star witness was Miss Jones. She spoke of Pollitt having been a regular visitor at Dennis's various homes in Richmond before the murder. (Pollitt denied knowing Dennis, but conceded he had heard of him.) Miss Jones insisted she had heard Dennis and Pollitt plotting Williams's execution. She even said Dennis had lured Williams to the house on one occasion so the Red Rat could get a good look at his intended victim. And once again Miss Jones was present when Dennis handed Pollitt a parcel 'in the shape of a gun'.

After the shooting Miss Jones was yet again on hand to take a phone call from Pollitt in which he allegedly said, 'Tell Dennis the job's done.' Dennis was most unhappy when he learned the wrong man had been shot, said Miss Jones, and refused to pay Pollitt his second instalment of $5,000. (It is believed the first $5,000 which Pollitt did receive was paid, knowingly by Dennis, with counterfeit notes.) Miss Jones also told of hearing Pollitt's explanation to Dennis of why he had shot the wrong man: 'I had to, he saw my face.'

Pollitt was finally sentenced on 20 June 1990, after the jury had deliberated for two days. Gaoling him for twenty-four years, Mr Justice Beach described the Red Rat as a 'truly evil man'. Simpson's wife Leonie, police involved in the case, and the Victims of Crime Assistance League all went public with their approval of the lengthy gaol term. The sentence, however, was later reduced to eighteen years by a full Supreme Court. It will be 2008 before Pollitt is a free man.

Kathy remains convinced that Pollitt is doing time for a crime he didn't commit. It is perhaps ironic that she believes Dennis was innocent of murders many policemen had him down for—like Pasche and Gouroff—but conversely blames him for the deaths of men like Simpson for which others have been convicted. In the case of Simpson, Kathy says she saw Dennis immediately after the murder and sweeps aside all the evidence pointing to Pollitt.

Kathy wasted little time after the trial in making her feelings public. The day after Pollitt's sentencing she told the Melbourne *Sun*: 'I remember the night very well. When Dennis came back from murdering Lindsay Simpson he said: 'I shot him.' Then he went inside and burnt his jacket in the forty-four-gallon drum.

And his overalls.' Today Kathy stands by her story:

I really believe that Dennis killed Alan Williams' brother-in-law. He wanted to do it himself. He knew the difference between Williams and Simpson, sure, but Simpson had seen what Dennis looked like. He killed him because of that. My son Peter said to me later: 'Dennis would have shot the wife and child as well.' I said: 'No he wouldn't have.'

I was there when he come back from the killing. The sheila that fucking was a friend of the Williams family was with him, and showed him where the house was. Dennis came back, the tyres were burning, he had the gun, her hair was up in the air like this from the ride, because she was scared stiff. She'd seen what happened. He told me he had done it. He said: 'I've just fucking knocked that fucking cunt. But I've knocked the wrong one.' I couldn't get up in court because I'd already done that once, in the Robinson case [see below].

Dennis was the sort of person who would rather do it himself. You've got to remember he'd already murdered. If you'd have seen what I saw down that street you would believe he did it, too. He had a witness with him, the sheila who took him. I know who it is, but you can't give her up.

I knew the Simpsons. Lindsay's mother was one of my best friends. I had to cut her off when I went to Stephenson Street. I didn't want her to come down there where I was involved in drugs. She, to this day, doesn't know why I'm not her friend. I had to cut all friends. But she still had the decency to come to my Jamie's funeral. I thought the world of Lindsay, and they saved for years to have that baby of theirs. That hurt me.

When Jamie Pettingill hurled his home-made bomb on the steps of the Melbourne Coroner's Court in the city centre in the early hours of 9 May 1985, he was acting on instructions from his brother Dennis. A few hours later an inquest was due to start into the death of a prostitute called Helga Wagnegg and Dennis wanted to issue a warning. There is little doubt that Dennis murdered the thirty-year-old heroin addict and, knowing he was obliged to attend the inquest, he felt a gesture was required to set proceedings off on the right track. Kathy makes no bones about it.

> It was Jamie did the bomb. He had it in his hand, and it was ticking loudly, but Dennis wanted the court blown up properly, and Jamie said, 'Aagh, fuck that, it's going to go off,' so he just threw it. It was dark, at night. Over the scanner they had monitoring the police radio it said, 'Go straight to Richmond,' and the next thing I see Jamie and The Enforcer jump the high fence at 35 Stephenson Street.

It is perhaps testimony to Dennis's arrogance, or even megalomania that he felt by this stage that he could blow up a building simply because the powers-that-be were about to use it as the venue for an inquiry into his handiwork. If Jamie hadn't panicked when the bomb started ticking, it would have caused serious damage. As the message that went out over the police radio immediately afterwards indicated—'Go straight to Richmond'—they had no doubt who was responsible. By the time the inquest got under way that morning extremely tight security precautions were in place. Everybody entering the building was searched and a number of witnesses had police escorts. The extra police on duty were taking no chances. They had few illusions left about Dennis.

Helga Wagnegg's story is only too typical of the human debris that washed up on Dennis's doorstep, and never made it off again in one piece. Like so many of the regulars who visited Stephenson Street for sex, drugs or guns, Helga's life was going nowhere. Her last known address was Pentridge Prison, she was hopelessly addicted to heroin, and she sold her body to supply her habit.

Two years earlier she had brandished a machine gun at the door of a brothel during a robbery attempt that never got off the ground. She had been out of Pentridge on temporary leave only nine days on 8 November 1984, when she made her fatal visit to Stephenson Street. Helga was known at the parlour at 108, and had no difficulty scoring heroin that morning. But she had already consumed close to 100 pills, possibly Serepax, and collapsed on the pavement a few metres from the parlour.

Kathy dragged her back into the parlour—it wasn't good for business to have customers collapsing in the street early in the morning—put her head under a cold tap, and began walking her. Everybody joined in to help, including two regular customers, hairdresser Scott Findlay and his lover Gary McKay, a nurse. Kathy then left, believing Helga was recovering.

Next I heard Dennis had sent someone down to the Yarra with buckets to fill up the bath at the parlour. He was putting her in there so it'd look as if she drowned in the Yarra. She died of an overdose—I don't know if it was the smack she bought, or whatever they say Dennis injected her with.

Coroner Mr Hugh Adams SM conducted the inquest on 9 May with Dennis sitting in the courtroom. He did not give evidence, and despite what other witnesses had to say about his role in Helga's death, was allowed to leave before the verdict was handed down.

Findlay's statement was read to the hearing. It detailed regular visits he had made to the parlour at 108 Stephenson Street to score heroin. About young Jason Ryan and his uncles, Findlay said: 'Jason Ryan would be approximately thirteen years of age. He has been present on numerous occasions when drug

THE MATRIARCH

dealings have taken place. I have seen this Jason carrying the same type of guns that the police carry. I have had a look at these guns and know them to be real. He has on numerous occasions pointed firearms at me.' Findlay said he had also seen Dennis, Jamie and Trevor with guns, 'usually in their back pockets or down the front of their pants'.

Findlay said that when he and McKay approached the parlour on 8 November they saw a woman they later learned was Helga. 'I remember her because she was off her face. She could hardly walk; she was staggering from side to side and smiling all the time. She was definitely not drunk. I can tell. Her eyes were really pinned. I did not consider this to be anything unusual.'

Later Findlay saw Kathy enter the building with Wagnegg saying: 'Quick, Helga's OD'd.' In the back yard of the parlour he and McKay then helped Kathy to walk Helga and apply mouth-to-mouth resuscitation and heart massage.

'I did this for about fifteen minutes. Dennis Allen then turned up and told us to stop and leave her and get away from her. He said: "I will give her a hit of speed to get her around." Dennis told me and Gary to piss off. Kathy Pettingill left when Dennis Allen arrived.'

Findlay said Dennis later told him: 'Leave her and she should come around in a little while.' Over the next twenty minutes McKay and Findlay checked on Helga where she was still lying in the back yard.

'I was of the opinion she was dead.' Findlay said in his statement. 'After about twenty minutes Dennis Allen came back again and decided to give her another hit of speed. When he walked through the kitchen past me I saw he had a needle.'

Denise Strongman, an employee at the parlour who was also present, then told Findlay that Dennis had injected Helga in the neck. Dennis had placed a large piece of wood over Helga, saying it should be left there so the police helicopter would not

168

see her if it flew over. Shortly afterwards Findlay and McKay left the parlour.

Findlay said he had decided to make his statement, although: 'I genuinely believe that my life would be worth nothing if any of these people found out that I was making a statement to the police about those matters.'

Under cross examination by Andrew Fraser, representing both Kathy and Denise Strongman, Findlay conceded that the two women and Dennis had been trying to help Helga. Findlay denied suggestions from Chris Dane, appearing for Dennis, that while making his statement police had provided him with drugs to relieve withdrawal symptoms from his heroin habit.

McKay said his attempts to revive Helga were interrupted: 'Dennis was there and he wouldn't let me.' McKay said he phoned from work later that night and was told by Denise that as far as she knew Helga was all right because she had gone by the time she (Denise) returned from a shopping trip.

Kathy's statement, also read to the inquest, included details of Helga's attempt on 8 November to get work at the parlour. 'She told me she had just got out of gaol, she was broke, and wanted a job badly. She was slurring her speech and stumbling. I told her I couldn't employ her at the moment. I was fully staffed.' Kathy's statement revealed that she had found Helga one hour later lying on the footpath outside The Cherry Tree. She had brought her into the yard of the parlour and splashed water on her face. 'I asked her what she had taken. She slurred that she had taken 100 Serepax.' Kathy said that after further attempts to revive Helga she had left the parlour to lie down at 35 Stephenson. 'I rang up 108 every ten minutes for the next hour to check on how she was. The boys (Findlay and McKay) said that she was all right. I told them that when she was good enough to tell her to go. I never saw her again. It was approximately one week later I heard that she was found in the river. I couldn't believe it.'

Some years later during an unconnected court hearing Jason Ryan said Dennis had ordered him to get a bucket of water from the Yarra. 'Dennis tipped it down her (Helga's) throat and held her head in the bucket for about half an hour,' he said.

But despite these efforts the inquest heard medical evidence from a pathologist indicating that Helga had definitely not died from drowning. Nor had he been able to find puncture marks in her neck. Further medical evidence revealed an absence of amphetamines in Helga's body, but morphine (heroin) was found in the blood and urine.

At this stage in the proceedings Dennis's solicitor asked for permission for himself and Dennis to withdraw from the hearing. The Coroner agreed after counsel for the Director of Public Prosecutions said: 'It would not in the circumstances be appropriate to call Mr Allen, for legal principles.'

Next witness was Detective Sergeant Paul William Higgins* of the armed robbery squad. He read from his own statement revealing that 'an informant of mine' had told him the day after Helga's visit to the parlour that she had overdosed on heroin and her body had been dumped in the Yarra. The informant said Helga had been in The Cherry Tree on the day of her death, and had injected herself with heroin in the toilet area, had consumed alcohol and then collapsed on the footpath outside the hotel. Higgins said that 'He (the informant) stated that he later learned that the body had been dumped in the Yarra. I asked him who placed the body in the Yarra, and he stated that he couldn't tell me for fear of his life. I asked him whether he placed the body in the Yarra, and he replied: "Definitely not me."'

Under cross examination from the Coroner, Higgins said he

---

* In April 1993 Higgins was jailed for seven years, with a minimum of five, on corruption charges, after a sixteen-month trial and an inquiry costing an estimated $30 million.

had had regular dealings with this informant, and that he had been 'very reliable'.

Was this mystery informant Dennis, playing a form of double agent role with the police? Was he passing on information about a crime in which he was deeply involved, knowing that his relationship with Higgins and other officers would ensure no awkward questions would be asked?

Next came evidence from a horse strapper named Jeremy Cassin, who said he was driving along the southeastern freeway by the side of the Yarra under a full moon at 4.15 a.m. when he saw 'three people standing on the embankment and one of the persons was in the water up to his waist . . .' Later when he heard radio news of an anonymous telephone call mentioning a body in the river. Cassin contacted police.

Helga's body was not recovered from the river until the Monday, 12 November, when a pensioner, John Sanders, was fishing under the freeway and saw what appeared to be material floating towards him.

Detective Senior Constable James O'Brien of Richmond CIB then told the Coroner of an interview with Dennis two months after Helga's disappearance. After speaking to Charles Nikakis, his solicitor, Dennis was asked to make a statement and replied: 'I don't know if I would or not. It's up to you, anyway. I don't give a fuck.'

After responding to further questions about Helga with a 'no comment', Dennis promised O'Brien he would contact him if he received any information about Helga's death. He was allowed to leave the police station shortly afterwards.

Announcing his findings, Mr Adams said: 'It is quite clear that the deceased was dead before she was placed into the river. The person or persons responsible for the disposal of her body into the Yarra could, if their identity is subsequently detected, face charges under the Victorian Coroner's Act re the unlawful disposal of a body.' His verdict read: 'I find that Helga Elfriede

Wagnegg died on an unknown date and place as a result of asphyxia caused by a reaction to an intravenous administration of heroin. On the evidence adduced I am unable to determine if the administration of this substance was self-administered or not, nor am I able to determine the identity of the person or persons responsible for the placing of the body of the deceased in the river.'

In a chilling aftermath to Helga's murder, in early 1996 I interviewed The Talking Bone, who was working at the Stephenson Street parlour at the time of Helga's disappearance. She remembers being summoned by Dennis to 49 Cubitt Street the day after Helga's death.

He asked me what I was going to tell the police and the inquest, and I told him I would say I didn't know the lady. He said that was good, and then he told me he was going to show me what would happen if I caused trouble.

He walked me into the bathroom, and it was completely lined with black plastic sheets—floor, walls and ceiling. I knew what that was for. There were two sides to Dennis, and all you had to do was push the wrong button.'

Kathy believes Helga's body was transported to the Yarra in a van, one of three vehicles owned by Dennis. This van had almost certainly been used earlier for the disposal of other bodies, and was to gain a certain, anonymous fame all of its own—in the movies.

Dennis had this van. It was all metal in the back so he could hose it out. It wouldn't fit under the bridge [on the way to the Yarra] *but he forced it under. It was just near the Rosella factory. It wasn't a small van. More like a small furniture truck, that's the only way I can describe it. It was all crumpled on top after he went under the bridge. Helga's in the back of*

it. He was taking it to the Yarra, and he threw the body in and
the police got it out.

Kathy isn't sure if Dennis was the mystery informer, but she does remember a scene shortly afterwards, almost too surreal to be credible.

Just after Helga, this morning me and The Enforcer have
decided to walk around Cubitt Street about nine o'clock. And
I see coppers everywhere. And I'm thinking: 'Aah, fuck, what's
he done now?' And I look over and there's film cameras. They
were making that movie Malcolm.* *It didn't jerry that the*
coppers weren't real. But when you're coming round, and you
see all that, and it's right near Dennis's ...

I go to see the movie, and here's this van, the crumpled
one, that he's got rid of because he don't want no-one to know
about it, it's gone all around the world. It's in the scene with
the car splitting in half in the fucking movie Malcolm. *I go*
back and I tell him. I said: 'It's in the fucking movie.' He said:
'Oh, don't talk shit.'

The next and possibly most keenly felt death in Kathy's life was that of Jamie, the second youngest of her eight sons, from a heroin overdose at the age of twenty-one. Jamie died on 14 May 1985, a few days after the inquest into Helga Wagnegg's death. Kathy still mourns Jamie, and misses him with a fierce possessiveness. She also believes the overdose that took his life was deliberately administered.

The theory among police at the time of his death was that

---

* Nadia Tass and David Parker's award-winning movie was released in 1986. Filmed in and around Melbourne, including Richmond, it tells the story of a slow-witted inventor and his entry into the world of crime.

Dennis committed fratricide because Jamie was angling for a bigger share of his empire. Kathy disputes this, saying it is highly unlikely Dennis was involved: Jamie had demonstrated his loyalty to his elder brother too many times—the shooting incident involving 'Snaggles' and Keryn Thompson, and another episode where Jamie did time for his brother after an armed robbery went wrong.

I met Jamie intermittently in his early teens, and can testify first hand to the charm that won him many friends, and a reputation as the warmest natured of Kathy's children. But as with Dennis, there was another aspect to Jamie's character. It was Jamie who demonstrated a cold, undeniably callous streak when he responded to his own father's death with the words: 'Well, I'm not bloody worried about him.' And when Kathy wept over the heroin-induced downfall of Victor Gouroff, Jamie said: 'I don't give a fuck, I've got the coat.' It was this darker side of Jamie that held sway when his life slid rapidly downhill during his final months in 1984 and early 1985. It seemed Jamie had the throttle on his life jammed wide open. There was an awful inevitability about his end.

Kathy's recollections of his birth are still special to her.

He came with such a rush that the blood vessels in his eyes burst. The nurses couldn't believe it. He's lying on his stomach and he's holding his head up.

Another early memory involves his sister Vicki.

These two, Jamie and Vicki, had a fight. I was laying in bed in the front room in Ross Street, Northcote, a big house. They fell in my bedroom door fighting. So I got up and I belted him. I said: 'Now you get up the street right now, and you buy her something, and you tell her you're sorry.' And he did, he went up and got her a bracelet. 'Don't ever let me see you hit your sister again,' I said. I was brought up like that.

By the age of twelve Jamie was an accomplished burglar, and by his early teens car theft was his passion. By now the family was living in Ross Street, Northcote, and local police estimated Jamie was stealing ten vehicles a week. By fourteen he was a runaway from Turana, and stayed briefly with Dennis, who was charged with harbouring him. During this period Jamie was regularly running away to South Australia in search of his father, Jimmy Pettingill.

Armed robbery has always been regarded by Kathy and her underworld peers as a crime requiring 'dash'. The theory goes like this: Anybody can break into an empty house, or sell a gram of heroin, but it takes a real man to stride into a bank, gun in hand. When you carry a gun you open a door to the unpredictable. It takes dash to remain cool enough to control the adrenalin flow at the height of the action.

Jamie had the necessary dash at a remarkably early age—by the time he was fifteen he had been charged with four armed robberies. For these crimes he served time in an adult gaol by the time he was eighteen. During this sentence Kathy threatened to burn herself alive outside Pentridge if anything happened to him while being transferred from D Division to the notoriously violent high security H Division. 'I know what Jamie can expect in H Division,' she told the Melbourne *Sun*. 'If it happens I will burn myself outside Pentridge. I want you to know what I feel, just in case something happens.'

Dennis's advice at the time was typically to the point. 'Use kero, not petrol,' he told Kathy. 'The kero'll work quicker.'

The robbery where Jamie took the rap for Dennis happened around this time. On 5 March 1980, Jamie and Dennis burst into the bar of the United Kingdom Hotel in Clifton Hill. Dennis fired a shot at point blank range into the leg of part-time barman Albert Caulfield, fifty-nine, who died three days later in Queen Victoria Hospital. The Coroner found at the subsequent inquest that Caulfield died from a stroke caused by a moving blood clot, but declined to say whether or not the shooting contributed to his death. Dennis fled the scene and was never apprehended for the shooting. Jamie wasn't so fortunate, but refused to give up his brother. It was some years before Kathy learnt the truth.

One of the family let it slip. But I always remember Jamie saying to the Supreme Court judge: 'I can't tell you who it was, your honour, 'cos it was a maniac.' But he wouldn't give him up, just like Victor did a five-year sentence for Peter, the only armed robbery on a bingo game. Peter did it and Victor got the blame. With Jamie, what sort of a brother would let a kid . . . Dennis knew he'd get a lighter sentence. I think Dennis thought the world of him.

Jamie appeared before the Supreme Court on 16 February 1982, facing four charges dating back to 1980: armed robberies of the United Kingdom Hotel, a TAB branch/supermarket at Ascot Vale, and two separate incidents involving bus drivers at Collingwood. Mr Justice King sentenced Jamie to four years' gaol, with a minimum of three, causing an uproar within both the police force and the Attorney General's Department. Both were appalled at the lightness of the sentence. Tom Rippon, secretary of the Police Association, commented: 'I don't think that punishment reflects anywhere near what the public would expect to be handed out in this instance.' The AG's Department sought advice on lodging an appeal.

Dennis was ensconced in Richmond by the time Jamie was released from his sentence, and a job was waiting for him as stand-over man on bad debts. Jamie was good at it, too. In November 1984, when an undercover policeman attempted to score heroin at the parlour at 108 Stephenson, Jamie punched him and then drew a knife, sending the policeman fleeing for his life. Jamie was duly charged with assault.

But all the heroin proved too much of a temptation. Jamie

had been introduced to the drug in gaol, but there were virtually unlimited quantities available in Richmond. He was, however, a comparative rarity—a user with such an aversion for needles he was too squeamish to inject himself. Jamie used to look the other way when a friend, or whoever else was handy, jabbed a needle into his arm. That's why Kathy was so shocked in late March 1985, two months before his death, when Jamie overdosed the first time.

Now I'd had an episode in Dennis's house at number 37 where some girl had locked the door and Jamie was nearly dead on the floor from an OD. And she was sitting there. So I called Wayne the builder. He come running up, and called the ambulance and everything. I'm trying to kill the girl because I thought Jamie was dead, and the ambulance brought him back. He came alive again.

Jamie was kept overnight in Prince Henry's Hospital on this occasion and was given psychiatric assessment. Less than two months after this near miss Jamie had recovered sufficiently to play a major part in the bombing of the Coroner's Court. But the writing was on the wall. Five days after the bombing he was dead.

They reckon Dennis murdered Jamie, got too big for his boots or something. He never. I'd seen him hours before he died. He was in a flat owned by one of his girlfriends in Northcote. By the time it came to the inquest [March 1986] I had to come from Fairlea, where I was doing time for smack, in handcuffs and everything. And I said just one thing to Hal Hallenstein the Coroner, and he knew what I was talking about. I said: 'Your Honour,' and Victor's tugging at me coat, I said: 'Your Honour, could you please tell me if there was anybody else in that flat?'
Jamie wasn't on his own, he couldn't stick a needle in his own arm. Jamie was given an overdose. If it had been Dennis's

177

smack I would have killed Dennis meself. I'd only left Jamie hours earlier. There was no depression or nothing. I know it wasn't an accident. Someone had a motive for killing him. It wasn't Dennis with the motive, it was the others. I know what I know, I know what I know. I haven't found out the 'why', but I know the 'who'.

Jamie was a heroin addict in the end. It was a man in prison that got him onto it. And that man was terrified for years. He'd sit in his cell and wouldn't come out because he didn't know which day was his. He was living in fear.

Me and my selfishness when Jamie was murdered, and I will say murdered, I didn't think about my other kids' feelings, right? I had my own grief. Victor called round to see if I wanted to go to the flat where Jamie was found, and I thought it'd be like last time, the ambulance would save him. It hadn't sunk in that Jamie was dead, because he'd only left me a couple of hours earlier. And I went to get up out of the bed, because the doctor came and gave me a shot. And I said to Dennis: 'I've got to go to the morgue.' And he said: 'No, you don't. Trevor's going.' So Dennis took that responsibility off me shoulders, which normally he wouldn't have done.

Jamie's funeral was a major event, and saw the blessing of 35 Stephenson Street by Father Peter Norden, a Roman Catholic priest. The same priest also officiated at the funerals of Dennis, Sissy and Gladys.

We had to make an amnesty with the police for Jamie's funeral because none of us were allowed in the same street. That was part of our bail conditions. So the coppers said it was all right. I wanted, being of Irish descent, the funeral cortege to go down Stephenson Street, and we stopped the cortege, and Father Norden blessed the house, 35, where Jamie lived with me and Trevor and Jason.

The bail conditions that barred family members from being in the same street meant that Dennis was prohibited from conversing with Kathy in any way, but no such restriction applied to Kathy. 'I could talk to him, but he wasn't allowed to talk to me. I had a lot of fun with that one.'

The death notices published in Melbourne's *Sun* newspaper immediately after Jamie's death were testament to the number and variety of friends he enjoyed, and the regard in which he was held. Dennis's message came first, typically cryptic and in an entire column by itself:

From the one another.
There could never be a better brother.
There all the way, so will they.
We love you always JAP
You were there
One million
So will I
DEN

Kathy translated the 'one another' as brother; 'there all the way' as a reference to Jamie's loyalty; 'so will they' is an obscure vow of revenge; JAP was Jamie's nickname; 'one million' means one million per cent, and 'so will I' is another promise of vengeance.

A joint notice from Dennis, Peter, Victor, Lex and Trevor read: 'Dear brother, we know you had a message for those that won't weep. We'll deliver that, our promise we keep.' Again Kathy believes this is a promise to track down and kill those ('that won't weep') responsible for Jamie's murder.

Other notices were less complex. Peter's said in part: 'I'll walk with pride knowing you belong to our family.' Jason wrote of having 'an uncle as wonderful as you'. Perhaps most revealing of all was the note from Carmel Duke, a former girlfriend who had been with Jamie on the day he died, and who lived in the flat where he took the fatal overdose.

'... in thirteen years there is not a bad memory of you. As I sit here on the bed where you took your last breath there is one of a million memories that come flooding back to mind: We were walking home from school and we were both freezing cold. You took your cardigan off for me to wear and swore you couldn't feel the cold.'

There were thirty-six notices in all, many of them revealing deep and sincere expressions of love and friendship. As Kathy observes, people in her world do not make a show of revealing their feelings to one another; most emotions are kept inside. The only occasion they are truly revealed and paraded for the world to see is at the time of death.

The aftermath of Jamie's death resulted in ugly family disputes, both at the wake and at the next New Year's Eve party. At the wake at Cubitt Street a relative who was convinced Dennis had murdered Jamie put a gun to Dennis's head and pulled the trigger. Dennis's luck held out once again—the gun jammed and the incident went no further.

At the New Year's party Lex was questioning a woman Kathy believed had played a role in Jamie's fatal overdose. Peter, during a rare spell of freedom from his almost permanent incarceration, was also present. Kathy had anticipated trouble and had hidden her gun earlier. Eventually Peter and Lex began arguing, and Peter ordered the bodyguard whom he had brought with him to fetch Kathy's gun. At this stage Kathy intervened.

The next minute I said: 'Right, Peter hit me with your best shot.' And he did, in this eye, the bad eye. But by this time Lex has kicked that woman straight down the passage, right onto the road.

At the inquest into Jamie's death on 11 March 1986, Coroner Hal

Hallenstein recorded an open verdict saying Jamie had died from an overdose of dextropropoxyphene, oxazepam and morphine.

'I am unable to say whether death was self induced, accidental, by misadventure or otherwise,' the Coroner added.

Evidence was heard from sisters Carmel and Deidre Duke, both of whom had known Jamie since the family lived in Northcote fifteen years earlier. Deidre had had an affair with Jamie, and Carmel regarded him 'like a brother'.

The sisters stated that on 14 May Jamie arrived at Deidre's flat at Hales Court, Northcote, at lunchtime when both were present. Jamie had been staying overnight at the flat intermittently during the previous three weeks, and because of his condition the sisters were starting to worry that he was using hard drugs. On the day of his death Deidre left the flat not long after Jamie arrived. He said that he was tired and wanted to lie down.

Carmel checked on him frequently over the next three hours as he lay on Deidre's bed. She noticed his breathing was irregular and his face was changing colour from purple to yellow. On her final visit to the bedroom Carmel realised Jamie had stopped breathing, and ran to the nearby flat of a friend, Lynn Williams, whom Kathy had known for twenty years. Williams called an ambulance while her boyfriend returned with Carmel to Deidre's flat. Despite their efforts to revive him Jamie was dead by the time the ambulance arrived.

In her statement Kathy acknowledged Jamie was using amphetamines on an irregular basis. 'In my opinion Jamie could not self-administer himself with an injection because he has a fear of needles.' She added: 'I believe that he was being injected by another person, but at this stage I do not know who that is.'

Kathy said Jamie had been renovating the house at 43 Cubitt Street to make a home for Deidre, her daughter and himself. 'He had everything to look forward to in life with his girlfriend.'

From evidence heard at the inquest it would appear that

Jamie did not inject himself after arrival at Deidre's flat. The police and ambulance officers who attended were unsuccessful in their search for any form of drug paraphernalia.

The one piece of evidence that supports Kathy's theory of Jamie having been injected 'by another person' was provided by ambulanceman Robert Bland, who said that while attempting to revive Jamie he had questioned Carmel and Deidre. 'They told us he had arrived at the flat three hours previously with an unknown female who had since left, and they [Jamie and the unknown girl] had just hit up on heroin prior to arrival at the flat.'

Neither Deidre nor Carmel mentioned this woman, but said Jamie had arrived alone. Nor did they say anything about Jamie having used heroin, but gave the impression they didn't know he was using hard drugs. The Coroner's open finding left the circumstances of Jamie's death a mystery that has never been solved.

Whatever the truth behind his death, there is no doubt Jamie died on 14 May 1985, unwittingly providing Dennis with an alibi for his alleged involvement in the heroin deal with Roger Rogerson. For it was on that date that Dennis was said to have sent 'Miss X' to Sydney to collect heroin from the soon to be disgraced detective (see Chapter Five).

The final footnote to Jamie's life came a few days after his death when Kathy was asleep in bed at 35 Stephenson Street. She woke to find the room uncharacteristically cold. As she looked up from the pillow she saw Jamie's familiar form in the doorway to her bedroom, the same doorway from which Dennis had summoned her downstairs to clean up Wayne Stanhope's remains. Jamie was wearing the greatcoat Victor Gouroff traded for a cap of heroin. He said two words in a voice that she remembers as half threat, half plea. 'Shut up.'

To Kathy, by no means a superstitious person, the message was clear—stop asking questions, let it rest.

It was six months after Jamie's death that the most publicised of all the murders in which Dennis was involved took place. The victim was Anton Kenny, a Hell's Angel. To be precise Kenny was a one-time president of the Nomads, a club so closely affiliated with the Angels world-wide that they wear the same winged skull patch on the back of their jackets.

During the 1970s and early 1980s I conducted interviews and wrote part of the script for a documentary film on the Melbourne Chapter of the Hell's Angels, and got to know a number of members. There are Angels and there are Angels—some are far more approachable than others, and are good company. Anton Kenny wasn't one of these. My memories of him are of a somewhat surly individual with an air of physical intimidation adopted by most club members to keep outsiders at a distance. At six feet and wearing his full colours, Anton was a daunting figure. But by the time he ran into Dennis in late 1984 much of that had changed.

For a start he had been kicked out by the Angels—for making a statement to police in 1982 when apprehended on drug charges. Kenny didn't implicate any of his brother Angels, but the simple act of making a statement was enough to cause his expulsion. Having witnessed first-hand the strength and permanence of the bonds that tie Hell's Angels to one another, and the support system which exists within the group, it is not difficult to imagine the sudden emptiness of Kenny's existence when he found himself on the outer. As their president Les Phillips used to say: 'Everybody wants to be an Angel.' And the only thing worse than not being an Angel is being an ex-Angel. So Kenny's decline was rapid.

He began using heroin, another offence that would have had him banned from the club. (Any use, except medical, of a needle is prohibited.) He lost weight and his appearance of physical strength gave way to a general sleaziness. Through his brother Wayne he met a convicted murderer, Peter Ian Robertson, and the pair began to spend time in one another's company. Robertson, or 'Robbo' as Kathy knew him, had known Dennis for some years, probably from their time together in gaol. 'Robbo' introduced Anton to Dennis and the strange world of Stephenson Street. During the first half of 1985 the former Nomad became a comparatively regular visitor to one or other of Dennis's properties.

On 8 November 1985, the day after Dennis's thirty-fourth birthday, Kenny became the latest in a growing list of people whose last breath would be taken in Dennis's company. Five people—Dennis, 'Robbo', Kenny, a Peter Hastilow, from the outer suburb of Chirnside Park, and the ever-present 'Miss Jones', were all involved in a post-birthday celebration drinking session at 49 Cubitt Street when bullets started flying. Kathy believes the fracas was touched off by 'Robbo' catching Kenny in the act of 'tampering' with Dennis's two daughters, Lindy and Jade, then living at Cubitt Street. While this is the type of incident that would have sparked Dennis's temper to the stage where bloody murder was a favoured option, it is also unlikely.

Hell's Angels, despite their carefully cultivated repulsive image, do not welcome pedophiles into their ranks. While Charger Charley the Child Molester may have been a celebrated figure in the early history of America's founding West Coast Angels, it is extremely doubtful that their Melbourne brothers of the 1980s would have allowed a man with a predilection for toddlers to rise to the exalted rank of president. And however far Kenny had fallen during the three years since his expulsion from the club, it doesn't follow that he acquired such a taste along with his appetite for heroin. Kathy's attitude to him may have been prejudiced by his indifference to her girls.

Anton'd been round the bloody parlour, but I don't think he had sex. I had a couple of towels with Mr D written on them. I said to Anton: 'Will you take these round to Dennis?' 'cos it was Dennis's birthday. And that's the last time I saw him alive.

The truth of what happened to Anton Kenny at Cubitt Street will probably never be known—there are too many conflicting accounts. Dennis's brother Peter, for instance, told a Supreme Court hearing into unrelated matters that both Dennis and Robertson had fired the fatal shots that killed Kenny.

In May 1987 Robertson told the jury during his trial for Kenny's murder that he had heard four shots and seen Dennis come out of the lounge with an automatic pistol. Robertson walked into the room where he saw Kenny kneeling on the floor holding his chest. 'I didn't call him [Dennis] a rat,' were among his last words.

Peter Hastilow gave a completely different version. In November 1986 he told the South Melbourne Coroner's Court he was in the kitchen at number 49 with Dennis when he heard four or five gunshots. He and Dennis entered the lounge where Kenny was lying motionless. Hastilow claimed he was told by Robertson: 'Get out of here, and keep your mouth shut.'

'Miss Jones' made an initial statement in which she said she had seen Robertson fire the fatal shots at Kenny. She later changed this story, saying the statement had been made on Dennis's orders. Her second version had her playing with Lindy and Jade in a room of the house in Cubitt Street. Dennis came in, she told the Coroner's Court, and ordered her 'to get out with the kids, because things are about to happen'. As she was leaving the house she heard four or five shots, she said.

Dennis summoned Kathy to the scene not long after the shots were fired. He had a special telephone code for letting his associates know when he needed help in disposing of a body. According to The Enforcer he would use the acronym MIA—missing in action. In Kathy's case he was more to the point.

And then I get a phone call: 'Get your arse around here, cunt.'

There was an arch [in the house at Cubitt Street] *so I've walked down and Dennis has said: 'Don't come any further.' But I did. And I was fucking mystified. If Anton's shot there was no blood. And I think: 'How can he be shot if there's no blood?' It was all internal.*

So I start to see his eyes roll back a bit. Now I know a lot about bodies. And I put a fan on him, thinking he's about to die, and he looks feverish. Dennis says: 'What are you fucking doin'?' I said: 'Well, I know what I'm fucking doing, Dennis. What happens if rigor mortis sets in?' Right? 'Cos it comes and goes. Right? I don't dispute that Dennis cut his legs off. No, no, no, I don't dispute that. There was no need to do that if they'd listened to me when I had the fan on him, but they didn't. Rigor mortis comes and goes after so many hours.

So with that he says: 'Get him in the fucking car.' Meaning his station wagon. 'And dump him outside Prince Henry's Hospital.' How could I've pushed him out the fucking car?

So then I see them take the bluey jacket off him, you know those workmen's blueys? Then I see Dennis undo Anton's pants, and I think: 'Aah what the fuck's going on now?' There's the bag of speed stuffed down his trousers. But then they put the bluey back on him to keep him warm. And I've got the fucking fan on him. So I leave, and that's the end.

So how the hell could I have got him in the station wagon? I mean, I knew we were under surveillance. This Robbo, he'd just got out after a murder blue.* I said: 'Who fucking shot him?' Just like I'm talking to you Robbo said: 'He tampered with the kids.'

What happened over the next few days represents a nadir of depravity even for Dennis and his circle. It began with Robertson's

---

* A reference to a murder conviction recorded against Robertson at the age of sixteen for shooting a young Lebanese man during a robbery. He served eleven years.

description of Kenny's final moments of life. This description was made in a statement to police on 21 October 1986 which was read to the inquest the following month:

> He was on his knees with his hands holding his chest. Anton collapsed on the floor on his back. I could see only spots of blood on his chest area. Dennis said: 'Give me a hand,' and we dragged him out to the kitchen. He was still breathing. He said: 'Am I going to die?' I told him: 'Don't be a weak cunt.' I grabbed him on his wrist and he was all cold and clammy.

Dennis then ordered him to pick up spent shells from the lounge-room floor, Robertson said. When he returned to the kitchen he found Dennis removing $900 in $100 bills and a bag of speed from Anton's person. 'I didn't realise, but Anton was dead by then.'

In an earlier interview with Detective Senior Sergeant Ian Dosser of the homicide squad on 19 March 1986, Robertson had provided gruesome details of the disposal of the body:

> Robertson: 'We carried him down the back lane to another of Dennis's houses [on Cubitt Street] and left him there. We boarded the house up.
> Dosser: The body had its legs chopped off. Where was this done?
> Robertson: No. 43.
> Dosser: Who chopped the legs off?
> Robertson: No comment.
> Dosser: What was used to chop them off?
> Robertson: A chainsaw.
> Dosser: Where is this chainsaw now?
> Robertson: In the Prahran tip.
> Dosser: Why did they chop the legs off?
> Robertson: I don't know. They reckon I was a weak cunt

THE MATRIARCH

because I couldn't stand the smell. I nearly vomited.

Robertson then spoke of putting the body in a forty-four-gallon drum and adding cement, lime and a form of acid used to clean bricks. Dosser asked him who drove the van containing the drum to the Yarra River, where it was finally dumped.

> Robertson: I did, I was pretty pissed though. I can remember drinking a bottle of Scotch ... on the way ... the van really stunk after we dropped it [the drum] in. There was also a hell of a smell in the house, and we had to go and get Pine-o-Kleen and splash that around to kill the smell. Shit it was off.

Two other men were mentioned during the interview. One was Jimmy Rizio, owner of the van used in the disposal.

> Dosser: Was Rizio there when Anton was shot?
> Robertson: No, he came later with a sheila, I don't know her name, but it was all set for Rizio to fuck her. I think he was going to hump her in the shower, but she had the rags on, so he left her. Fred [the second man mentioned by Robertson] finished up fuckin' her anyway.
> Dosser: Do you want to say anything about the incident?
> Robertson: I didn't shoot him, that's all. If I say too much then I'm off. I'll be knocked ...

Robertson's second October 21 statement went into even more detail. It began with the stripping of Kenny's body down to his underpants and the burning of his clothes. It was shortly after this, according to the statement, that Jimmy Rizio and 'a blonde-headed sheila' arrived and made their abortive attempt at having sex in the shower, while Kenny's half-naked corpse lay still warm nearby. 'Jimmy came out and said he hadn't had a fuck because the sheila had the rags on.' Jimmy then left.

The Enforcer was there at the time, together with Lynn Williams, who called the ambulance when Jamie overdosed, and Vicki Ward, who was to become another murder victim. While Miss Jones and the 'blonde-headed sheila' cleaned the lounge carpet with Pine-o-Kleen, Dennis, Robertson and The Enforcer carried Kenny's body from 49 Cubitt Street to number 43. They returned to 49, drank for two hours and then returned to 43 and placed Anton head first into the forty-four-gallon drum taken from the back yard of 49. Dennis added the lime and acid to the drum and plugged in the chainsaw. While The Enforcer and Robertson boarded up the windows, Dennis went to work. Robertson's statement continues:

> He started to hack at the legs of Anton around the knee area. There was bits of flesh and bone flying everywhere. I spewed up. Dennis cut off one leg and poked it in next to the body. Dennis said: 'Fuck this, let's have a drink.' He turned off the chainsaw and we all went back to 49. Dennis had bits of shit, bone all over him. I had some on me. When Dennis was sawing off the leg you could hear the bone hitting the tin in the building.

Dennis and Robertson returned to 43, where Dennis made an abortive attempt with the chainsaw to remove the second leg. He then went back to 49 and returned with a meat cleaver. Robertson stayed at the front of the house.

After the second leg was severed all clothing was burnt and the following morning the lime bag and acid bottle were also burnt. Later cement was added to the drum. Another day went by and still the body had not been removed. By now thirty to forty bottles of Pine-o-Kleen had been used in an effort to get rid of the stench of rotting flesh. Finally Robertson and The Enforcer took the drum, weighing 265 kilos, in Rizio's van and rolled it into the Yarra, from where it was recovered by police four months later in a metre of water. According to The Enforcer, during the four months before its discovery the barrel was used as a regular jumping-off base for people swimming in the Yarra.

When it was opened at the city mortuary the legs were still in the barrel and the lime seemed to have had little effect in hastening the decomposition of the remains. Three bullets were recovered from the upper part of Kenny's body.

Not long after this, on 19 March 1986, Kathy made a statement to the police, something she would have avoided at all costs in normal circumstances. But Dennis was putting on the pressure.

> *I was in gaol for drug offences. Dennis comes out with the homicide squad. Now I won't talk to the police if I can help it. The screw takes me over to the office, and this is in front of them* [homicide squad officers] *Dennis says to me: 'If you don't tell them that Robbo did it, they're gonna charge me with the murder.' So I did. I made a statement.*

Kathy told the police that when Dennis summoned her to witness Kenny's dying moments she asked Robertson: 'Who did it?' Her statement continued:

> He said: 'I did. He tried to tamper with the two kids.' I knew Anton was gone, but I didn't really believe it until I saw it on the telly where someone was found in a barrel in the river. I was told by Robbo that he had put him in a barrel and dumped him in the river, but I didn't believe it. I thought it was all bravado. I thought they had taken him to the hospital.

The inquest opened on November 1986 and quickly became an ordeal for all concerned—for Kathy because of her dawning realisation that her statement to police was likely to produce a murder conviction against Robertson, breaching her dedication to the criminal code; for Coroner Hal Hallenstein in attempting to select the truth from the wildly conflicting evidence put before him; for the police due to the savage mauling they received over their investigation; and lastly for relatives of the dead man who had to listen to the horrifying descriptions of the disposal of his body.

Dennis was called before the coroner early in proceedings so that his options could be explained to him. Hallenstein told him that he was implicated in Kenny's death, and that he could remain during the hearing and give evidence if he wished, or he could leave the building. Dennis chose to leave.

One of the early witnesses provided a unique insight into how Dennis appeared to outsiders on first acquaintance. Daryl Stewart, a Noble Park rigger who had driven Kenny to Dennis's home in Cubitt Street one evening, had this to say: 'As I walked through the house I saw a guy with all gold chains around his neck. It was unbelievable all the chains. I couldn't believe it.'

Various police witnesses then described the discovery of the body and tendered photographs showing Kenny's corpse and its severed legs immediately after recovery from the Yarra. The autopsy report began: 'The entire body was covered by greasy, greyish brown and crusting, white, foul-smelling material ...' Amazingly, Kenny's tattoos were still largely intact. They included a heart with scrolls, 'a fierce head surrounded by golden wings and snakes entwined, and a skull with large teeth'. The right leg was severed just below the knee and the left leg twelve centimetres below the knee.

Peter Hastilow, who had sold Dennis much of the furniture he bought for his various properties, then gave his version, describing being with Dennis in the kitchen when he heard the fatal shots fired, and being warned by Robertson to keep his mouth shut.

'Miss Jones' was the next witness, and her first statement describing the shooting was read to the inquest:

> I saw Robbo sitting down at the table pointing a gun at Anton. Robbo seemed to be off his head. He had a terribly angry look on his face. Robbo's arm was straight out, pointing at Anton, and he fired once. Anton said words like: 'Fuck mate, what's going on? I thought we were just mucking around.'

Under cross-examination Miss Jones altered her story, saying she had been at the house when an argument broke out. Dennis had told her: 'Go and grab my kids and take them around to my brother's house because something's happening here.' She said she had been kept prisoner for two days after this and Dennis had placed a gun at her head, ordering her to tell police that she had witnessed Robertson shooting Kenny. In truth she did not see Kenny shot, she said.

The coroner then ordered suppression of Miss Jones's identity, and adjourned the hearing to 19 December. This was when Detective Dosser underwent his ordeal in the box.

He spoke of being present when the forty-four-gallon drum was opened and seeing 'what appeared to be the left ear, hair and left cheek of a human body set in concrete.'

During cross examination by Mr T. Forrest, appearing for Robertson, the name of Senior Sergeant Paul Higgins cropped up. This was the same officer, later to be gaoled on corruption charges in one of Victoria's costliest and most celebrated trials, whose tip-off from a regular but unidentified informant (almost certainly Dennis) had led to the discovery of Helga Wagnegg's body.

Forrest asked Dosser if Dennis was Higgins's informant. After objections and legal argument he again put the question, 'Do you know whether that information that was relayed to Sergeant Higgins was via Dennis Allen?'

Dosser replied: 'I believe it may have been, yes.'

So five months before his death here in a public forum was first-hand evidence that Dennis was supplying information to the police. What came next provides a rare insight into the murky business of what can happen when police are obliged to weigh the merits of an informer against the gravity of the offences he may be committing.

Forrest: Were any forensic examinations made of Mr Allen's house, at that time, that is before the body was found?
Dosser: No.
Forrest: Why not?
Dosser: I can't give a reason.
Forrest: You had information that a murder had been committed, you knew the name of the deceased, you knew where it was supposed to have been committed, but no forensic examination took place for some months afterwards?
Dosser: That's correct.
Forrest: Who was in charge of this investigation?
Dosser: I was.

Questions about the offences Dennis was facing at the time were then raised. Then:

Forrest: Has Dennis Allen been interviewed in the form of a record of interview about this offence?
Dosser: Not by myself.
Forrest: Has he been interviewed by anyone, in the form of a record of interview?
Dosser: He refused to partake.

The subject then turned to Higgins's role.

Forrest: To your knowledge was that information [about Kenny's body being in the Yarra] relayed to Mr Higgins by Dennis Allen?
Dosser: I couldn't answer that.

Forrest: What connection did he [Higgins] have with this investigation?

Dosser: None.

Forrest: And yet he seemed to be the only source of leads that you had?

Dosser: He was a source, yes.

Forrest: Is Mr Higgins giving evidence here?

Dosser: No.

Forrest: Has he made a statement?

Dosser: No.

Forrest: So here is a man who is dealing directly with a major witness, or indeed a possible accused in this matter, Dennis Allen [yet] he [Higgins] has not taken a formal statement from him, that is correct?

Dosser: Yes.

Forrest: He is not even in the homicide squad, and he has nothing to do with the squad that would have anything to do with this investigation?

Dosser: Yes.

Under further examination Dosser conceded that Robertson had not been asked to sign the notes of the interview conducted with him, was not asked to read the record of those notes, and was not tape-recorded despite the facilities being present.

Forrest continued to pile on the pressure. He elicited from Dosser the fact that Dennis and Kenny had fallen out over a drug deal in which Kenny supplied poor quality drugs. Dosser conceded this could have been a motive for Dennis murdering Kenny, but said the matter had not been investigated, and would not be investigated. Pressed by Forrest, however, he changed his reply: 'Yes, it—yes, it will be investigated.'

Forrest: That is not what you said a minute ago.

Dosser: No, I'm sorry, it will be investigated, yes.

Coroner Hallenstein then summarised his dilemma:

> One has a statement by [Miss Jones] and a statement by Hastilow, who identify Robertson as the person who killed Kenny. We have a third witness, Pettingill, who says that, by way of admission, Robertson has indicated to her that he has killed Kenny. We then have the other side of the coin. [Miss Jones] has recanted on oath, there are aspects as to the credibility of a number of witnesses, and there is a statement by Robertson which specifically and in detail implicates one Dennis Allen as the person who killed Kenny. Now, what do you say I do with those two sides of the story?

Coroner Hallenstein's finding was that Kenny died from 'gunshot wounds to the abdomen unlawfully and maliciously inflicted by Peter Ian Robertson'. He then formally charged Robertson with Kenny's murder. Robertson pleaded not guilty, and was refused bail and remanded to appear at the Supreme Court.

By this stage Kathy was racked with guilt that the statement she made in gaol on Dennis's orders was going to condemn Robertson to a lengthy sentence.

> *Dennis dies in the meantime* [April 1987, before Robertson's trial]. *Now I'm ready to commit suicide, right? Because I'm not going to be the one that sends a man to gaol. Right? That's the criminal code. You can't. I had to retract the statement, because I would have killed meself rather than send Robbo to gaol. I can't ... I've got to live by our code.*

So Kathy stood in the witness box at Robertson's murder trial and told of a deathbed confession by Dennis of having murdered Kenny, and thus secured Robertson's acquittal. The circumstances in which she made this court appearance were extraordinary.

I got a phone call from————* of the police. He's blind drunk. This is about seven o'clock on a Saturday night. And he said: 'If you're a good Catholic, rah, rah, rah,' and he's rambling on, 'and we'll fix you.' It was a death threat. So I'm having a bit of a cry after he's said that.

Monday morning I walk into the Supreme Court building. There's a jack there, a jack there, and a jack there. I had been spat on in the corridor by Anton's relatives, his brothers. And I had the police ready to kill me. And I think: 'I'm trapped.' Right? So I call the tipstaff out, right? And I said to him:— ————has threatened my life and I want you to tell the judge.' And he comes back out, and he says: 'Mrs Pettingill, the judge said he's aware of the situation, but please do not say anything in front of the jury.' The police threatened my life.

Despite her fears Kathy still managed to tell the jury, just one month after his death, of Dennis's confession and on 28 May 1987, Robertson was acquitted of Anton's murder, largely on the strength of Kathy's evidence. He was immediately charged with unlawfully disposing of a body, and on 29 June was gaoled for four years. Passing sentence, Mr Justice Murray said Robertson, then aged thirty-one, was lucky not to have been charged with being an accessory after the fact or murder, which carried a maximum penalty of fifteen years.

The judge described the disposal of Anton's body as 'the most horrifying set of circumstances which I have had occasion to deal with.' He added that the manner in which Dennis and Robertson had acted would 'certainly live in my memory for a long time.'

Today, eight years later, it is difficult to work out the truth of Dennis's deathbed confession. If Kathy was lying in court, and there is no reason to suspect she was, she is unlikely to admit it now and face perjury charges.

---

* Name omitted for legal reasons.

Anton Kenny was the last of the seven victims most widely believed to have been murdered directly or indirectly by Dennis. The other six were Greg Pasche, Victor Gouroff, Lindsay Simpson, Wayne Stanhope, Helga Wagnegg and Jamie Pettingill. Kathy's view is that, of these, Dennis murdered Simpson, Stanhope and Wagnegg. But the real truth of how many slayings can be laid at his door is now almost certainly beyond uncovering. A series of other killings and disappearances linked to his name still remain on police files.

On 18 August 1986 a woman called Elizabeth Shaw died of a suspected 'hot shot' in a flat in St Kilda. Shaw was a heroin addict and people in Dennis's circle suspected her of also being an informer. So when Dennis's name appeared on one of the death notices in the *Sun*, police suspicions again turned to Stephenson Street.

The notice listed nearly twenty names including Dennis, Victor, Trevor and Kathy. It read, in part: 'Sadly missed by those she worked for. She inspired some by the stories she told ... Vengeance is mine, said the Lord.' One theory suggests the notice may have been placed by police, hoping to flush out a suspect. But there is something very familiar about the cryptic sentiments expressed. Kathy has only the vaguest of memories of Elizabeth Shaw, and knows nothing about the death notice.

Four months later, in December 1986, the body of Vicki Ward, a thirty-four-year-old unmarried mother of two young daughters, who was present during the disposal of Anton Kenny's body, was found by three road workers dumped in a ditch in a remote area of Campbellfield, with a bullet wound in the back of the head and another in an arm. She was wearing a grey jumpsuit and gold chains around her neck and ankles—so robbery was an unlikely motive.

Early evidence suggested she had been at a restaurant with friends on the evening of her death, but had left around midnight. The friends told police a vehicle had pulled into the restaurant car park and the occupants had sounded the horn. Vicki went out to the car, saying she would be back in twenty minutes. She was never seen alive again.

Initial police theories centred on an impending murder trial she was due to appear in as a key witness. But there was something else. Vicki had been one of Dennis's lovers and had even lived with him in Stephenson Street for a period. As a result of one of the many raids on his properties Vicki had been charged, along with Dennis and Jamie, with trafficking and possession of heroin. There was also evidence that the relationship between Vicki and Dennis occasionally ran off the rails. Police had watched unseen one night as Vicki cowered in her car in Stephenson Street as Dennis systematically smashed every window and light on the vehicle. So had Vicki become just another of his victims?

Keith Iddon and William Crocker, the two men eventually charged with her murder, desperately wanted this to be believed—so desperately that they offered money to Kathy to come up with a second deathbed confession from Dennis.

Vicki Ward was Dennis's girlfriend, but he didn't kill her. I was offered $50,000 by the two that murdered Vicki to say that Dennis did it. But you see they wrote that in a letter to someone else who gave it to Homicide, so no way known was I going to get up and say Dennis did it. But I wouldn't have acted for them anyway. They were fucking idiots, right off the planet.

Kathy's refusal didn't stop Iddon and Crocker telling the jury at their trial that Dennis was the culprit. Both spoke of his reputation as a killer and of his sinister nickname, Mr D. It didn't do them any good. They were convicted and sentenced to life with no minimum term. This was later reduced on appeal to twenty-two years with a non-parole period of seventeen years.

Another victim was Albert Caulfield, the barman at the United Kingdom Hotel, Clifton Hill, who died from a stroke caused by a moving blood clot, after being shot when Jamie and Dennis attempted to rob the hotel in March 1980.

And then there was Victor Frederick Allard. He was a Painter and Docker, a threatening figure who, police believed, dealt heroin. Allard was hit in the stomach by three bullets in February 1979, while walking down Fitzroy Street, St Kilda, one evening. Who was with him at the time?

> *Dennis and Sissy were standing beside him on the street talking to him when he was shot dead. Nobody knows, nobody told. Later that night I rang the homicide squad and I said: 'Listen to me. If Dennis isn't home within half an hour I'm coming in there.' They said: 'Just because we've got him in here doesn't mean we think he did it.'*

John Geary was the son of a close friend of Gladys and Harry. He was murdered in his bed in the mid-1980s. Kathy remembers his sister sitting on Dennis's knee at 106 Stephenson Street some time after the murder.

> *I never liked her. She said: 'I've been going out with the homicide squad trying to find out who murdered John.' Her brother. He* [Dennis] *just tipped her on the floor. I just looked at her and shook me head.*
>
> *Dennis did John's eulogy at the funeral. Wore a good suit, and it was hard for Dennis to dress up in a suit. But he was a suspect. I don't know what to think.*

There was another, unnamed, woman who died in 1983. Police believed she had evidence connecting Dennis to Victor Gouroff's murder, and had been killed as the most effective method of ensuring her silence. Kathy refers to her briefly.

There was also other women that they thought Dennis had murdered. There was one that came from Fitzroy. I can't remember her name. She's never been found since.

In his book *Walsh Street*, former *Age* police reporter Tom Noble refers to a Maori who stole Dennis's watch and was murdered and had his hand chopped off. Kathy believes this is a reference to a heroin addict who would regularly leave his watch as security against later payment for the drug.

There was a junkie come in with a watch his father gave him for his twenty-first birthday, and we used to have it hanging up on credit all the time, and Dennis got sick of him and got the axe and just chopped the watch in half, and the bloke nearly had a heart attack. The junkie cried.

And then there were the deaths by overdose of up to six unnamed heroin addicts, quite possibly caused by Dennis's failure to ensure his supplies were sufficiently cut. The Enforcer remembers an incident when Dennis and another soldier both believed the other had diluted the drug when, in fact, neither had. What hit the streets shortly afterwards was lethal. The six deaths from overdose which occurred over the following weeks may, or may not, have been caused by Dennis's heroin.

Lastly there were the near-misses, like the bashing of the young man whom Kathy helped escape in his underpants and a similar incident she recalls from the same period.

There was a girl kept prisoner there. Sue Guy. She gave up Jason, something to do with a car. So Dennis gives Jason a pick handle and he made Jason hit her over the head, and it stunned her. And Dennis had the black and white confession [Sue Guy's statement implicating Jason]. *I thought he was going to kill her, and I left. He didn't kill her, but she was there about*

four days with no food or water. They kept hitting her on the
head with the pick handle. I put her on the bunk in the bedroom
and I think she stayed in there about four days. She was out
of it.

As Kathy said, she became almost blasé about murder in the end.
And Dennis, through the distortion of paranoia and rage, saw it
as a performance. The little boy who loved running down live
rabbits and jumping off forty-foot bridges had found a new way
of capturing an audience.

But by the end most of that audience, and his friends, had
deserted him. His horrendous abuse of speed had alienated all
but the most desperate or the most loyal. Addiction had cost him
something else as well—his good luck and his health. Before the
end of April 1987 Dennis was gone—dead (literally) from a
broken heart.

CHAPTER EIGHT

Strange Screams
─ of Death ─

IT IS LATE AFTERNOON IN THE BACK GARDEN OF A LUXURIOUS HOME
in the affluent suburb of Lower Templestowe. February 1986.
Two adolescent Alsatian dogs have the garden to themselves,
and are frolicking on the lawns surrounding the waterless, in-
ground swimming pool. A man in bib and brace overalls, gold
jewellery and tattoos, slips quietly into the garden. The dogs
obviously know him, and as one approaches him, the man
kneels and appears to pet it. He produces something long and
thin from his pocket. Carefully, he places it against the dog's
neck, his favourite place at times like this, and, gently at first,
applies pressure. The dog stiffens, but does not seem unduly
concerned. After a few seconds the man releases the dog and
repeats the procedure with its mate. Next the man catches both
dogs and gently lowers them, one by one, into the shallow end
of the pool. He leaves the garden as unobtrusively as he
entered.

Over the next two hours the dogs run and maul themselves,
literally, to death. They have been injected with carefully calcu-
lated dosages of high quality speed, and the confines of the
empty pool become an inescapable arena for their agony. The
playfulness of late afternoon is replaced by a frenzy of snarling,

frothing savagery as they tear themselves, and each other, to an inevitable end.

Dennis has done it again. He's overdosed Peter's two pet Alsatians in their master's den. Sibling rivalry? Jealousy over a shared woman? Partly, but also Mr D doing what comes unnaturally. Peter and the family don't always see eye to eye, and if there's a message needs delivering, Dennis knows just how to package it.

I t was in August 1985 that her second son Peter was finally released after serving twelve years in gaol for his rampage through the suburbs in 1973. Kathy visited him faithfully all that time, but at one stage while he was in Pentridge her visiting rights were curtailed, bringing a predictably outraged reaction.

I told Dennis: 'I'm going to chain myself up so I can get to see Peter.' It was about eight at night. He takes me up there to Pentridge with this friend, Arthur, and they chain me and this Colleen up, she was Arthur's ex-girl, and he wanted to get rid of her for the night. They chained us up through the holes in the besser brick wall outside the prison.

So the screws were trying to tell me to disperse and that. How could I? Somehow Colleen smashed part of the wall, and they called the police. They got the bolt cutters, and took us away to the Coburg lock-up. Couple of weeks later I go to court at Coburg on a drunk and disorderly.

I said to the magistrate: 'Listen to me your honour, I've been punished enough. I'm barred from Pentridge now, and I can't get to see my son, Peter, and he's doing years.' He said: 'Fined $40, and in default one day.' But then he gave me back all the chains and padlocks, and I had to walk down the court with them all, and I felt such a fool.

THE MATRIARCH

Prison offered little hope of rehabilitation for Peter. He came out in 1985 with no regrets for what he had done, and no intention of settling down. This statement of his philosophy, quoted by Tom Noble in his book *Untold Violence*, makes that abundantly clear.

> The soldier ants, they go to work for their three or four hundred a week, collect their pension and home, right. Pay their car. Say five hundred a week right, this is one off. I earn five hundred a week what do you earn?
>
> Well I paid a hundred and fifty off the house, I paid a hundred off the car, buy food, what are you left with, forty dollars, that's what he earned a week, forty dollars. That's to live on ... I don't feel remorse. I don't feel remorseful, you know why? Because they choose. That's what they choose.

Peter obviously didn't consider himself an ant, or a mere soldier. For the next eight months he behaved as if he was determined to make up for the wasted years behind bars. If he had wished he could have joined Kathy, Dennis and the rest of the family in Richmond, becoming part of a flourishing and influential circle.

No-one knew better than Peter how powerful the family had become, as he vividly described in a secretly taped conversation, again quoted by Tom Noble, this time in his best-selling *Walsh Street*.

> The protection is created by the fucking psychological wall brought by the fucking family's actions, right? People won't dare go against ... the family. Won't move against me—oh, repercussions from the other brothers. Won't move against them for repercussions from the other brothers. Then, so, all the murders, the fucking bashings, the shootings and the victories ...

Even so Peter was determined to strike out on his own without 'the protection'. Additionally he had ties in Sydney, where his daughter from an earlier relationship with a model gave birth to the first of her three children, making him a grandfather at the age of thirty-five and Kathy a great-grandmother at the age of fifty-two.

One of his first steps back into the real world after release was to persuade Kathy to go guarantor on a sports car, a Mazda RX7 worth close to $20,000. Next he found himself a girlfriend— a woman called Rhonda Meehan, who was separated from her husband and living in Brunswick with their son. Soon after they began living together, Peter ran into his first problems with the police since his release. He had begun dealing heroin and a raid on Rhonda's flat caught him in the act of preparing a relatively large quantity of the drug for sale. After a couple of nights in the familiar surroundings of Pentridge he organised bail and was back on the streets.

But things suddenly went wrong on the personal front when, characteristically, Dennis stepped in. He and Rhonda had an affair. The details and duration are hazy, but according to Kathy it had a devastating effect on Peter. Whatever the circumstances, he moved into the Fitzroy flat of Vicki Ward, ironically one of Dennis's former girlfriends. However, this was simply a convenient business arrangement which enabled him to use her flat as a base for preparing his drugs for sale. Before long he patched things up with Rhonda and their relationship steadily grew closer.

Peter had now established a wide and lucrative ring of sub-dealers to whom he was supplying drugs. He might not have been making quite the fortune Dennis was enjoying, but police have estimated his income around this period at $30,000 a week. His ambition was to buy his own house so that he, Rhonda and her son could live in some degree of comfort and security. But being Peter he wasn't going to be happy with anything but the best, and set his sights on the upwardly mobile suburb of Lower Templestowe. He found a suitable house shortly before Christmas, complete with in-ground swimming pool, and by March 1986, seven months after his release from gaol, had paid the $170,000 asking price. He and Rhonda spent an additional $30,000 on furnishings, most of it, according to Kathy, with cash.

And then there was the incident with the dogs:

Dennis killed the dogs out of spite and over Rhonda. The pool was empty and they couldn't get out. They run round and round and round in a frenzy with the speed. Peter was destroyed over Dennis's affair with Rhonda. He used to fall in love too quick. He used to call them his Charlie's Angels, they were all the same fucking type, scrawny blondes. I don't know why Dennis took her off him, he could get anybody, even before the jewellery. He killed the dogs to hurt him. I think they got jealous of one another, because it didn't take long for Peter to go back to gaol, and Dennis was still out, with all his money and his gold.

By now Peter was dealing in firearms as well as drugs, and allegedly sold a number of machine guns stolen from an army base. He boasted that one of these ended up with Pavel 'Mad Max' Marinof, who was shot dead by police early in 1986, some six months after a rampage which put four policemen in hospital.

Police interest in Peter was predictably increasing and the Templestowe house was under virtually constant surveillance. Then one night in April a squad of armed officers smashed in the front door, dragged Rhonda out of bed, handcuffed Peter while he was still naked and stood around him, guns at the ready. Peter was at his most vulnerable and therefore at his most vicious and threatening. His response is reprinted from *Untold Violence*:

Be warned. I'm telling you, you aren't bulletproof. Be warned,
I'm telling you right now. You touch one hair on her and I'll
kill you all. I'll hunt you down and I'll kill you all. I won't fuck
around with you, right. It's pretty hard to prove if you're
waiting up a driveway . . .

As a result of the raid Peter was charged with dealing heroin
and marijuana and conspiring to commit armed robbery. This
time he didn't get bail. Kathy won't accept Peter's accusations at
the time that the family was against him, but confirms the bad
blood between him and Dennis quite possibly had something to
do with the arrest.

As usual Peter defended himself, with Victor's wife Wendy
acting as his 'clerk' at the subsequent lengthy trial, which ended
in 1988. Despite his allegations that police had set him up he was
found guilty and sentenced to thirteen years with a minimum of
eleven. His pride and joy, the Templestowe house, was also confiscated, along with other property police said he had obtained
as a result of illegal activities. So, after just eight months of
freedom, during which he was said by police to have made more
than half a million dollars, it was back to square one for Peter—
and for Kathy as well, as she dutifully resumed her weekly visits
to him.

She was having her own run of bad luck. For several years since
her last spell in gaol in 1980 she managed to keep out of the clutches
of the law, apart from being fined $125 for indecent language and
using premises for prostitution. Then in March 1983 she was
sentenced to twenty-eight days on five charges of assault and
'assault by kicking', but the prison term was reduced on appeal to
a fine. It arose from the incident at the outer-suburban municipal
baths recorded in Chapter Four. In March 1984 she was fined for
possession of an unlicensed pistol, a magnum, and three months
later she was fined $150 for assault on police.

THE MATRIARCH

In 1986 she was sentenced twice, for possession of a firearm and drug dealing involving the eight ounces of heroin, with a street value of $200,000, dug up by police in the back yard of 35 Stephenson Street. She spent around five months behind bars, both at Pentridge and Fairlea. When she got to Pentridge it was almost like coming home, and she soon earned the grudging respect of the warders for her efficiency as head of the prison cleaning brigade, swabbing the bluestone floors spotless and gleaming.

When she was released after finishing the second term in 1987, she came home to find the family's affairs in disarray and Dennis sinking into decline. As time went by Kathy became more and more uneasy about the way things were going at Richmond.

Number 106 had a smell of death, danger, and fear, the house, and I'd had enough, and I wasn't going to go back in there. I handed the keys to The Enforcer and a woman I knew and they could go in there if they wanted to, but I was never going back.

There was heroin in the house when I shut the doors for the last time. I gave them the keys, I wanted nothing to do with it. They went back and got the stuff. I'd had enough. I was too scared to go back into that house, I knew something would happen.

TELEVISION COVERAGE OF THE ONE-DAY INTERNATIONAL BETWEEN the Australian and English cricket teams is due to start any moment. It's Sunday, 19 January 1987, and the warming rays of a beautiful summer's day are filtering through the industrial grime and haze which seem permanently to choke light and life from the back streets of Richmond.

Sunday is visiting day at Pentridge and most of the other prisons scattered around Victoria, and normally Kathy would be

208

off somewhere with a carton of cigarettes to bring one or other of the family some temporary respite from the tyranny of boredom which is their life behind bars. But not today. She's left visiting duty to Trevor, Victor and the rest of the boys. Today's for the cricket. Kathy is an obsessive follower of the game and today promises to be particularly sweet, with victory over the Old Enemy on the cards. She has settled down on a banana lounge on the patio of 35 Stephenson Street, the TV in front of her, a long lead running back in through the window. No drugs, no bodies . . . just cricket.

On the box commentators are licking their lips at the prospect of an exciting day's play, and pre-match pitch appraisals are under way. Then Kathy hears the noise for the first time. Initially she's not sure where it's coming from, or what it is, but it has every hair on the back of her neck standing on end. But then, just as quickly as it comes her first bristling fear is gone, and she relaxes back in her seat. It must have been some glitch in the TV set. Then, halfway through the opening over, there it is again— unmistakably close this time, coming not from the screen but from next door, a low, guttural growling of something or someone in terrible pain. There's also an edge of menace in there somewhere. But is it menace, or just terror?

Kathy is now bolt upright, the cricket forgotten. That's Dennis. Next door. Who's in there with him, and what are they doing to him? She's out of her chair, through the gate and onto the patio at 37 as the sound builds to a high, keening wail. As she rattles the front door handle the awful voice of her son coming from the other side has changed to a crazed gibbering. She should have known Dennis's door would be locked. As far as she is aware he is alone, no Enforcer on hand, so of course he would have locked up.

She races back to 35, half sobbing in her panic, and frantically searches for the bunch of keys that will let her into 37, but they are nowhere. The extent of Kathy's fear forces her into something that would normally be unthinkable. She grabs the phone and dials Richmond police station, a familiar number from all the bail and other arrangements she's had to make over the years. Within minutes a couple of plainclothes detectives have arrived, and by now Kathy has located the keys. As the three of them enter the front gate at 37 all is suddenly quiet. Somehow it's worse than the screaming. Kathy's hands are trembling as she undoes first the front door, then the security grille, and leads the way inside. One of the detectives pushes past her and heads for Dennis's bedroom, as if he's been here before and knows where to look.

Almost unwillingly Kathy cranes over his shoulder through the open door, not wanting to see, not wanting to know. The first thing she takes in is the rumpled sheets at the foot of the bed. Then Dennis's half-naked form. His torso is twisted across the top of the bed, but his head and shoulders have somehow come to rest on the little bedside table, looking away from her. There's no blood, no sign of violence, other than the strange, twisted line of his body. Kathy hears the detectives muttering something about 'faking it'. Dennis is due in court next day, and he's been known to find a way out of such inconveniences. But then one of them takes Dennis's head, almost tenderly, in his hands and turns it face upwards. His mouth is half-open and drooling spittle across the pillow, his eyes glazed and sightless. At first Kathy thinks he's dead, but then words intrude into the turmoil in her head. 'I reckon he's had a stroke,' says the officer. 'Quick, get an ambulance.'

Three hours later Kathy is by his bedside at St Vincent's Hospital in the city. Dennis's still unconscious form is shaking and jerking spasmodically beneath the cover, but the nurses and doctors have come and gone, doing all they can for now. Then suddenly his eyes flicker open and take in the surroundings. She sees his hand, outside the covers, on the side where the doctor says the stroke has hit. It's as if he's trying to clench and unclench his fist, but nothing happens other than a strange twitching. His eyes seem to focus on her and he starts to groan, the sounds finally forming into words. Slurred and unsure, but still words.

'Jesus it's hard to me, this,' he mumbles. 'Go out every night working, get all this money, and I bought this hospital.' With an enormous effort his eyes fix on Kathy's. 'You've got to get on to Charlie and Andrew to bring the papers in.' And then the mouth and eyes close again.

Charlie Nikakis and Andrew Fraser. At least he remembers who his legal representatives are, Kathy reflects as his head lolls back onto the pillow. An hour later he wakes again, and this time appears more lucid. Kathy puts down the book she has been reading: 'Do you know that you bought this hospital?'

Dennis looks at her, and there is a flash of something familiar about the eyes: 'You fucking idiot, I only bought this fucking room.'

The last eight months of Dennis's life were marked by tragedy, further deaths and increasing pressure from police. The officers he had been paying for information and warnings of impending raids were themselves becoming subject to scrutiny, and the Richmond empire seemed under siege. Dennis's friends were becoming fewer and the list of his enemies was becoming unmanageable.

I knew Wayne and Sandy were going to give him up. I said to Wayne: 'Why are you a friend of my son's? What's in it for you?' He said to me: 'Can't he just have a friend?' I said: 'No, he can't.' On his last birthday I asked all the soldiers: 'Can we all put in together and buy him one of those double fridges?' You got the freezer and fridge for about three grand. They wouldn't be in it. And he used to give them a grand for their birthdays. Always. Because Dennis died with no friends, and

211

in the hospital, when I thought he was lucid, I said: 'You
haven't got any friends.'

August 1986 was a particularly difficult month. First there was
the suicide of Sissy inside Pentridge, which hit Dennis harder
than most people, other than Kathy, realised. Lindy and Jade
were removed into the care of Sissy's mother, and Dennis began
drinking even more heavily than usual. This and his ever-
growing dependency on speed were taking an inevitable toll on
his health.

After his stroke on 19 January Dennis entered St Vincent's, and
Wayne, Sandy and Miss Jones began to see an end to their nightmare. His empire clearly on the wane, the trio negotiated witness
protection deals with police, and began to sing. But Dennis was
getting sick of hospital and Kathy wanted him home. The unspoken feeling was that he had only weeks to live.

Doctors had found Dennis was suffering from an extremely
rare bacterial infection, causing pieces of his heart to break off
and be transported into his bloodstream. One had lodged in his
leg and another, much more seriously, in his brain. His massive
addiction to speed almost certainly contributed to his condition.

He'd been starving himself in hospital to punish me, and it did
punish me. Then he started hounding us to take him home.
Well I got Kim Nelson and her husband, and Lex was there,
and we were going to hire the wheelchair, and Kim was going
to nurse him and everything. But unknown to us the homicide
squad told the hospital, if Dennis was to be signed out to ring
'em. Well they rang 'em. So the two homicide squad jacks get
out the lift. Now this is approximately 12.30 in the day. As
one of them comes towards me I could smell the grog. So they
wheel Dennis past me, and I think Lex had a blue with one of

them in the car park, a physical fight, because he was there to help us, Lex.

This was 11 March 1987. Dennis was taken by police car to the homicide squad offices where he was charged with Wayne Stanhope's murder, largely on the testimony of Miss Jones, Wayne and Sandy. He was then taken to Melbourne Magistrates' Court, where the charge was formally put before magistrate Brian Clothier. Dennis had become visibly emaciated and had lost several kilograms through his illness. His gruff speaking voice had dropped to a barely audible whisper and, too weak to stand, he was pushed into court in a wheelchair. The man police once said was an untouchable, because no witness would live long enough to testify against him, had become an object of pity, rather than fear. He was remanded to 11 June and sent back to the security wing of St Vincent's. Dennis was never to appear again in court. Less than five weeks later he was dead, at the age of thirty-five.

The day he died I was in that hospital really early. I don't know why ... instinct? Thirteenth of April, thirteen his lucky day? By this stage he'd been in the prison ward at St Vincent's a few days. And I used to take him in a Serepax, just one. So this night, the night before he died, he said: 'I don't want one.' And that worried me. And I come back real early the next morning. And they were wheeling his bed out. They put him in the St Ann's Ward.

He didn't die in the prison ward, like most people think, and they had him all hooked up to these monitors, right? So Charlie and Andrew, his lawyers, came in about quarter to six at night, and he said to them: 'I'm that bloody tired.' He said: 'I haven't been to sleep for days.' And one of them said: 'But you go twelve or fourteen days without sleep anyway, Den.' So with that, they leave.

Now I had two screws, because he was in custody, and I wanted the confession about who put this heroin in my back yard at number 35 that we were charged with, me and Trevor. So I asked the screws to witness it. I said to him: 'Dennis, who put that heroin in my backyard?' He said: 'That fucking Wayne did.' Not meaning Stanhope, the other one. Now I got that confession.

At six o'clock I'm sitting there alone and then all of a sudden as the minutes tick, I could see the monitor going down, and he closed his eyes. And the alarms went off. Well the nurses went to rush in, and I said: 'You're not coming in. That's it. Leave him be.' I said: 'To spend the rest of his life in gaol? No.' So he died officially at five past six. I stopped them from reviving him. He was thirty-five. He died in agony, Dennis.

And I made him pay while he was dying. I said all I wanted to say to him while he could hear. 'How do you think I feel?' And 'What did you think about when I wanted to kill you, Dennis?' But he couldn't answer me back, he was too feeble. But one day I said I was going to kill him, and Jason was there, and his face was white, and I said: 'I'm going in next door to kill him.' The kid nearly died. Because I couldn't see any end to the murders. I had to stop the killings, I'd had enough of the killings. I think it was after Wayne Stanhope's murder that I'd had enough. I just wanted to kill him.

Kathy was torn between grief and anger at the realisation that Dennis had been betrayed—particularly by Wayne and Sandy.

So this Wayne and Sandy had bought him a tile picture made of tiles, called 'The Family'. As soon as Dennis died I went back to 37 and I got the fucking thing, and I smashed it to smithereens. And young Jason's watching me. I was in a

*terrible, terrible temper, and I think it was Victor restrained
me. I had to get me anger out.*

Once again the back pages of the *Sun* were used to express
all those feelings that could never be hinted at during Dennis's
life. There were messages from family members, including
Gladys and Harry, his brothers, Jade and Lindy, Vicki and Jason.
Kim Nelson was there, and his legal representatives, 'Charlie N.,
Chris D. and Andrew'. Their message read: 'Denny, sorry we
missed the turn. When we get together again, we'll get bail down
there.'

A discordant note was struck by four or five notices pur-
porting to come from police officers Brian Murphy and Paul
Higgins. Although Higgins's name was linked with Dennis, it is
unlikely either of the two men actually inserted them. Kathy
checked and discovered they were lodged by a tattooed man at
a Footscray newsagency. Another notice was signed TJF, police
slang for an aborted mission—'The Job's Fucked'.

Missing from the death notices, almost without exception,
were the names of the rich and famous who visited Stephenson
Street during Dennis's reign. They included leading barristers,
well-known Catholic priests, a prominent rock star, and on two
occasions members of an international cricket side and a visiting
American basketball team.

*Father Peter Norden, who did Jamie's funeral, used to come
down the hill jogging, and call in and have a drink with
Dennis. Father Brosnan, the chaplain at Pentridge, used to
come down quite a fair bit, once a month or something like
that. He liked Dennis. Must have had a lot to do with him in
gaol. I believe they all went to the chapel, but I don't think it
was just to say prayers. A bit of gossip, a bit of this and a bit
of that. Dennis thought he was all right.*

Brosnan gave me $100 for food for Victor and Wendy's

kids when I was looking after them in the early 1990s and I got them crayfish and prawns. Did Dennis believe in God? No, I don't think so. I think he thought he was God. But I remember one time Father Brosnan was on a special diet, and I had to poach him some fish. He used to eat in 37.

Father Brosnan's memory of his relationship with Dennis and the family was not so clear-cut when I interviewed him for this book. Early in the conversation he acknowledged: 'We got on very well, Dennis and I, we always were good friends.' But later he amended this to a 'passing friendship'. Father Brosnan added that he generally found Dennis pleasant, but added: 'But that was because he could afford to be.' He never saw Dennis's violent side, because—'I didn't see him in action with his mates'.

He declined to pass any judgment about the way Kathy's family turned out, other than to say: 'There were a lot of reasons, the circumstances and the environment they lived in, and Kathy would not have been the greatest example for them. As kids there would have been a lot of confusion in their little minds, and this would have stayed with them.' Although he couldn't specifically remember the poached fish, Father Brosnan said: 'I wouldn't deny it, though, it would have been quite possible.'

Among the barristers who visited on occasion were Bob Kent QC and Chris Dane QC, both of whom represented family members. Mr Kent said in an interview for this book that he remembered attending Stephenson Street for conferences with his client. Kathy recalls a few incidents:

Chris Dane, he was down there in his black coat and striped trousers. He came down over that police surveillance.

I do remember there was basketballers, black ones. How did he get to know them? How did he get to know a lot of people?

The reputation of where to get things. They were huge, they were black, maybe they wanted a smoke. 'Hey, man, what's doin'?' I had the Pakistani one-day cricket team come down to the parlour at 108. I was walking up the street and I noticed the tracksuits going in, about half-a-dozen of them. We used to advertise in the Truth.

Then there was Stevie Wright from the Easybeats, he was there all the time. Dennis was going to promote him, so Stevie flew down with his books. Dennis must have paid for the ticket. Dennis thought 'fuck that' in the end. Before Dennis died Stevie sent him an album to St Vincent's, a special album, not released normally. During the Bi-centennial in Brisbane he came booming out onto the stage, and the very next day he was down at Stephenson Street. I said: 'Dennis is dead.'

Not surprisingly, Dennis's death became a major media event. The *Age*, the *Sun* and the *Sunday Press* all ran significant stories detailing his drug empire, the killings of which he was suspected and the indignity of his final days. 'Peaceful death of a violent man', 'Dealer avoids justice a final time', and 'Death pays a dealer one final call' were three of the choicest headlines. Kathy also remembers the Channel Ten news crew trying to film the coffin coming out of number 37.

A few days after Dennis died Kathy made an ill-advised appearance on Derryn Hinch's 3AW talkback radio program. Hinch understandably wanted to discuss the murders and the drug dealing. Kathy, also understandably, wanted to talk about Dennis's tragic life, Sissy's suicide, the birth of his two daughters addicted to heroin, the murder of his brother. There wasn't much common ground between the two. 'He's dead. Can't you let him rest?' was Kathy's final word.

At the time of his death Dennis was facing more than sixty serious charges ranging from murder to mild misdemeanours. During the last nineteen years of his life he received twenty-six separate terms of imprisonment ... but spent less than seven years in all behind bars.

Contrast this with the appalling custodial history of his younger brother Peter. He has been before the courts on only three occasions since the age of nineteen, but has spent all but a few months of the past twenty-one years in prison.

CHAPTER NINE

Walsh Street

KATHY'S DAUGHTER VICKI IS IN THE WITNESS BOX IN MELBOURNE'S Supreme Court before Mr Justice Vincent, who is presiding over one of the city's most celebrated trials of this century. In the dock across the courtroom from Vicki sit four men, including two of her brothers, Victor and Trevor. The four are accused of the cold-blooded execution of two young police officers late one night in a back street of one of Melbourne's wealthiest suburbs. Along with her seventeen-year-old son Jason, Vicki is giving evidence against Victor and Trevor, helping the prosecution in a case which, if successful, will certainly see them gaoled for the rest of their lives.

Sitting upstairs in the public gallery is Kathy, looking on in shame and horror at this public destruction of her family. She knows her sons are innocent, but the spectacle of her daughter, her own flesh and blood, playing a leading role in this drama is too much for her. The one principle by which she has always lived, and which she has instilled in her children, is the placing of family loyalty above all else. And here, in open court, Vicki is driving a stake through the heart of that principle. Kathy knows Vicki has been told by police that she must choose between her son Jason and her two brothers. She knows detectives have worked their poison, voicing Vicki's worst fear, that Victor and Trevor are planning to have Jason murdered if he continues his evidence against them. But to Kathy this is ridiculous—Vicki should know that in a family like theirs, such an act would be unthinkable. Why can't she see the detectives are seeking only to attack from within? To weaken the family's strength and resolve from the inside?

Suddenly Vicki turns and flashes a look of pure, venomous hatred across the courtroom towards the dock. There is no mistaking at whom it is aimed. Victor and Trevor seem almost to wilt before the intensity of their sister's loathing. Kathy leaps to her feet from the hard wooden bench in the gallery and, tears washing down her face, stumbles down the stairs. It is the last time she will ever set eyes on her daughter.

The life and crimes of Dennis Allen were undoubtedly the impetus behind the emergence of Kathy Pettingill's family as the most notorious criminal dynasty in Australian history. Eighteen months after Dennis's death the involvement of three of her other children, Victor, Trevor and Vicki, her grandson Jason, and Victor's wife Wendy in events surrounding the Walsh Street murders became the second chapter in the saga of the family's enduring infamy.

But in many ways Walsh Street was also part of Dennis's legacy. Kathy believes the string of unsolved murders and other crimes he left behind, and perhaps more importantly, the allegations that he had a number of police officers on his payroll, convinced many of Victoria's so-called finest that they still had a score to settle with the family. Without Dennis her other children would never have been caught up in Walsh Street, she says. Or, as she put it in a much publicised television interview at the time: 'We're still paying for Dennis's sins.'

How true this may be is difficult to say, but the fact remains that the family will forever be connected in the public mind with the murder of the two young constables, despite both Victor and Trevor having been acquitted. For Kathy the supreme irony is that their acquittals are seen today as almost irrelevant, and in the minds of many police officers have simply added to the enormity of the score left to settle.

The killing of a policeman is never lightly undertaken by even the most desperate criminals. In only the most extreme circumstances—escaping from custody, or avoiding capture during commission of a major crime—would such a step be contemplated. Even then the consequences are so predictable that the bullet is likely to remain in the breech. This is borne out by the figures: since it was formed in 1853 the Victoria Police Force has lost twenty-nine members in the line of duty. Of their killers, all but the Walsh Street assassins have been brought to justice.

Besides, all the underworld hates a cop killing; it brings too much heat. And Walsh Street wasn't the murder of a single officer in the turmoil of battle or the frenzy of flight. It was the ice-cold extermination of two young men selected at random and killed for revenge. A Holden Commodore car had been abandoned in the early hours of the morning of 12 October 1988, in the middle of Walsh Street, South Yarra, the innocuous bait in a savage trap. Any patrol car could have been summoned to check why it was there but Prahran 311, carrying constables Steven Tynan, aged twenty-two, and Damian Eyre, twenty, was the first on the scene.

The two officers parked their car close behind the abandoned Commodore and approached on foot. Tynan climbed into the driving seat and Eyre stood or squatted beside him on the road. At least two men came out of the darkness, getting to within a metre of their quarry before the first shot was fired. Tynan fell across the front seat, his skull shattered. A second shot hit Eyre in the back, and a third and a fourth missed their target, presumably because the stricken policeman was able to struggle with his attacker. Then Eyre's police issue revolver was jerked

221

from its holster, placed against his head and fired at pointblank range. At that moment the course of Victorian criminal history changed forever.

The sound of the shots woke many people living nearby, a number of whom at subsequent court hearings described hearing voices and seeing figures running from the scene. Interestingly, two witnesses, independently of one another, said one of the voices they heard was a woman's. Others spoke of hearing cries of anguish, presumably from one or other of the two victims. Unfortunately none of them were at their windows when the murderers sprang their trap.

Whoever those men were who stepped out of the shadows, they must have realised they would have the state's entire police force baying for their blood, and half the underworld anxious to turn them in to cool things down. But did the four men ultimately charged—Victor and Trevor and their two co-accused—fit the bill?

At least one person thought so. Immediately after their acquittal Detective Inspector John Noonan, head of the TyEyre taskforce which investigated the murders, gave voice to the outrage of his colleagues when he bitterly observed: 'The verdict brought down by the jury says not guilty. They're certainly not saying that the four people who were charged are innocent, and neither am I.' He was wrong, of course. Under our system of law the four were innocent from the start, until proven guilty, and their acquittal merely reinforced this innocence. Noonan was supported by the secretary of the Police Association, Senior Sergeant Danny Walsh, who said: 'I, together with the rest of the police force, am totally devastated with the result. I can't believe it.'

At around the same time Inspector Noonan was making his statement, a radio message was going out from police headquarters to all units: 'The verdict in the Walsh Street trial was all four not guilty, repeat not guilty. All units are warned, keep yourselves in control.'

Chief Commissioner Neil Comrie was to observe seven years later, in November 1995, that the aftermath of the Walsh Street period was still dictating the manner in which the war between his force and the underworld was being conducted.

An examination of the extraordinary sequence of events leading to and following the Walsh Street murders will help to explain why they made and changed history.

11 October 1988: Career criminal Graeme Jensen is shot dead in a car in the outer suburb of Narre Warren. It is later revealed that Jensen and his associates, including Victor Peirce, had been under surveillance and that the police had allegedly made threats against their lives. Detectives would also claim that underworld circles had decided that the next time police killed a criminal, the death would be doubly avenged—two of their number would pay the penalty.

12 October, 4.45 a.m.: Constables Tynan and Eyre shot dead in Walsh Street. Police immediately claim link with Jensen killing.

12 October, afternoon: Victor Peirce's home at 86 Chestnut Street, Richmond (Dennis's former house) raided. His wife Wendy, nephew Jason, and Jason's close friend Anthony Farrell taken in for questioning. Farrell later becomes one of the four put on trial for the murders.

12 October, later same afternoon: Police raid the Brunswick flat of Vicki Brooks, Kathy's daughter, minutes after Victor has fled over a back fence. Peter McEvoy, an old friend of the family and tenant in the flat, is questioned but not arrested. McEvoy is to become another of the four defendants.

12 October, later in day: Having been warned by friends that police are likely to shoot him first and ask questions later, Victor goes with his solicitor to police headquarters to give himself up, but is told there is no officer available to see him.

13 October: Victor again visits police headquarters, and this time

is charged with the murder and armed robbery of Dominik Hefti, a security guard killed during a raid on 11 July 1988 at a supermarket in Brunswick. Police have had Victor under surveillance, suspecting him of the robbery, and Jason Ryan has implicated him in the killing of Hefti in a statement made immediately after the raid on Chestnut Street. Eventually the Hefti charges against Victor are withdrawn, and charges of murdering Tynan and Eyre are laid. He spends the next thirty months in custody.

Next few days: Police raid the habitats of known criminals across the state as officers drop current inquiries to help with the manhunt. Police refuse to attend routine calls without back-up, requiring two cars for all but the most innocuous of assignments. The state government offers a reward of $200,000, and Police Minister Steve Crabb describes the killings as cold-blooded and despicable.

14 October: Damian Eyre buried.

17 October: Steven Tynan buried.

21 October: TyEyre Taskforce formed. Initially, and probably for political reasons, senior police have decided to treat the slayings as ordinary murders, despite Walsh Street being the first multiple killing of policemen in Victoria since the days of the Kelly Gang in the late 1870s. The entire 130-strong Bureau of Criminal Intelligence, and surveillance experts from the drug squad and the National Crime Authority, are made available to the taskforce.

21 October: Jason provides police with his first version of the killings, naming those allegedly involved, including family friend Jedd Houghton, during a lengthy interview.

24 October: Jason taken on a four-day tour of country Victoria by three detectives, leading to allegations of police intimidation aimed at gaining further information from him.

27 October: Jason names career criminal, Gary Abdallah, as the man who provided the get-away car for the murders.

28 October: Jason enters witness protection scheme. He is to remain in the scheme for close to three years at a cost of more than $2 million.

31 October: Jason incriminates Anthony Farrell and another friend, Emmanuel Alexandridis, in events leading up to the killings, and gives further information about Farrell, Houghton, McEvoy and his uncle Victor. Jason himself becomes the first person to be accused of the killings and is charged with murder. At a midnight hearing in the Supreme Court he is bailed into the custody of the protection squad.

1 November: Anthony Farrell becomes the second accused and is charged with murder. Police carry out the second of nine raids on Victor's home in Chestnut Street, and charge his wife Wendy with possession of a firearm, assault on police, and indecent language.

Early November: List of suspects numbers twelve, later to grow close to 100. The state government passes legislation allowing bugged phone conversations to be admitted as evidence in court.

16 November: Jason again changes his story for police, naming Houghton, McEvoy, Farrell and his uncles Victor Peirce and Trevor Pettingill as the murderers.

17 November: Police trace Jedd Houghton to a caravan park in Bendigo. Houghton has become aware he is under surveillance as a Walsh Street suspect and, allegedly, is heavily armed. Police storm the caravan in which he is living, and he dies instantly after being hit with two shots. Police say he pulled a gun on them. Evidence will later be given that Houghton confessed his role in the killings to his girlfriend's father.

29 November, early hours: Trevor is kidnapped outside his Fitzroy flat by four masked men, bundled into a car and driven to the bush, where he is severely beaten with a sledgehammer. His assailants repeatedly order him: 'Tell the police

the truth.' He is dumped by the roadside and spends the next two weeks in hospital recovering from his injuries. In a newspaper interview Kathy initially claims the kidnappers were police officers, but subsequently retracts, saying it was a rival gang of criminals. Still later, after the acquittals, she goes back to her original opinion that the culprits were police.

23 December: Wendy Peirce stabs a woman in the face with a broken glass in a pub brawl in Richmond, causing serious injury. She is charged with attempted murder and spends Christmas in custody.

30 December: Victor is brought to court from Pentridge where he is on remand on the Hefti murder and robbery charges, and is charged with the murders of Tynan and Eyre. He is remanded back to Pentridge.

5 January 1989: Police carry out their final raid on Chestnut Street, reducing the house to matchwood with the aid of massive earthmoving equipment. They also excavate the site to a depth of two metres and remove many spent bullets, presumably dating back to Dennis's occupation. The search takes place with the permission of the Taxation Department which now owns the property, having seized it from Dennis's bankrupt estate.

13 January: Victor carried bodily down Russell Street into court by four police officers flanked by six detectives. Defence counsel refers to it as 'a show for the media circus'.

9 April: Gary Abdallah repeatedly shot by police while being questioned in his Carlton flat. Two officers present say he pulled an imitation pistol on them.

26 April: A rusting sawn-off shotgun, believed to be one of the murder weapons, found buried at Royal Park Golf Course by a gardener. Police trace the history of the gun, an unusual make, imported from Japan, through painstaking research.

Late April: First signs of conflict between two heads of the task-force, Detective Inspectors David Sprague and John Noonan.

The rift is to worsen, virtually splitting the investigation into two warring camps. Both men admit retrospectively that their failure to get on, exacerbated by problems with Wendy Peirce, irreparably damaged the inquiry.

3 May: Peter McEvoy appears on television, after being interviewed by Inspector Noonan, saying he is afraid police are planning to kill him because they believe he was involved in the murders.

10 May: McEvoy arrested and charged with murders.

19 May: Abdallah dies in hospital without regaining consciousness. Inquiries into the police shooting will include an inquest, an investigation by the Ombudsman and a trial. Allegations will be made that police shot Abdallah after tying him up but all charges are eventually dismissed.

Early June: Wendy, now on bail on the attempted murder charge, has a series of meetings with police, during which she is shown love letters from Victor to other women, and agrees to enter witness protection scheme.

15 July: Before police arrive to take her into witness protection, Wendy has a number of visitors to her Cheltenham home and claims to be forcibly administered heroin as a 'hot shot' intended to kill her. Among those alleged to be involved are Trevor, Peter McEvoy's girlfriend, and a man who had been sharing a prison cell with Victor.

Mid-July to late August: Wendy provides the police with a series of video-taped interviews giving information on various crimes, including murders and armed robberies, involving members of Kathy's family.

Late July: Split between Inspectors Sprague and Noonan worsens. Wendy refuses to have any dealings with Noonan and two other taskforce officers who were previously involved in raids on the family during Dennis's reign in Richmond. As a result Noonan is kept in the dark about vital information supplied by Wendy. The two other officers are temporarily removed from the taskforce, to the outrage of their colleagues.

Later in July: The Department of Public Prosecutions (DPP) declines to help the taskforce prepare its final brief for court, presumably because the DPP does not believe the case is yet strong enough. Pressure is also coming on the taskforce from Chief Magistrate John Dugan to get the committal hearing under way. The job of compiling the brief is immense, involving 230 witnesses, 700 exhibits, 900 witness statements, 6,500 information sheets, 700 audio tapes and 12,000 telephone recordings. Close to 3,000 cab drivers alone are seen during investigations.

28 July: Split comes to a head in prolonged public row between members of the taskforce.

Early August: Taskforce numbers are reduced from fourteen to six, and Sprague and Noonan move their remaining teams into separate offices. Little or no communication follows between them.

Mid-August: Charges of murder against Jason Ryan withdrawn. He is granted immunity after agreeing to testify against the accused.

31 October: Committal hearings begin against Farrell, McEvoy and Victor. Prosecution alleges the three accused, plus Trevor, Jedd Houghton and Jason, gathered in a South Yarra flat to plot the death of the two police officers in revenge for Jensen's killing.

November: Committal hearing continues with allegations by fellow inmates that Victor has confessed in gaol to the murders. Another prisoner, Lindsay Rountree, tells of an alleged attempt by Victor to recruit him into an underworld group pledged to murder two police officers each time a criminal is killed by police. Kathy's daughter Vicki also gives evidence, leading to a permanent estrangement between them.

8 December: Wendy begins her evidence, which will include details of an affair she says she had with Graeme Jensen, and much about Kathy's family during the Richmond days. Most damning of all, she tells of Victor saying, the night before Walsh Street, that he was 'going to kill the jacks that knocked Graeme'. When he returned the next morning, she alleges Victor told her that he, Jedd Houghton and Peter McEvoy had killed two policemen in South Yarra.

22 February 1990: Committal ends with Victor, McEvoy and Farrell being sent for trial on charges of murdering Tynan and Eyre.

9 July: Trevor charged with the murders and ordered to stand trial, after limited committal proceedings, with the other three defendants.

21 January 1991: Voir dire preliminary hearing in the Supreme Court to test evidence Wendy is due to give before the trial. It soon becomes clear she is no longer prepared to provide the same evidence she gave at the committal, and later that day she signs herself out of the witness protection scheme. Thus, eighteen months, $2 million and thousands of hours of police work after she has become the main hope for the prosecution, Wendy walks away from the case, effectively destroying its chances of securing convictions. The prosecution is now left to rely almost entirely on the evidence of Jason, who will admit to continually lying and changing his version of events on five occasions. The jury must also be aware he has been granted immunity from charges.

Early February: Kathy's daughter Vicki enters the witness protection scheme. She has already informed police that McEvoy has allegedly confessed his role in the murders to her.

Mid-February: Trial begins. Various prosecution witnesses fail to give same evidence as at committal. Jason, as the main Crown witness, comes under heavy fire from the defence. His background with Dennis in Richmond is probed in depth, leaving the impression of an unstable and unreliable witness.

Early March: The four accused make unsworn statements from the dock, on which they cannot be cross examined. Their evidence is likely to be viewed by the jury as less credible than if they had taken the oath, allowing their versions of events to be put to the test of close questioning. Trevor says he spent the night of the murders at home in North Fitzroy, sound asleep under the influence of sedatives. Victor says he was in a motel room with Wendy and his three children. McEvoy says he spent the night in Vicki's flat in Brunswick. Farrell says he also spent the night there, on the settee, under the influence of drugs and alcohol.

Mid-March: With the evidence completed, the jury retires to consider its verdict.

26 March: After six days of deliberation jury returns not guilty verdicts against all four accused. Media estimates of the total cost of the case quote a figure of $30 million. This includes $800,000 in legal aid for the defendants, who have been represented by one Queen's Counsel, five barristers and eight instructing solicitors. Of this $800,000, a total of $600,000 came from a State Government grant. The six-and-a-half-week trial is estimated to have cost $65 a minute.

If the above represents an objective account of how the events of Walsh Street unfolded over a period of two and a half years, what follows is Kathy's view of proceedings, based on her unshakable conviction that police decided immediately after the murders that the family was responsible, and set about making the facts fit the theory.

Firstly Kathy believes—and it was alleged at the trial—that when Graeme Jensen was killed on 11 October 1988, he was shot in mistake for Victor. Victor and Jensen had been under surveillance for some time before the shooting, and had been filmed together. Evidence was given that two days before Jensen's death Victor was warned by a woman named Penny Rountree that the police were gunning for him. She was the wife of Lindsay Rountree, who testified that Victor had approached him with the 'kill two cops for one of ours' proposition. Rountree had been arrested by the armed robbery squad at Euroa on 6 October, and claimed they told him they were going to kill Victor. Police later denied this, but Rountree passed the alleged threat onto his wife with instructions to inform Victor. Peter McEvoy told the committal: '... Victor had learnt that there was a squad of police gunning for him, and that they intended to kill him on sight when they found him.' Anthony Farrell similarly claimed: 'Well, Victor was in fear of his life and what I believed to be murder by certain members of the police force.' Farrell said he had difficulty understanding why police had refused to see Victor on the first occasion he tried to give himself up and 'next thing you know you've got a gang of police running in his house looking for him. At that stage I came to the conclusion that the police were out to murder Victor Peirce.'

Sandra Faure, the woman with whom Jensen was living at the time of his death, claimed that when she was taken by police to the scene of the shooting a policewoman asked her: 'Are you Wendy?' She believed this was a reference to Victor's wife, Wendy, and indicated that the policewoman believed it was Victor who had been shot. When Sandra's fourteen-year-old daughter approached the scene, wanting to see her 'Daddy', an officer allegedly told her: 'Well, he's fucking dead, fuck off. There's nothing to see, fuck off.' This came from Peter McEvoy, describing the shooting during a secretly taped conversation on 15 January 1989. He said: 'Drivin' down the fuckin' shop and they've just fucken pounced on him. (Jensen) ambushed him ... Went straight into his fuckin' head in the side. That side there, just above his ear, came out the front, straight out his forehead, pulled the fucken part of his fucken skull out, mate. Size of a fucken cigarette packet in his forehead.'

Kathy's opinion of Jensen, who first became known to the family through his close relationship with Jamie, contrasts strongly with that of police, who regarded him as a vicious career criminal with a long record of convictions for violence and dishonesty.

I knew Graeme Jensen very well. He was beautiful, he was gentle, he was kind. Very quiet, amiable, I never heard him swear. I knew him through Victor. Known him a few years. I met him regularly at 86 Chestnut when Victor was there. I was talking with Graeme in the lounge one time, and next minute Victor's thrown a penny banger in, and there's Graeme, he's hit the roof, scared stiff. Victor says: 'How rude you are. You talk to me Mum, but you won't come out here and talk to me and me wife.' But Graeme didn't like her. And Graeme hated me bloody scones. I was going to put one in his coffin, but I didn't. We were filmed at the funeral, me and Vicki.

I invited him down to Venus Bay but he didn't come. It was a couple of months before he was shot. He didn't get the chance, did he? We went down to the funeral parlour in Boundary Road, and Peter McEvoy was keeping watch over him. I put a flower in Graeme's coffin, and when we got to the church I looked around and I thought: 'Which one of you boys is next?' I thought: 'Jedd Houghton's next' and I knew Gary Abdallah was going to be murdered. He was a friend of Trevor's. The rumour on the street was that he was going to be murdered.

Within twelve hours of the murders of Tynan and Eyre on 12 October the homes of two of Kathy's children, Victor and Vicki, were raided. What information had police received during this twelve-hour period suggesting the family were the most likely culprits?* Or were they acting on an educated guess, as Kathy thinks, that her sons must have been to blame? This theory, she believes, became the driving force behind all subsequent actions of the taskforce.

An insight into how quickly police connected the murders of their two colleagues with the shooting of Graeme Jensen came from a Mr W.J. Wesson, whose flat, close to the murder scene, was used by police as temporary headquarters immediately afterwards. Mr Wesson said he heard officers in his loungeroom making the connection with Jensen's death between one and two hours after the murders. But Detective Senior Constable Col Ryan said at the committal that the idea to raid Victor's home at Chestnut Street, hours after the double murder, came from Chief Inspector Brendon Cole, who had received information connecting Jensen's death with the Walsh Street shootings.

Only hours before the raids, down at Venus Bay, Kathy was listening to the early morning radio. The murder of the two young police officers came as a complete shock:

I heard on the morning news two policemen had been shot in Walsh Street, and I thought: 'What a dreadful thing.' Not thinking anything else, just how terrible. I didn't see no connection with Graeme. I hadn't heard about that two for one. I was doing the dishes that night and Derryn Hinch said to a police officer he was interviewing: 'Do you think it had

---

* Even Lex Peirce was seen by police during the immediate aftermath of Walsh Street. Lex has had the least involvement in crime of any of Kathy's children, and must have been an extremely long shot as a Walsh Street suspect. The statement he made to police at the time provides a saddening insight into what life must have been like during Dennis's reign for a disenchanted family member. 'I didn't really like Dennis when he was alive,' read Lex's statement, 'because he was kind of arrogant towards me. He was more or less my big brother and looked down on me as if I was a shitman, as if I didn't really matter. It's not that I cared about this, I just didn't like him.'

anything to do with the Pettingill, Peirce, Allen family, as a payback for Graeme?' I dropped the dishes.

We got blamed for Dennis because they never got him for all the things he done. And Victor's knowing of Graeme Jensen. I cried at the funeral of the two cops on TV. They should never have died.

After the raids of Victor and Vicki's houses I spoke to Victor on the phone, and said: 'Victor, if they think it's you, I want you out of that house.' I was crying. Victor said: 'Where will I go?' Andrew Fraser and Charlie Nikakis [solicitors] *took Victor to the police on 12 October but they wouldn't see him.*

Jason gave Victor up for Hefti [the security guard slain in an armed robbery] *because he was scared stiff. I was happy when Victor was arrested, because he was safe and sound in gaol, and I knew he couldn't be shot.*

During the raid at Chestnut Street a shot was fired, the noise causing sufficient trauma to kill two pet budgies owned by Victor's daughter, Katie, then aged three. On hearing of this Kathy immediately bought Katie replacement birds. Kathy alleges that the second time police raided Chestnut Street an officer spotted the two new arrivals and wrung their necks in front of Katie. Kathy made an official complaint, but got nowhere. If this incident is true, it indicates how hot police feelings were running at the time.

On 13 October Kathy was approached by the *Sun* for a story which must have come dangerously close to libel. Amazingly, it began with the paragraph: 'A woman connected with a group of criminals suspected of the South Yarra ambush killings last night denied any of them was involved.' Kathy said: 'I hate coppers, but those boys [Tynan and Eyre] didn't do anything. Our family wouldn't do that. We were not involved. You don't kill two innocent coppers. If you want to get back, you would kill the copper who killed Graeme.'

234

The following day the *Sun* ran a front-page story quoting unnamed police sources who claimed that associates of Jensen planned the murders at his wake, saying in part: 'It could have been a spur of the moment thing,' a senior policeman said yesterday. 'They could have said: "They've killed one of ours, we'll kill two of theirs." '

This apparent idle speculation, aired here in the *Sun* for the first time, was to become one of the cornerstones of the prosecution's case.

By 21 October Jason Ryan had been interviewed by police a number of times, and had allegedly been bashed. (In a conversation with the author Wendy Peirce described him as looking 'like the Elephant Man' after one alleged beating.) He had also started naming names. Kathy believes Jason's weakness planted the seed in the minds of the taskforce that their best chance of securing convictions against the family was to attack and divide from within. Jason was the first in the bag (the witness protection scheme) and singing like a bird. The next targets were Wendy and Vicki. Pressure would need to be applied.

Then, between 24 and 27 October, Jason was driven around the bush by police while they were awaiting a decision on his suitability for the witness protection scheme. Kathy alleges police broke one of Jason's arms, smashed his teeth, fired shots over his head and held him upside down in a creek, threatening to drown him, during these four days. Vicki was not told of Jason's whereabouts and at one stage actually made inquiries through missing persons. This was the start of pressure on her.

On 1 November Anthony Farrell was charged with the murders, becoming the first of the four men who eventually stood trial. Jason had already been charged with the murders, but the charges were later dropped. At this time Anthony and Jason were still in their teens, and Jason had already demonstrated a propensity for opening his mouth to police in a crisis. This is one of the strongest points in Kathy's argument. There is no dispute that her two sons, Trevor and Victor, were hardened and experienced career criminals. If they were contemplating the cold-blooded execution of two police officers, and the enormity of the consequences involved, would they take along a couple of inexperienced young boys, one of them already known for his lack of discretion? Or, as Peter McEvoy put it during an interview with Inspector Noonan: 'Who would be fuckin' stupid enough to do a job with Jason or Anthony, they're only fuckin' kids.'

Pressure now mounted on Wendy with her arrest for illegal possession of a firearm, assault on police, and indecent language charges that resulted from the 1 November raid on Chestnut Street. This pressure intensified over the next two months. First she was charged with attempted murder following the pub brawl, leaving her in custody and separated from her children over Christmas. Then, a few days later, Victor became the third person accused of the killings. Finally there was the demolition of her home in Chestnut Street.

In the meantime Jedd Houghton was shot by police in a Bendigo caravan park. Allegedly a bag was placed over the head of Houghton's girlfriend during the raid, an action which was later justified as normal practice. A few days later Kathy made a gesture in response, pursuing a member of the taskforce down the street outside the court and handing him a folded paper bag.

I found out the truth about the shooting in the caravan. What happened was Jedd and his girlfriend had a smoke. He was laying down with her and they shot him dead and then they put a paper bag over her head. So I go to court the day after the shooting, and I've got a folded up paper bag and I handed this to Colin McLaren [a member of the TyEyre taskforce, but not present at the shooting of Houghton] *and I handed it to him, to let him know I knew. I chased him down the street*

236

to give it to him, and do you know where it is now?
wall at St Kilda police station. Alison Niselle [joint producer
of the ABC's *Janus* series, which was loosely based on
Kathy's family] *told me.*

Indirect confirmation of a paper bag being placed over the girl's
head came from Detective Inspector Noonan. Giving evidence
before an inquiry into Houghton's death in June 1990 he said:
'Any person in a premises that is raided is bound and has a hood
placed over their head ... (the officers) are entitled to do that
because of the briefing I gave them.'

Kathy continues:

I didn't know Jedd Houghton that well. He seemed such a nice,
fit young man. The heartache his mother's been through. I
didn't know Gary Abdallah. Trevor did because his wife Debbie
lived near him. The day Gary was shot I got a call from a journo
on the Herald–Sun *to say Trevor had been shot, but I knew*
Trevor was at the Children's Hospital with one of the kids, so
I knew it wasn't him.

She believes that it was in direct retaliation for her action with the
paper bag that Trevor was kidnapped and bashed. Kathy claims
that overhead streetlights where he was seized were removed
immediately before the attack, and describes other tactics used
during the kidnapping as similar to those employed by police
during raids. It was for fear of further reprisals that she withdrew
her original allegation that police were responsible.

Some time early in the evening Trevor and Debbie got a call
that they were going to be raided. She was heavily pregnant
and he wanted to get her out. Whoever it was had taken all the
streetlight bulbs out, and as they've walked out the door four
men with shotguns came up.

237

'Don't move, don't move, don't move.' They tied Trevor
up with masking tape around his hands, left her and hustled
him across Merri Creek, through a gap in the fence. They put
him on the floor of a Commodore, he could tell it was that.
They stabbed him, iron-barred him, sledge-hammered him. They
left him for dead on the side of the road in Glenroy. He told
me: 'Mum, I heard the click of the gun. I knew it was going
to be quick, and all I could think of was it's going to be over
soon.' He managed to crawl across the road to a service station.
He was on his way to the operating theatre and his thumb was
hanging off, and he was crying. And he said: 'Mum, I'm not
crying because I'm hurting. I'm crying because I'm so glad to
see you.'

He's fucked for life. The spine and that, the stab wounds.
The arthritis and everything. He's thirty years of age. It was
cops. Who else would take the lights off the street? I changed
the story to say it wasn't them to get them off my back. If I
hadn't said that, they were going to do something else. I asked
the cops for their running sheet [record of activities] for that
night, but they wouldn't give it to me.

After a relative lull over the next few months, in April 1989 Gary
Abdallah went down in a hail of police bullets in his Carlton flat,
becoming, after Jedd Houghton, the second suspect named by
Jason to be shot.

In the following weeks Inspector Noonan spoke to Peter
McEvoy on a number of occasions, leading to McEvoy's appearance on television expressing concern. Thus the pressure
continued on Vicki—McEvoy was an old friend and tenant of
her flat.

Like Jason and Farrell, McEvoy was charged with the
murders, shortly after his television appearance. Victor's charges
were to follow a month later.

Anthony [Farrell] was just a young lout, a bit weak, not capable of killing two cops. Macca [McEvoy] I'd known a long time, and he'd come down to Venus Bay with Vicki. All I know of Macca is he's a rapist* and they've not got that much dash. He's out now after doing seven years for a robbery after Walsh Street, but we've not been in touch. There's no need to. What have we got in common?

On the night of the murders Victor had dinner at a friend's. Victor was a vegetarian so she cooked it specially, the friend's wife. And she booked the motel where Wendy and Victor and the three kids stayed. Victor loved Graeme Jensen, but Trevor couldn't have given a fuck. When Vicki phoned Trevor to tell him about Graeme's death he had taken a tablet, and he said: 'I don't give a fuck,' and went back to sleep. Nothing interferes with Trevor's sleep.

Victor saw his daughter born and fainted. Trevor went 'eerrgh' when one of his kids was born. I can't imagine them blowing anybody's brains out. They'd be laying on the ground. They didn't kill any of Dennis's mates. Neither of them have the killer instinct like Dennis had.

Even though there was widespread speculation that Trevor would be the fourth man to be charged with the murders, the move took Kathy by surprise.

I didn't expect Trevor to be charged. I went into St Paul's Cathedral in town when I heard. I think the paper boy was yelling it out. I bought the paper and there's Trevor, and I went into the church to say a prayer. Yeah, deep down I'm religious.

---

* A reference to rape convictions recorded against McEvoy when he was barely out of his teens. He and a group of youths terrorised and sexually assaulted more than twenty girls in the Heidelberg area of Melbourne during the mid-1970s. McEvoy was convicted on two rape charges and gaoled for three years.

THE MATRIARCH

*I was crying and praying it wasn't true. I phoned H Division
at Pentridge and a screw said: 'It's been on the news for hours.'
He didn't give a stuff. After the committal I said a prayer for
them all at St Francis Church.*

The youngest of Kathy's children, Trevor, had a long list of convictions going back to 1979 which included charges of burglary,
conspiracy to commit robbery, escaping from custody, drug
offences, and driving offences. He had first met Peter McEvoy in
1982 and formed a close friendship with him. Trevor moved to
Richmond shortly before his nineteenth birthday and began living
with Kathy at 106 Stephenson Street. After a year he moved out to
live with a girlfriend and her family in the affluent suburb of Cam-
berwell for the next two years. After Dennis's death Trevor moved
back to Richmond and began living alone at 37 Stephenson Street,
evidently unconcerned with the house's bloody history.

Then, early in July, the taskforce played its final trump card
with Wendy by showing her a set of love letters written by Victor
to her best friend. Where the destruction of her home, separation
from her children, and the gaoling of her husband had all failed,
this finally succeeded in cracking Wendy.

For different reasons Vicki too began to weaken and eventually gave way. According to Kathy, police had told her that
Victor and later Trevor, despite being behind bars awaiting trial,
were going to organise to have Jason killed rather than allow
him to continue testifying against them. Kathy believes Vicki
should have seen through this and stood by the family, knowing
her brothers would not take such a step. It is quite likely police
would have told Vicki of such a fictitious threat. Setting one
criminal faction against another is a common tactic, and often
bears fruit. Telling Jason the lie years before that his Uncle Trevor
had implicated him in a burglary helped police secure a statement from Jason blaming Trevor, so why not try it again? Vicki

confirmed the police threat, telling the committal on 17 November that she had taken an overdose of pills in a suicide attempt after a member of the TyEyre taskforce had told her she must choose between Jason and her family.

By late July, ten months after the murders, pressure was also mounting on the taskforce, through Chief Magistrate John Dugan, to get the committal under way. The DPP declined to help the taskforce prepare its final brief, and Kathy believes this is when the squad should have realised its inquiries were heading in the wrong directions.

On 31 October the committal began with complaints from the defence about treatment of the three accused. On the opening day the court was told that Anthony Farrell had been woken at dawn in the remand centre in the middle of town where he was being held five blocks from the court. He was then driven out to Pentridge and back into the city, being strip-searched four times during the process. A month later Geoff Flatman, for Victor, spoke of Victor and Peter McEvoy being brought to court via a 'very circuitous route under very trying conditions and taken over bumpy roads in the heat.'

For Kathy there were a number of revealing signs demonstrating the inadequacy of the prosecution case. The first of these involved long term criminal Lindsay Rountree's evidence that Victor tried to involve him in a pact to murder two police officers the next time a member of his (Victor's) circle was killed by police. Rountree's evidence at the committal may have passed muster, but by the time of the trial, Victor's counsel Geoff Flatman was able to produce recorded evidence of a conversation between Rountree and police giving the distinct impression that Rountree was prepared to testify against Victor in exchange for a more lenient sentence on armed robbery charges he was facing. In his final address at the end of the trial Flatman said Rountree had come up with his evidence against Victor only 'after he got some sort of undertaking that he could get something said on his behalf . . .' and had perjured himself by claiming he had never asked for favours from police.

Then there was the farcical evidence of a pair of Pentridge inmates, Harold Martin and Michael Warner, two middle-aged conmen, with 600 convictions between them. Kathy claims they shared the same ill-fitting suit, provided by police or the witness protection scheme, for their court appearances. Both men suggested Victor had given them detailed confessions of his guilt while they were in gaol together. The court clearly preferred the defence version that Victor had barely met either man, let alone put his liberty on the line by confessing to them. After Martin admitted under cross examination during the trial that he had given evidence of similar prison cell 'confessions' in half a dozen cases in various states in the past, the prosecution wisely advised the jury to accept neither him nor Warner as witnesses of truth.

Kathy argues that if the prosecution had had a half decent case they would not have needed to fall back on such transparently obvious fabrications from doubtful witnesses like Rountree, Martin and Warner, who attempted to impute motive and confessions to Victor. She has a point. The lies of Martin and Warner, particularly, must have caused considerable damage to the prosecution's case, and it is difficult to understand why an ageing conman like Martin, with his record of regularly trotting out cellblock confessions, would have been placed on the stand during such an important trial. It is even more difficult to believe that nobody in the prosecution camp had done the same homework as the defence, and discovered details of Martin's previous, embarrassingly similar appearances. If they had, and decided to go ahead with Martin anyway, this is indeed evidence of a certain desperation.

Kathy has similar doubts about the South Yarra flat where, according to the prosecution, the killers of the two young police officers allegedly met and discussed tactics only hours before the slayings. Depending on whose version is believed, up to seven men met in this flat, occupied by Anthony Farrell's girlfriend, and smoked and drank coffee before leaving. Yet no evidence of dirty cups or ashtrays was ever found. In addition a nearby neighbour, Eleonora Cundari, testified that on the night of the murders all was peace and quiet at the flat, whereas normally she was unable to sleep for the banging of doors and loud voices, causing her to complain regularly.

Kathy was not alone in her scepticism. On 23 February the *Age* published an article summarising the committal hearings. It was strongly critical of the Crown case, and observed: 'In the first fortnight the prosecution's account of the events of 11 and 12 October started to blur with contradictory statements, allegations of police harassment and the questioning of witnesses' credibility. Residents of Walsh Street and the surrounding area often gave conflicting stories ... doubt was cast on the alleged motive for the killings.'

Eleven months later the prosecution suffered its greatest setback at the voir-dire hearing where Wendy made it clear she would not be repeating her committal evidence at the trial, and opted out of the witness protection scheme. Kathy maintains Wendy had been planning this move for some considerable time, and six months earlier had informed Victor of her intentions through her mother who was visiting him in Pentridge. Wendy confirmed this in a subsequent interview with the *Herald-Sun*, saying she had given evidence at the committal only after pressure from taskforce members. 'I told them months before the trial I would not give evidence against Victor. From day one I was never going to give evidence. Jason was not going to give evidence either, but he was too scared to go through with it.' The same story quoted an unnamed 'senior' policeman as describing Wendy's life expectancy as 'limited', and predicting she could be marked for death. Eleven years later she is still very much alive.

The trial duly ended with the four men being acquitted, but in the process Kathy's family was irrevocably split with no chance of a reconciliation with her daughter Vicki. Kathy believes that without Wendy, and with the unreliable Jason as their main witness, the prosecution had no hope of securing convictions, and justice was done. Mr Vernon, counsel for Peter McEvoy, summed up the prosecution's malaise when he began his closing address at the trial by listing a number of factors which had 'poisoned the well of justice'. These included: 'Falsely alleged verbal confessions, harassed and frightened witnesses, courtroom rehearsed witnesses, proven liars, self-confessed liars, witnesses abandoned by the Crown—you may think because their dishonesty was shown plainly—witnesses who have changed their tack more often than the yachts in a twelve metre race, witnesses who have personal matters at stake.'

The *Age* agreed in a story written by its chief court reporter, Peter Gregory, headed: 'The fatal flaw in the Walsh Street case.' The first paragraph read: 'The Crown case in the Walsh Street trial was flawed from the start.' Gregory's story also stated the Crown's case left the jury 'with no other option' than the acquittals.

If Steven Tynan and Damian Eyre were the most tragic of all the victims of Walsh Street, and Graeme Jensen, Jedd Houghton and Gary Abdallah made up the second group, then the third must have been the three members of Kathy's family, Jason, Vicki and Wendy, whose evidence failed to obtain convictions for the prosecution, despite the millions of dollars spent safeguarding them.

Jason Ryan, now twenty-five years old, is possibly the saddest figure of all in Kathy's immediate family. By the time he was five his mother Vicki and father John Brooks, a normal law-abiding citizen, had separated. In 1983 when he was thirteen he ran away from home for the first time because his mother was getting bashed by the man with whom she was living—one of Dennis's soldiers.

Jason went to live in Richmond with Dennis, possibly the worst choice he could have made among all his relatives. He also first met Anthony Farrell, whose mother Susan Parkinson was having an affair with Dennis. Both mother and son were regular visitors to Richmond. But whatever kind of monster Dennis may have been to outsiders, he was loyal, at this stage, to his immediate family, and he counted Jason as one of these. According to Kathy there was a genuine bond between the two—they wore the same Japanese headbands, Dennis lavished gifts and money on Jason, and regarded him as something of a protégé. It was even said at the committal hearing that Dennis was thinking of grooming Jason to take over from him as head of the family.

Jason was also supposed to have been in charge of the family arsenal, looking after the guns and hiding them on the nearby railway embankment. Kathy says this is an exaggeration of his role, but she does not dispute that he was entrusted with large sums of money, and regularly carried thousands of dollars on his person. He sat in on drug deals, and would 'playfully' point guns at some of Dennis's more vulnerable customers. This no doubt seemed like high adventure and an exciting kind of grown-up game to the impressionable thirteen-year-old. But the game soon turned sour.

First a gun was found under Jason's pillow during a police raid on Stephenson Street. Dennis was asked who owned the gun. 'He's old enough, he can wear it,' he replied. Next came the nightmare of Wayne Stanhope's death, which Jason witnessed from a few feet away. Soon afterwards it was happening again. Three months after Jason brought his uncle the gun that killed Stanhope, he brought the drugs, and then the bucket of water, that were used during Helga Wagnegg's last minutes on earth.

His descriptions of the two incidents, provided some years later, were masterpieces of understatement: 'Watching people shot when I was thirteen, it was frightening,' he said of Stanhope's death.

245

And of Helga: 'Dennis told me to grab a bucket and get some water from the Yarra River. Dennis tipped it down her throat, and held her head in the bucket for about half an hour.'

If nothing else these two incidents taught Jason a great deal about violence. Concerned at his behaviour police obtained a court order removing him, albeit temporarily, from Dennis's influence, and placing him in the care of champion footballer Fred Cook and his wife, who were running the Station Hotel in Port Melbourne. But after only six weeks he fled back to Dennis after being caught stealing from behind the bar. Once back in Richmond the violence began to escalate. He sliced off the tip of the nose of the soldier who had been involved initially in kidnapping Kathy; he pulled the gun on the truck driver who parked in the wrong spot in Stephenson Street and was warned his vehicle would be blown up; and, on Dennis's orders, he beat the captive Susan Guy with a pick handle.

When Dennis tired of his precocious nephew, Jason lived for periods with Kathy and his other uncles, Peter (during his short spell of freedom), Victor, Jamie and Trevor. When Dennis died and everybody was thrown on their own resources, Jason was no exception. 'I had to do drugs and burgs (burglaries) for survival.' One of the burglaries was pulled off in company with Trevor, the occasion when Jason was tricked by police into informing on his uncle—the first sign of a talent that, had it been more credible during the Walsh Street trial, may well have put Trevor and Victor away for life. Also in 1987, when he was breaking into factories and warehouses, Jason, now a cocky sixteen-year-old, stabbed a man in the stomach with a knife in a brawl in an inner suburban hotel. He received a six-month good behaviour bond.

So by 1988 and the early stages of the Walsh Street saga, Jason was well on the way to a career in violent crime. But however streetwise he had become by the age of seventeen, nothing could have prepared him for what was to follow. He was, after all, the first defendant to be charged with double murder in the most notorious crime in Victorian history. His constant tears and general demeanour during the weeks after his arrest were proof that even the brutal learning curve of Richmond had left him unprepared for this. His trauma must have been compounded when first Jedd Houghton, and then Gary Abdallah, both names he had provided to the taskforce, became the victims of police bullets.

There were also the allegations that police were putting barriers between him and protection, both legal and spiritual. In July 1989 Jeff Giddings, a Fitzroy Legal Service solicitor, described as outrageous the lack of legal representation made available to Jason by police during the previous eight months. Earlier Chief Magistrate John Dugan had described the situation as 'intolerable'. And Father Peter Norden, who officiated at the funeral of four family members, publicly protested at the same time as Giddings at having been denied access by police to Jason.

Inspector Noonan said at the committal, in the absence of the jury, that Jason had told him he did not wish to see Father Norden, because: 'He (Jason) said he had good grounds to believe that he (Father Norden) was a regular associate of that family.'

But much more serious were the allegations surrounding Jason's earlier trip to the country with four armed robbery squad officers from 24 to 27 October, less than a fortnight after the Walsh Street killings. Kathy and other members of the family have always seen it as the pivotal stage in Jason's decision to give evidence against his uncles. In court it was described as the catalyst for the prosecution case. Kathy has charged that during those four days Jason was tortured and that he was never the same person afterwards—she even described him as a 'robot' in the witness box. Because of this she has forgiven him for what was to follow, and says that even now she would welcome him back into the family circle with no repercussions.

Jason himself has never confirmed the torture allegations, and told the trial he was either not frightened of the police who were with him on the country trip, or couldn't remember whether he was frightened. Whatever the truth of this bizarre outing, it seems odd that the officers should choose to indulge in target practice with shotguns during a barbecue with Jason near Bright on 26 October. According to Detective Col Ryan, giving evidence at the trial, it was his colleague Brendon Cole who decided on the trip. Under cross examination it emerged that one of the officers who accompanied Jason was Detective Rodney Grimshaw, who had been present when Jensen was shot, and who had been convicted for contempt of court over an attempt in 1990 to threaten a Crown witness in an unrelated case. During legal argument in the absence of the jury, Geoff Flatman, Victor's counsel, said of the excursion: 'The taking of (Jason) Ryan to the country for a period of time between interviews ... is a very bizarre feature of the history of Ryan becoming a witness, and the history of this case generally, because it is really the catalyst of the Crown case getting off the ground.

Even Mr Justice Vincent was clearly not entirely happy about it, saying on the same occasion: '... the witness was taken away by a number of police members in circumstances which are, to say the least, not commonly encountered, that all deny that there was any improper behaviour during the trip, nevertheless it wasn't very long after the return from that trip that the witness started to provide versions of involvement of persons in a very serious ciminal offence.'

Defence counsel at both the committal and the trial made much of Jason's five separate versions of the murder of the two police officers, and described him variously as 'a cunning, street-wise little urchin of no morality', 'a liar of epic proportions' and 'a dreadful witness, an unreliable witness'. Kathy especially remembers the jury watching him talk through a video of one of his visits to Walsh Street with Inspector Noonan.

He was wearing a pinstripe shirt and trousers with a short back and sides. It was about quarter to four, and the video was on, and Jason's there, and it's the first day of his evidence, and the jury's scribbling down everything he says, and the judge adjourns for the day. And the next morning Jason gets up in the box, and he says: 'That video yesterday was a pack of lies.' And I watch the jury. It was like he'd punched them all in the stomach. They went 'oooh', like that, couldn't believe it.

Another memory involved a man in the public gallery.

There was old men used to come upstairs to the gallery and bring their lunch for the day. And on the video Jason's standing in the rain in Walsh Street during one of his re-enactments for police and he's got his spiked hair at the time, and you can see he's scared stiff of Noonan, and he's saying this: 'And this is where Victor was standing.' And Noonan's saying: 'Are you sure about that, Jason?' And the old man said to me: 'You can tell that boy's been bashed.' And I looked at the old man, and I thought to meself: 'You're just a stranger, and you've picked it up already.'

Once the trial was over, and the jury had delivered their thumbs down verdict on Jason's constantly changing versions of the events of the night of the murder, he remained within the witness protection scheme for three years. But there were disturbing reports of how he was faring.

The only journalist to be allowed access to him, *New Idea's* Bill Ayres, had a secret meeting with him late in 1991, when he learned Jason was no longer under protection and was desperately trying to stay out of trouble. His police minders had spoken earlier of the metamorphosis that had taken place in him. The surly, smart-mouthed punk who hadn't known enough to clean his own teeth had begun to take on responsibility for his appearance and surroundings; had expressed a desire to learn a trade, and had taken courses in English and mathematics to supplement the education that was cut short at thirteen. But Bill Ayres picked up the first signs that all was not well. Jason told him of the near impossibility of trying to lead a normal, productive life while looking constantly over his shoulder, waiting for the bullet he knew would come one day. He also had this to say of Kathy: 'She's a very dangerous old lady, wicked. She was my nanna, but she certainly wasn't the kind of nanna who'd sit around and do the knitting.' However Kathy believes police must have encouraged or persuaded him to provide this type of comment.

Ayres remained in intermittent contact with Jason for a year after the interview, and does not believe there will ever be a reconciliation between him and the family. 'Because of his experiences and well-honed knowledge of the family, I doubt he would ever trust them sufficiently to renew relationships. He also seemed frightened and unhappy that his police protection had disappeared entirely.' Ayres passed Victor's phone number to Jason during this period, with a request from Kathy that he resume contact with the family. Kathy says Jason duly made the call and spoke to Victor, breaking down and crying during the conversation, and indicating he wanted to return to the fold.

In April 1994, according to a somewhat critical review of the witness protection scheme, Jason was said to be unemployed and mixing in criminal circles again. He was also reportedly bitter about being abandoned by the police officers he had previously learned to trust. More recently Kathy has heard on the grapevine that Jason has become a father. She describes as rubbish the dire warnings made by police and others about the bullet waiting for Jason, if he ever does re-establish contact with the family.

Another day after the committal Trevor and I were driving along in Clifton Hill. We see Jason in a car, Trevor spots him.

What do we do? Nothing. We just let him drive. Don't forget he was my first grandchild. I idolised him, I minded him, I babysat him, and I still love him. He was living with me, not Dennis, most of the time, when he was thirteen. He wasn't rough, like they say. I saw the quiet Jason. I'd call him for his tea and get him up of a day. I knew he stayed up late next door. He was wonderful with Dennis's two little daughters, with anyone's kids. Take them out and get ice cream and stuff like that. There was a huge bond with Dennis, he idolised him. I couldn't blame Jason for going against the family. My first instinct was, I thought: 'Aggh I'll kill that little bastard.' But deep down, I wouldn't have.

He's welcome here at Venus Bay any time he likes. He was only seventeen at the time of Walsh Street. I knew what he went through up the bush. We didn't know where he was. We had to go to missing persons. They smashed his teeth, they broke his arm, they put his head in a creek, and tried to drown him. They shot over his head. And then they said he fell over a chair. We can't get the medical records. At the same time they were threatening to charge him with being an accessory to the Wayne Stanhope murder.

Why then, if all this is true, did Jason tell the trial he was not frightened of police? Kathy responds:

Because by then he'd done the deal, he was like a robot, he looked like a policeman. He kept laughing, even at the committal. He'd look at the boys in the dock, and laugh. They must have give him a smoke [marijuana] in the room outside, because he'd look across at them and just burst out laughing, smiling. That's when Anthony Farrell cracked and cried in court and said: 'Jason, just tell 'em the truth, Jason tell 'em the truth.' He was crying out to him.

THE MATRIARCH

If Jason emerges as the saddest member of Kathy's family, Wendy must, and always will, remain its ultimate enigma. She had a criminal record dating back to 1976 for burglary, theft, resisting arrest, possession of stolen property, possessing marijuana and other offences. She had been an integral part of the inner circle since 1977 when Kathy first brought her home to stay. She soon became deeply involved in a relationship with Victor, eventually bearing him three children, and lived with him in Albert Park and through the Richmond years, most of them in Chestnut Street. She even sat behind Peter as a kind of acting unpaid law clerk during the weeks of his trial for heroin and cannabis dealing in 1988, making notes and looking up references. Peter never suffered fools gladly, and to entrust Wendy with a task as important as the fight for his liberty must have required considerable faith in his sister-in-law's intelligence. But then nobody has ever claimed Wendy is stupid—just dangerously unpredictable and a dauntingly committed hater, as she was described at one stage during the committal. She has long been known within the family as Witch, a not entirely affectionate nickname, first given to her by Jamie, and some indication of the fearsome vindictiveness of her behaviour when crossed.

So after twelve years within the bosom of the family, it clearly took considerable pressure to force Wendy into the ultimate betrayal. She knew only too well what happened to informers, having witnessed first-hand, so she said at the committal, four of Dennis's murders. She had also seen the wrong side of Victor's temper. On one occasion, Wendy told the task-force, he was in a rage and brought a revolver out of the bedroom to the table where they were sitting. 'Get up and dance, cunt,' he told her.

'I said I wouldn't, and then he shot twice at me between my legs. The bullets missed my legs ... I was terrified of him,' she said.

Wendy also warned the police that a defence tactic at the trial

252

would be to suggest that if Victor had failed to avenge the shooting of his own mother, when Kathy lost her eye, he would hardly be likely to avenge the death of Graeme Jensen by taking the lives of two policemen. Wendy said that in fact Victor had got hold of Keryn Thompson, one of Kathy's two assailants, in The Cherry Tree one night and was going to shoot her, but Dennis stopped him.

Kathy remembers first meeting Wendy back in 1977.

I was introduced to her by a friend, and I brought her back to stay with us in the flat at High Street, Northcote. Victor had just got out of gaol, and we all went out there, but he got out earlier and took a taxi and we must have passed one another. He runs into the flat, and I've done it all up, and he thinks he's in the wrong joint. And there's a sheila in the bed and he wakes her up and asks her for the money for the taxi. That's how he met Wendy.

After seven years together Wendy and Victor moved to Richmond, where Wendy tried to rear a young family in an environment in which murder, drug dealing and prostitution were more commonplace than kindergarten, nappies and baby food. Dennis's death may have brought a short relief from the mayhem, but what was around the corner was, for Wendy, much harder to deal with than Mr D's evil empire.

Immediately after the killings in Walsh Street the raids on her home began. Police say there were nine, but Kathy disputes this, saying that Wendy and Vicki kept count of how many times their respective homes were subjected to raids—Wendy won, thirteen to eleven.

By the time police had finished with Chestnut Street, one observer commented, there wasn't a piece of the house too big to fit into two cupped hands. And these weren't visits which began with a polite knock at the front door and the showing of warrants. More often than not the raids involved members of the Special Operations Group (SOG), whose speciality was breaking down doors in the early hours of the morning. Kathy recalls Wendy's horrific version of the first two raids on Chestnut Street, and the incident involving three-year-old Katie's budgies.

> Wendy, Jason and Anthony Farrell went to 86 Chestnut Street to feed the dogs. They burst in, the SOG, right—they were looking for Victor the day after Graeme Jensen was killed, but I had told him to go. They fired over Katie's head, three years old, and the sound of the gunshot killed her two little budgies I'd given her. Beside that she wet her pants.
>
> Wendy's laying on top of her, Jason's on the ground, and young Anthony Farrell's there, right. So the raid's over, looking for Victor. So I give Katie two more budgies. She's three don't forget. So they come in again. Do you know what they did in front of her? They strangled 'em. You wonder why we hate 'em. They're sicker than us. Wendy said a classic: 'They're gangsters with badges.' I reported it to internal investigations but nothing happened to my knowledge.

A second incident which Kathy claims Wendy related to her would, if true, have had an even more terrifying effect on her—and even more so on her little daughter Katie.

> Do you know what the police did to her to make Wendy change? They put Wendy and Katie in the boot of a cop car and took them up the bush and dug a grave and dragged Katie up by the hair at three years of age. They took them up there, and dug her a grave, Wendy said. And they held Katie up by the hair, and went to put her in the grave.

This is similar to an episode Wendy mentioned at the committal when she allegedly agreed to show police where Wayne Stan-hope's body was buried, and travelled with detectives to an unnamed national park where parts of a belt and shoe were discovered after hours of digging. If these two events are one and the same, and Wendy had volunteered to go, it is hard to understand why Katie would have been taken along and syste-matically terrorised. Today Kathy suspects elements of Wendy's story may have been invented to gain Victor's sympathy as he was utterly devoted to Katie and, when present, the only adult who ever put her to bed.

So by November 1988 Wendy and the children were living in a splintered ruin, waiting for the next time the door would come crashing through. Victor was in gaol, charged with the murder of a security guard. And the pressure on Wendy was growing. Two days before Christmas 1988, in a Richmond pub, Wendy gave some indication of how close to the edge she had come. A woman called Glenys Wills had allegedly been claiming Wendy and Victor were police informers. Wendy repaid this ulti-mate insult with a broken glass in the face. She was charged with attempted murder.

As if that wasn't bad enough, she learned that Vicki had pro-vided the information to police which led to her arrest—the sisters-in-law were hardly close. Wendy was refused bail and spent Christmas inside separated from her children. Five days after Christmas the screws were tightened still further when Victor became the third person to be charged with the murders of Tynan and Eyre.

The early months of 1989 brought no respite. Chestnut Street was finally destroyed, family friend Peter McEvoy became the fourth man to be charged with the murders, and Gary Abdallah, another family friend, succumbed to police bullets.

By July Wendy had been granted bail on the attempted murder charge and was reunited with the children, living in a commission house in Cheltenham, well away from the pressures

255

of Richmond. She also started a dialogue with certain police officers. One of them, Detective Colin McLaren, met her in the New Orleans Hotel in Prahran and delivered what was the final blow which broke any resolve she had left. McLaren showed Wendy love letters from Victor to Julie Crabtree, her best friend, and to a second woman, another friend. The words Wendy used during the committal to describe these letters indicate something of the effect they had: 'I read through little bits and pieces of filth . . . I just felt sick.'

Wendy, finally, had reached breaking point. Again, her own words at the committal best describe her feelings: 'I was sick and tired of running . . . I was sick and tired of the hassles, of the police, I was sick and tired of what I had on my conscience. I'd had enough. I had my children to rear, and I had just had enough, I'd had a gutful. I was literally just going downhill. I'd been in prison. I'd missed my children for ten weeks. I had missed Victor for ten weeks. I was at that breaking point. I couldn't stand it any longer. I had to come through and tell the truth.'

So she agreed to enter the witness protection scheme, and give evidence against the family. The date set for the move was 15 July, when police were due to pick up Wendy and the children from the Cheltenham house. But before they arrived Wendy was visited by Trevor and his wife, Peter McEvoy's girlfriend, and a man called Tim Neville, who had been sharing a cell with Victor. According to Wendy they gave her a hot shot in an effort to silence her. But Kathy believes differently. 'It wasn't a hot shot, I'm sure of that,' she says.

Whatever it was, the police arrived that evening in time to avert any serious consequences and took Wendy and her three children into protection. Over the next five weeks she spent every day telling police what she knew or wanted them to know about the family, armed robberies, Dennis's murders and Walsh Street. Much of this information she then repeated during her five days in the box at the committal. The most damning evidence she gave against Victor was an alleged conversation she said she had with him during a contact visit at Pentridge. Wendy claimed Victor had whispered in her ear that he, Jedd Houghton and Gary Abdallah had shot the two young police officers.

She also detailed the events of the night of the murders, saying that she, Victor and the children had stayed in a motel in Tullamarine, because of Victor's fear that police were gunning for him. Under cross examination she said she would not have been surprised if the Armed Robbery Squad had shot Victor when he went to give himself up at police headquarters. 'I wouldn't put anything past the Armed Robbery Squad,' she said. Wendy said Victor had left the motel late at night saying he was going to get the policemen who had shot Jensen. When he returned next morning he told her two police officers had been shot.

During her eighteen months under protection Wendy was moved to the Australian Capital Territory and Queensland, and, according to the officers who were guarding her, was difficult and demanding. 'It got to the stage where she was picking the police she wanted to guard her,' one officer told the *Herald-Sun*. 'If she didn't like a particular policeman, she would demand he be replaced.' One car was allocated for police guarding Wendy, but in the end she had the car, and the officers went on foot, the same source claimed.

There is little doubt Wendy's behaviour, and particularly her refusal to deal with Inspector Noonan, contributed to the highly damaging split in the taskforce. In a later, unconnected Supreme Court trial Inspector Sprague, by then Detective Chief Inspector Sprague, head of the police detective training school, admitted he and Inspector Noonan communicated only by passing notes through a third person. Wendy's own view of her eighteen months under protection was hardly positive. She also spoke to the *Herald-Sun* about her suicide attempts in Townsville and Canberra.

She denied she had ever intended testifying against Victor, and maintained the police had made her tell lies. In an interview with *Truth* newspaper at the time of the trial, she spoke openly of her plans to marry Victor at the Melbourne Remand Centre—hardly the attitude of a woman whose evidence at the committal had seemed destined to have Victor sent down for life.

Strangely, in view of their often stormy relationship, Wendy described Kathy in the *Herald-Sun* interview as 'a very kind-hearted woman who has helped me a great deal.' But Wendy and Kathy had not seen eye to eye for years. Wendy was asked by Victor's counsel, Geoff Flatman, if she hated Kathy. She replied: 'Yes, and the feeling would be mutual.'

Kathy has no hesitation in confirming this. 'She was never allowed in any family photos.'

No matter how great the strain Wendy was under in the witness protection scheme, Kathy will never forgive her for things she said during the committal. In an interview with the TyEyre taskforce's Detective Col McLaren, Wendy gave the following description of the family: 'Disgusting, the worst family in history that I can think of. The worst people I've ever come across. All they care about is drugs, guns, murdering people, disposing of dead bodies, shooting at you ... they're pathetic.'

Kathy's reaction was just equally venomous.

Listening to Wendy's evidence when she was in court talking about my family, I thought: 'What a dog.' But I swore, I swore I'd get her. If she hadn't changed her mind I would have done. I would have tracked her down. I've got friends in every state. I would have got her.

So, having made the momentous, desperate decision to turn against the family, and having gone through the hardest part, giving evidence at the committal, why did Wendy do an about-turn and refuse to repeat that evidence at the trial? Kathy has her own theories on this.

The cops had told Wendy there was one way they would lose the case for sure and if that happened she was history. So that's why she came out of witness protection. At the voir dire she stands in the dock like a fucking big cow and said: 'I don't see why my husband has to pay for his brother's sins.' And out she went. She had been convincing Victor for months through her mother that she was coming out. Her mother was visiting Victor. Wendy'd come to the Supreme Court for the voir dire, she was about seventeen stone, and they'd died her hair black. They must have something against blonde hair in the protection scheme. They did Vicki's hair and another girl's. Even after Wendy come out, I didn't trust her even then. I thought she might go back again.

Almost perversely Kathy prefers to disbelieve evidence about Wendy's alleged affair with Graeme Jensen, the man whose death at the hands of police sparked the entire Walsh Street saga. During the committal Wendy detailed the relationship right down to answering questions from defence counsel dealing with descriptions of Jensen's penis. But Kathy maintains Jensen detested Wendy and would go to any lengths to avoid her.

I don't know why the cops told her to say she was having an affair with Graeme. They even told Victor Wendy and Graeme used to meet outside Myers [department store in the centre of Melbourne]. *Everybody meets outside Myers, so is everybody fucking everybody outside Myers?*

In December 1992, three years after giving evidence at the committal, Wendy was convicted of perjury by a County Court jury.

The offence involved her statement at the voir dire, not the committal, that she had never seen guns at Chestnut Street. She was gaoled for eighteen months, with a minimum of nine months. For much of the period Wendy was in gaol, Kathy lived at her and Victor's home in the outer Melbourne suburb of Rowville and looked after their three eldest children. The youngest, little Vinnie, went into prison with his mother. It was during this period that Kathy became involved in a series of events which led to her last appearance before a court.

Today an uneasy form of peace exists between Kathy and Wendy. They communicate irregularly by phone, generally about the children, to whom Kathy is devoted and sees on a regular basis. It is largely for their sake that Kathy has anything to do with her daughter-in-law.

The third family member to be involved in the witness protection scheme, and the most hurtful from Kathy's point of view, was her daughter Vicki. The two have not met since the trial, and Kathy's last sight of Vicki was in the witness box.

Vicki, possibly, was in the most difficult position of all when she opted to go into protection. In simplest terms she was faced with an unthinkable choice—between her son and her brothers. The police had allegedly told her Victor and Trevor were plotting from inside prison to have Jason killed before he could give evidence against them. Inspector Noonan admitted during cross examination at the trial: 'I told her she would have to choose between her son and the family.' If one accepts that Vicki was also told her brothers were plotting her son's murder, could she be blamed for believing it? She was under similar pressure to that being brought to bear on Wendy—her home was being raided on a regular basis, her two brothers, and her tenant and friend, Peter McEvoy, had all been charged with the murder. And, worst of all, her son was in protection with rumours flying thick and fast about both his wellbeing and his likely fate.

Despite these circumstances Kathy refuses to give her daughter the benefit of the doubt.

The last time I saw her she was standing in that witness box. I don't want to ever see her again, because I saw the looks of hate she gave her brothers when she was standing there, and I knew she was lying her eyes out. She looked at the boys with hate, pure hate, because of what the cops told her about Victor and Trevor having Jason knocked. They told her we would do it. They said: 'It means you've got to choose between your son and your brothers. Your brothers are going to have him knocked.' And don't forget we knew where Jason was at times. Taxi drivers told us, they know everything. We knew the street and all that he was in, in Fitzroy. Vicki knew that. We could have gone there any time and got him. I never forgave Vicki. She's old enough, she could have stuck by her guns. She had a mind of her own, whether to believe the police or not. She knew we wouldn't touch Jason, we wouldn't kill Jason. Her own commonsense would have told her that.

The most damning items of evidence Vicki provided to police were an alleged confession to her from Peter McEvoy, and her refusal to confirm the alibis of McEvoy and Farrell that they spent the night of the murder at her flat. Kathy says Vicki had told her long before going into protection that the alibis were truthful, and she would back them up. It wasn't until the day Vicki moved into the protection scheme that Kathy realised something was terribly wrong.

This day I rang from Venus Bay and I said: 'Vicki, you've won the jackpot, we're all coming to stay.' We [Kathy and other family members] *pulled up at the back of her house in Davies*

261

Street, Brunswick, and we're sitting there waiting for her. We look through the window at the back, and the furniture's all there. A couple of hours later we look through again and they've moved her out the front. There was no furniture. If I never see her again I don't want to.

Going into protection cannot have been easy for Vicki. Even more so than Wendy and Jason, she had spent years within the bosom of the family, and had clocked up a number of convictions for crimes including theft, forgery and uttering, assault on police, driving offences, and drug offences including possession of heroin.

Even after she went into protection, Vicki clearly had doubts about what she had done and, like Wendy, more than once attempted suicide.

When she was in the scheme she rang me at Venus Bay and said she was dying, she'd taken an overdose. I didn't know whether she was telling the truth. The only thing I could think of was phoning Noonan at the TyEyre taskforce. I said: 'I don't know where she is, but somehow she's rung me and told me she's OD'd.' And then he goes straight and gets her, and takes her to the hospital, and saves her.

Kathy's memories of the Walsh Street committal and trial are understandably vivid. She was allowed by Magistrate Hugh Adams to pass notes between the accused and their counsel at the committal, despite police objections. This gave her a unique insight into the tensions and interplay that went on between police and the accused during the fifty-nine days of the hearing. She did not miss a single day of either the committal or subsequent trial, earning the grudging respect of court officials and even the odd policeman. She remembers more than one officer asking her how she was bearing up under the strain.

One unpleasant incident from the trial has remained in her mind:

Justice Vincent had just got up to leave the bench for lunch, right? Well there was a sergeant in charge upstairs in the public gallery in case anything happened. So before the boys were led away from the dock a policeman come in in plain clothes, and he had two girlfriends with him. And he leaned over the balcony and he said to the boys, 'I ought to piss on you,' like that, showing off to his girlfriends. The sergeant said: 'Get out of my court. Get out.'

Not surprisingly most police were anything but supportive. Kathy remembers, particularly, one exchange with Inspector Noonan which upset her greatly, immediately after her daughter Vicki had given evidence at the trial. But she was determined not to let him know this.

When Vicki gave her look of hatred at her brothers that's when I went down the stairs from the gallery crying. And Noonan laughed at me. The boys' barrister had his arms around me. I'm coming down the gallery stairs and I'm crying. I'd never seen that look of Vicki's before. Noonan walks out of this room at the bottom of the stairs and sees me crying, and does a double take and smirks at me. Didn't say anything, but he's got me. I went to Anthony Farrell's mum and said: 'Listen, I broke down a bit downstairs. Noonan saw me crying. When we go downstairs at the lunchbreak will you walk past with me and we'll just laugh our heads off?' And we did, and Noonan saw us. We made it obvious. It was important to me that he didn't think he'd got me. I hate Noonan because he's an arrogant son of a bitch, and won't be told the truth. Why does he hate my family? Ask him. He's in Frankston now. I won't go near Frankston.

263

Noonan at the committal said I was sitting around the table when the pact was made about killing two coppers for one of ours. I go outside the court and I said: 'If I was sitting around that table and said that, why haven't you charged me with the murder?' And he said: 'I'm seriously thinking about it.' And I said: 'Don't think about it, fucking do it.'

Living under the strain of the court hearings for months on end took its toll on Kathy, and was not helped by the emergence, in the middle of the committal, of two of her lost children (see Chapter Two). An important factor that helped her survive, sanity intact, was her ocean-side cottage in the remote Gippsland township of Venus Bay, two hours drive from Melbourne. By no means the type of retirement home one would expect for a major crime figure associated with the massive profit-making of Dennis's Richmond days, Kathy's hideaway cost her only $70,000. It was worth its weight in gold, however, as a peaceful sanctuary from the turmoil of Walsh Street.

The other factor that kept her going during the committal was her certainty of Victor's innocence, and her need to provide him with moral support. Each morning as the prison van approached the court Kathy would wait until it came into view and run into the road shouting Victor's name.

He couldn't see me, but he could fucking hear me. I made sure. Every morning I did it. But when they went to the Supreme Court they put 'em in a white van like a baker's van. They'd take 'em to the remand centre, which was only a few yards away, so you know what I used to do? Wait until the van nearly got to the lights and hit the pedestrian stop light and shout: 'How you goin' Victor, Trevor, how you goin', hoo roo roo.' I needed to show them I was there.

When Kathy first began to feel, at the trial, that her sons were going to be acquitted, she was sitting upstairs in the public gallery next to Anthony Farrell's grandmother, Patsy. She motioned to where Trevor was sitting in the dock, closest of the four accused to the door.

I said: 'How's Trevor's foot?' And she said: 'How the fucking hell would I know how Trevor's foot is?' And I said: 'Well, one foot's out the door now.'

When the time came for the four accused to make their unsworn statements from the dock, Kathy claims the police were determined to make things as hard as possible for them. Chris Dane QC, counsel for Trevor, requested that police not crowd behind the accused during their testimony.

Here they are facing the jury and all the jacks that have charged them are right behind them saying things to them like 'You maggots', and that while they're trying to give their evidence. By the time it got to Trevor's turn Chris Dane said to Justice Vincent: 'Your honour, could you make them stop saying things behind the prisoners' backs.'

During the six days the jury deliberated over their verdict Kathy and Wendy, both broke and in an uneasy alliance, were living with Wendy's three children in a halfway house provided by a charity organisation. 'When I went to bed the wallpaper was hitting me in the head, it was a terrible place. Wendy used to lock me out at night if I got back late,' she says.

The verdicts came at 10.35 on the morning of 26 March, the day before Kathy's fifty-sixth birthday.

Hugh Rimminton, a journalist covering the case, was sitting next to me. He was wonderful, 'cos they were pulling faces at me, the police, as the jury come in, they thought it was going to be guilty. I asked Hugh to come and sit with me, just to make 'em stop, and they did.

Eight times I hear not guilty. The first one must have been Victor. Not guilty, not guilty. Then Macca, not guilty, not guilty. Trevor's crying his eyes out, right? It gets to Anthony, not guilty, not guilty. Then Trevor tells me [later] I'm crying me eyes out, and they haven't got to me yet, and I'm thinking oh, fuck, what if it's me?

I was too emotional, me head's ringing with eight not guilties, and I hear all this clapping downstairs, and I think: 'Who's clapping who?' It's the boys clapping the jury.

Immediately after the verdicts Kathy called out in open court: 'I knew they were innocent. I'll see you downstairs, Victor!' and raced down to the corridor below crying. 'Hip hip hooray, three cheers for the boys.' As the various defence counsel filed past in the corridor, Kathy and other relatives of the four accused thanked them. Kathy then turned to the media: 'I didn't hear the press say hip hip hooray for the boys. You're very biased, you're very biased.'

Well they were, weren't they? If you'd have seen them crawling all over me for those six days when we were waiting for the jury—'Can I get you a cup of coffee?' 'Are you warm enough?' And one girl she come up to me and she had shoes on and the heels were all split, and I said: 'I wouldn't even let you work in my parlour if I had one now.' I said to her: 'Who do you work for?' She said: 'Derryn Hinch.' I said: 'Well, if he was laying in the gutter on fire I wouldn't even piss on him.' And she said: 'Well, I don't like him either, I'm going to tell him.' I had the whole crowd around me, and they wanted my family history, and I'm thinking: 'No, you're not, you're not getting it.'

Kathy, despite her position in the underworld, is not privy to any information on who could have committed the murders of the two police officers. Her theories include someone avenging the death of Joshua Yap, a Chinese armed robber who died seven months after Steven Tynan shot him during a TAB robbery in South Yarra, only ten days before Tynan's death. (The police have effectively ruled out this possibility.) Her other theory is a widely and understandably discredited story involving a rogue New South Wales policeman who wanted Victor out of the way and killed two police officers knowing Victor would be a suspect.

> *Then a detective was supposed to have come down from Sydney and done it. I don't know what the motive was. I don't know what happened, but I hope to God one day that pistol is found, and then we'll know for sure who did it.*

Kathy believes it was this gun that was the subject of a bizarre episode, shortly after the murders, involving a police search of her home at Venus Bay.

> *I wasn't home. I reckon they were looking for the gun. But the thing was I bought a bug catcher at the hardware in Brunswick and I left it on the table at Venus Bay. And I hear about a raid. I was sitting in the kitchen at Wendy's at 86 Chestnut Street, so she rings up the TyEyre taskforce and that Brendon Cole said: 'Yeah, we turned her house over.' The kids got in the car and they came down with me. There was an inspector sitting here in his car, and he was going to secure the house and I said: 'Who the fuck are you?' And he said: 'Well, who the fuck are you?' 'I happen to be the owner of this place.' So he helped me put the toilet lid back on. They didn't get anything, but they stole the bug catcher. You know why the bug catcher was taken? They told me later on it was because they put a bug on*

the phone, that was the cryptic hint ... that was their bloody
sense of humour.

At the conclusion of the trial Victor made his own gesture from
the dock. 'Standing bolt upright and looking straight ahead,'
according to the *Herald-Sun*, he asked Mr Justice Vincent if he
could speak. Granted permission, he said: 'Now we have been
proved not guilty I would like to demand an inquiry into Mr
Noonan's investigation and the way he conducted the police
investigation.'

Victor remained in gaol for three weeks after the acquittal,
waiting trial on another armed robbery charge which had been
adjourned pending determination of the Walsh Street case. (The
charges involving Dominik Hefti had already been dropped.)
On 16 April 1991 he was granted $100,000 bail on charges
involving the theft of $212,000 from an ANZ bank in Ringwood
in January 1988. The case came to trial in August 1991, with
the two main prosecution witnesses being Lindsay Rountree
(whose evidence against Victor had already failed to secure a
conviction during the Walsh Street trial) and a Paul Anthony
Prideaux.

Rountree refused to sign his statement to police, and was not
called to give evidence. Prideaux told the court his statement to
police was untrue, and was 'all part of a conspiracy. I am not
guilty alone of putting this document together. I am as guilty as
those two detectives who signed the statement.'

At this stage Victor's counsel, Geoff Flatman, successfully
applied for the charges to be dropped. As Victor walked out of
court a free man with no charges hanging over his head, a policeman approached him and shook his hand.

I couldn't believe it. He must have been close to retirement or
very game. As he walked away Victor said to me: 'Mum, I've
got to convince 9,000 other policemen I didn't do it.'

Victor then gave a statement to the waiting media, saying he feared for his life. 'All of the offences I have been charged with, three murders and six armed robberies, I have beat them all. I was an innocent man from the start. I knew my innocence would be proven in the end. It was a matter of time. But to this day I still fear certain members of the Victorian Police Force. All I want is to live a family life. I have got children and a wife, and I just want to be left alone to work and to prove to the community that I am not as bad as police and the press have made me out to be. I wish they would catch the real killers of the Walsh Street policemen, because that would help clear our names.'

Victor then called for an inquiry into 'a handful of corrupt police'. Senior Sergeant Paul Mullett responded immediately on behalf of the force, describing Victor's allegations of corruption as 'absolutely preposterous. If Peirce just lives a life of an honest citizen he will have no problems from us.'

But that was perhaps easier said than done. Not long after Victor and Wendy moved with their children to Wheelers Hill, an outer suburb, during the period Victor was awaiting trial on the ANZ Bank charges, they became the victims of harassment stemming from Walsh Street. The couple told the *Age* they were ostracised by neighbours, that children walked past their house screaming 'cop killer', and that police surveillance stopped only after Wendy complained to her local Member of Parliament. Victor spoke of leaving his home every morning in overalls pretending to go to work to satisfy neighbours' curiosity about his movements. In reality he had found his background made it impossible for him to obtain work.

In the years following Walsh Street, Victor failed to stay out of gaol (in addition to the sentence he received for his role in Peter's prison drug cartel [see Chapter Ten]). He also received convictions for stealing a jar of coffee from a supermarket, and for trafficking in a drug of dependence. During the latter trial his counsel, Mark Rochford, spoke of the legacy of Walsh Street. 'He was notorious for something that he legally hadn't done.'

Victor brought civil charges against police involving an episode which allegedly took place in 1989, while he was awaiting trial on the Walsh Street charges. Victor claimed that eight plainclothes policemen removed him from Pentridge on a legal warrant and drove him around the city to different locations including a Walsh Street in Coburg (there are around a dozen listed in the Melbourne street directory). Wendy claimed during her evidence at the committal that Victor was bashed and spat upon during this episode. The allegations were the subject of an internal police inquiry. Victor was dissatisfied with the results and began his civil action.

Trevor has fared little better since his acquittal. He already had thirty-two convictions at the time of Walsh Street for a wide range of offences, and since the trial he has been before the courts on drug and burglary charges. In March 1995, he was gaoled for five years and three months, with a minimum of three years and nine months, on charges of trafficking in cannabis and amphetamines.

The three brothers: Peter, Victor and Trevor, were all released from gaol in 1998 and 1999, managing to stay out of serious trouble—at least initially. Victor obtained employment in the Footscray fruit and vegetable market, and later on the Melbourne docks as a stevedore. His four children remained the focus of his life up to the day of 1 May 2002, when he was gunned down in the streets of Port Melbourne. Typically he had been with Katie, then aged 16, and Vinnie, aged nine, minutes before his killers pulled up beside the parked car in which he was sitting, and fired the fatal shots.

Everybody had their own theory over the identity of the two assassins. Kathy had always predicted the police would one day take Victor and Trevor's lives in revenge for Walsh Street. And there was an eerie similarity between the car used by Victor's killers and the abandoned vehicle which lured officers Tynan and Eyre to their deaths. But Kathy quickly abandoned this line of thought, preferring instead the 'word' she received that a young up-and-comer was responsible, keen to make a name for himself as the man who knocked off Victor Peirce.

Predictably, no tears were shed by police. Detective Inspector John Noonan, who had led the Walsh Street inquiries, commented: 'It's just nice that people pay for their sins. Certainly I don't view it [Victor's death] with any sadness.' However, Chief Commissioner Christine Nixon vowed Victor's killers would be pursued with the same vigour as in any normal murder hunt. Encouraged by this, Kathy wrote to thank her, and to complain about Noonan's comments.

The funeral was in many ways a graphic illustration of the extent to which Kathy's life and outlook has changed in recent years. As she stood outside the Church of St Peter and St Paul in South Melbourne on a grey and blustery afternoon at the end of the service, the cream of Melbourne's underworld lined up to pay homage. A series of shaven headed men in dark glasses and sharp suits embraced her in turn, murmuring their condolences into her ear.

Standing at the centre of this menacing gathering, Kathy looked like what she had become—a middle-aged woman up from the country for the day, feeling slightly lost and out of her depth in the city. As the last of the murderers, armed robbers and drug lords released her from their embrace, I asked her if she needed a lift to the cemetery.

'I'm not fucking going to the cemetery, love,' she responded. 'I'm off back to Venus Bay right now. I've had enough.' Contrast this with Kathy's performance at the wakes for Jamie and Dennis, where she was in the thick of the blues and violence which characterise such underworld functions, and some idea of her new priorities emerges.

THE MATRIARCH

By the evening of the funeral Kathy was safe back home, still deeply traumatised by the death of a third son, possibly the one she loved most dearly of all. A group of neighbours were there to greet her, sitting up with her until the early hours offering comfort and friendship.

'That's my life now, that's what's important to me,' she said.

Kathy has become almost a pillar of the Venus Bay Community, receiving—along with hundreds of other Victorians—a framed citation from Victorian Premier Steve Bracks in 2001 for voluntary work she had performed. It is interesting to theorise over whether or not Kathy would have received her citation had those making the selection been aware of her life as Granny Evil.

By then bingo had replaced prostitution, violence and drugs as her main interest. For years she used her broken down old Datsun to ferry a group of middle aged women from Venus Bay to Inverloch, 30 kms away, for their weekly bingo sessions. Kathy didn't expect, or particularly want, any recognition. She was simply putting something back into a community which had demonstrated, in a thousand ways over the years, they were prepared to accept her for what she had become, rather than what she had been.

CHAPTER TEN

‑ Venus Bay ‑

Trevor Pettingill and his wife Debbie are staying down on the coast at Venus Bay with Kathy in her hideaway cottage. Debbie's mother Yvonne, who knows Kathy well, has set out to join them, and for the last leg of the journey has caught the local bus from Wonthaggi. It stops at the hamlet of Tarwin Lower, a few kilometres outside Venus Bay. It is early evening as Yvonne, a squarehead, and the only passenger, climbs aboard at Wonthaggi. The driver, a local called Ray, asks Yvonne where she's headed. 'Venus Bay eventually,' she replies. 'Ah,' says Ray. 'I'm from around there. We've got a wicked woman down there. Moved in a few years back. Her name's Kathy Pettingill. You know, Walsh Street and that.' Yvonne says not a word, but listens instead as, for the remainder of the journey, Ray regales her with tales of the family's terrible doings. As the coach approaches the stop at Tarwin Lower, Ray spots a diminutive figure standing beside a parked car. Someone's come to meet Yvonne off the bus. As they draw closer there's something terribly familiar about that head of curly grey hair. And as he finally draws up and Yvonne climbs down the steps, his worst fears are confirmed: 'Hello Kathy, love,' says Yvonne. And turning to grin back over her shoulder at Ray: 'I've heard so much about you.'

THE MATRIARCH

Kathy chuckles as she relates the story.

That was over eleven years ago, and I've been on that bus with Ray the driver. He knows who I am, and he speaks to me just like he would any of the other passengers. He's a friend.

The township of Venus Bay lies two hours' drive from Melbourne. The six-lane freeway out of the city soon becomes a highway, cutting through little farming communities with names like Inverloch and Wonthaggi. Occasionally a great sweep of the Southern Ocean comes into view, lines of breakers surging onto a curve of beach half-hidden behind a dark headland. This is Gippsland, the name given to the southeastern section of Victoria, an area of rich pasture land and sleek, drowsy cattle. The further Melbourne falls behind the greater the feeling of security, as gently rolling paddocks that somehow remain green all through the year replace the concrete and clamour of the city. The last half-hour of the journey flattens out onto a plain that could have been the ocean floor a million years ago. By now the highway has become twisting and narrow, the River Tarwin flowing beside it for company. Venus Bay, with its collection of weekenders, three or four shops, and year-round population of a few hundred, marks the end of the road. The only way on is by boat on the open ocean.

Kathy first heard of Venus Bay in 1988 when she was being held on charges of conspiring to traffic heroin, trafficking in heroin and possession of heroin. It became the place of her dreams.

When I was inside Wendy used to send me these books about houses for sale, 'cos I wanted to leave Richmond as soon as I got out of gaol. I wanted to sell Dennis's house. Young people had moved in at 37 Stephenson Street and it sounded the same as if Dennis was still in there. So then the Taxation took my house, which was in his name.

There was a house in these books in Venus Bay. I kept thinking: 'Why can't this bloke sell this same house?' I said to the screws: 'When I get out of gaol I'm going down there to buy this house.' And they used to take it with a grain of salt, 'cos junkies say this and junkies say that, but I've never been a junkie. So I said to Wendy: 'When I get out I want to go down to this Venus Bay and have a look at this house.' What sold me was the view of the ocean as you drive over Kilcunda on the way down from Melbourne. So I came down here. The house wasn't like this, I brought me own doors and chandeliers and stuff.

So I come down and the owner was sitting there, and they're Germans and they were Seventh-Day Adventists, linen press downstairs full of food for forty days or whatever their religion is. As soon as I saw the drive and come upstairs I said: 'I think you're sitting in my house.' I gave the estate agent $20 deposit to hold it, but the rumour around Venus Bay was I opened the trunk of me boot on the old Torana and I gave 'em $80,000 cash. It didn't cost that, it cost $70,000. For half an acre and this house. What made me laugh was Charlie Nikakis said to me: 'What about the water rates?' I said: 'There's no fucking water rates. I've got tanks.' I moved here in July 1988, just before Walsh Street. I bought it because I wanted the kids to come down.

People here didn't know who I was 'til Walsh Street. I was a bit of a hermit, I didn't go anywhere. When I first got down here I didn't have no money, just out of gaol. And I had to go to Tarwin to the welfare to get money for food. My car wouldn't start, and I didn't know the people over the road from a bar of soap, but they ran me there. I spilt water on me stove, and it *catches fire, and me neighbour Ray—not the bus driver—put the fire out for me. He didn't know me, and at the time I went to Melbourne and when I came back he'd mended the fire, and put the down lights and a fan in, and floodlighting outside. One day I went there and his wife Jean was sitting there knitting, and I said: 'Do you ever go to the bingo?' and she said: 'No.' And I said: 'I go every Wednesday.' Now I take Jean to Inverloch shopping every week 'cos she doesn't drive, and then we go and play bingo. Since I've known those two I've never got to know so many people in me life as in their house, and they all accept me.*

One of Kathy's new friends, Pat, another neighbour, had a typically unorthodox introduction to her. Pat kept missing shoes from outside her house until after a while all she had left was a set of single shoes, none of which made a pair.

Eventually Pat spotted the culprit, Kathy's dog Julie, Dennis's old guard dog, jumping over the fence with the evidence in his mouth. Jane hadn't met Kathy and knew her only by sight as the middle-aged, grey-haired woman living nearby. So she approached the matter somewhat diplomatically. 'You wouldn't have seen some odd shoes lying around, would you?' she asked when Kathy responded to her knock at the door. Without a word Kathy led her to a corner of the yard: 'Take your pick,' she said, pointing to a small heap of shoes. Pat thought Kathy's manner a little rough and ready, but over the next two months the women became good friends, spending considerable time in one another's company. At last Pat learnt the truth of her new friend's identity.

I was leaving her place one night, and she stopped me. She went very serious, which isn't like Kathy, and she said: 'Come back in, there's something I've got to tell you.' Well, she sat me

276

down and she said: 'I'm Kathy Pettingill.' I'd never heard her
last name, and she said it as if it should mean something to
me. It didn't and I said so. You see I don't read the papers, and
I wasn't in Victoria when Walsh Street happened, so I was
probably the only person in the State who didn't know about
it. So she had to start at the beginning and tell me about Dennis
and everything. Over the next twenty minutes I could feel my
hair standing on end. I couldn't believe it, never heard anything
like that in my life. I was just terrified. When she'd finished
telling me she said: 'Okay, that's it, now it's up to you. You
don't have to talk to me ever again if you don't want to, but if
you still want to be friends, that's okay too. Up to you.' She
even told me to think about it overnight. Well I did, and we're
still friends.

When I repeated this story later to Kathy, her only comment was:
'Well, it wasn't fair to keep it from her. Anyway she might have
heard it from someone else, and that would have been worse
than coming from me.'

But it hasn't always been sweetness and light among the
townsfolk of Venus Bay. Shortly after the Walsh Street trial
Kathy's son Lex and his family came to live in the town for a
while and Lex's two children began attending the local school.
According to Kathy other children regularly abused her grandchildren and even spat at them because of what they had heard
about Walsh Street. Eventually Lex, and later Kathy, went to see
the headmaster. Education Department officials were called in
and rumours began to spread about Lex threatening the
headmaster. There was even a story about the teacher being
transferred to another school because of his fears.

Eventually the rumours spread to Melbourne and in May
1992 the *Sunday Age* sent a reporter down. The president of the
school council, Lindsay Marriott, put him right, explaining that
if anything it was Kathy's family that had been intimidated. Even

ice sergeant, Bill Waller, concurred: 'Basically they just want their privacy respected,' he said.

Life was starting to return to normal for Kathy when she had another unpleasant reminder of Walsh Street.

I saw Shane Richards [one of the prosecution's protected witnesses who gave discredited evidence against Trevor] *at Inverloch one night. His mother was living up here. I was going to the bingo. My first reaction was to jump out of the car and get him. But I was in someone else's car, and he had two young blokes with him, and he was walking the opposite way to where I lived, so I didn't.*

I also saw Lindsay Rountree up at the Stud Park shopping centre when I was up in Melbourne one day. He was going into K-Mart. Well, him and Wendy were talking like old time buddies from the witness protection. I just sat outside and thought. 'I'm not talking ever to that dog again.'

It was during this period the ABC ran the first of two highly regarded crime series, *Phoenix* and *Janus*. Kathy became an avid fan of *Phoenix*, and wrote to the producers over a technical mistake—they used the wrong robes for a judge during a court scene. As a result of her letter the producers contacted Kathy when they were beginning research for the second series, *Janus*. Kathy agreed to help out as an 'authenticity consultant'. 'It meant telling them what crooks wear, how they talk, what they eat, all of it,' she recalls. 'They knew nothing. They didn't even know you never send a crook a card with a dog on it.'

Kathy was paid the princely sum of $240 and two cab fares for her help on *Janus*. But what annoyed her even more than the ABC's tight-fisted attitude was the hidden agenda she believed was going on. While producers and researchers asked her questions about criminals in general, they also pumped her for information about Dennis and Walsh Street, but gave her no indication *Janus* was to be based loosely on her own family.

When she sat down to watch the opening episode, which included the murders of two police officers, she realised immediately what was happening, and got straight on the phone for legal advice. She was told there was little she could do, even though the central characters, Shirl and Mal Hennessey, clearly relied heavily on her and Dennis for inspiration. Mal wore a similar collection of gold jewellery to Dennis and Kathy firmly believes other characters in the series were based on Jason and Wendy.

When the words, 'The persons and events portrayed in this drama are fictitious. Any resemblance is coincidental and unintended,' came up on the screen at the end of the first episode, Kathy laughed out loud. She strongly believed the producers should have told her they were basing their series on her family, and she would then have made her decision on whether or not to help them.

The most Alison Niselle, joint creator and producer of *Janus*, will say is that it was 'inspired by recent Australian history, but all characters and events are completely fictitious'. Strangely, given this explanation, not one of Kathy's underworld friends failed to make the connection.

A major disruption to Kathy's peaceful life by the ocean came in December 1992 when Wendy received her nine-month minimum sentence for perjury. Victor was already in prison, so there was nobody to look after the three eldest children. (Vinnie, the baby, went into gaol with Wendy, too young to be separated from his mother.) So Kathy faced the alternative of seeing her grandchildren being taken into care, or coming to the rescue. She chose the latter and moved up to Melbourne and Victor and Wendy's home in outer-suburban Rowville, rather than disrupt the children's lives by moving them down to Venus Bay. Unknown to her Kathy was almost immediately placed under surveillance and, she believes, was set up.

They called it Operation Earthquake, and it turned out to be Operation Tremble. Supposed to be a huge conspiracy only we didn't know the other people arrested at the time. They pulled in thirty people, but we didn't know the rest. We were supposed to be a big gang, drugs, heroin, everything. I was supposed to have done all these drug deals.

Two ladies moved in round the corner in Rowville and one of them I'd been in gaol with. Another neighbour rang me and said her kid, only fifteen, had bought a hot video off them and didn't have enough money to pay for it, and they were threatening to cut her throat or something. Because I knew this woman from gaol I went round and stood outside and said: 'Get out here, you're cutting nobody's throat. If anything happens I'll cut your fucking throat.' Little did I know this was part of the set-up. One evening I was dishing up the kids' tea and one of these women comes round and says someone's knocked on her door to score some drugs and wanted to know where Kathy Pettingill lives. I didn't want to know. I wasn't dealing. I never got any drugs for 'em.

Then an undercover copper came round for drugs with one of the girls. And one said: 'Can you get us some smack?' and the other said, 'Speed' at the same time. I gave him a phone number to score. I made him take all his clothes off to make sure he wasn't taped but it was her, she had it in her handbag.

A few days later Wendy was released from gaol and Kathy moved back down to Venus Bay. Not long afterwards, on 16 September 1993, came the aftermath.

It's a quarter to six at night and I've just had a shower, hair in rollers, hair all wet and everything. I've got two little potato pies, tiny little potato pies, in the oven, and I'm waiting for the news. I hear a noise, then: 'Police, don't move! Police, don't move! Police, don't move!' as they go from room to room downstairs. I'm sitting here on me own. One runs up the stairs with a big screwdriver, the other one comes up with a bulletproof vest, and he's got a pump action shotgun, and he says to me, I'm sitting there, 'Get on the floor! Get on the floor!' I laid down like this on the floor, and he's got the shotgun at me neck.

The one with the screwdriver comes towards me and he turns me over and starts fiddling with me, and I think what's he doing? 'Cos there's four lady detectives down there, which I didn't know at the time. Why didn't one of them search me? So he says: 'I've got the gun, I've got the gun.' And then they all run upstairs. There's fifteen of them, looked like a car yard outside. And he's got this silver pen pistol. I've never seen this gun before, and he says: 'How many bullets are in it?' And I said: 'How the fuck would I know? You brought it, you know. Don't insult me.' I wouldn't have a gun like that—I always had Magnums.

Later on I get the trembles, and he says, the one with the gun at me neck: 'I think you'd better sit up.' I was handcuffed behind me back. Well, they wrecked the house, but the worst was when they came in. They said: 'We've just shot Trevor, by the way. We've just killed Trevor, he's up there talking to Dennis. And you won't be coming back here for years.'

They had been to Trevor's place. They had an ambulance outside his place ready, but Debbie saved his life. She was heavily pregnant and was going to Safeway to do some shopping, but she didn't feel up to it, so she stayed home, and saved his life. They maced him, same day as they raided me.

The resulting court hearings didn't end until March 1995, by which time Kathy had spent a considerable period in custody on remand. She finally admitted to three of the original fifteen charges and was sentenced to eighteen months, nine of them suspended for two years. Because of the time already served on remand she was freed and left immediately for the sanctuary of Venus Bay.

Meanwhile, by June 1991 her oldest surviving son, Peter, was serving his second sentence in Geelong gaol, when he became involved in an incident which caused his transfer back to Pentridge. His incarceration had done little to curb his main skill, drug dealing, and when a fight broke out over who ran the gaol's very efficient drug cartel, an inmate named Andrew Caddaye finished up with thirty stab wounds. He received a punctured lung and almost had a hand severed in the attack. Peter was one of eight prisoners moved to Pentridge in the aftermath of the assault.

Two months later, possibly as a result of this incident, police began an investigation into Peter's activities behind bars which was to last until September 1992. The result of their inquiries was a million-dollar five-month trial which ended in October 1994 with Peter getting an additional seven-year sentence.

The trial, before Mr Justice Francis Walsh in Melbourne County Court, heard of Peter's role as the mastermind behind an audacious drug ring which supplied heroin, amphetamines, marijuana and Rohypnol to gaol inmates throughout the Victorian prison system, principally Pentridge, Geelong and Bendigo.

Peter's system was based on a network using a corrupt prison officer code-named The Postie, five TAB accounts, three women couriers, and Victor as banker and supplier. For much of the period he ran the syndicate Peter worked in the F Division laundry in Pentridge, from where he spent up to two hours a day on the phone. Unknown to Peter police tapped the laundry phone and recorded a total of more than 17,000 calls, 2,000 from the gaol and the remainder from other tapped phones, including Victor's, on the outside.

The system was deceptively simple. Prisoners wanting drugs had to have relatives or friends on the outside who would pay money into one of the five TAB accounts, including one in Victor's name and another in Wendy's. The drugs were then brought into the gaols, either by The Postie or the couriers, and passed to Peter.

As a result of the break-up of Peter's syndicate, the entire system of phone use within the state's gaols has been changed. Prisoners are now allowed to phone only pre-approved numbers.

Kathy maintains that the horrific amount of time Peter has spent in prison since his twentieth birthday has done less damage to him, both physically and mentally, than would be expected.

He's just like you or me. He's well adjusted, happy, you'd be amazed. At the end of the last ten stretch he did, he told me: 'I've done a quick ten.' Doesn't affect him. All he does is play cards. He's learnt Vietnamese when he was in the yards. He's in the slot at the moment because they reckon he's running the gaol, which he probably was. Victor reckoned Peter's the untidiest person in his cell. Victor was meticulous. You could eat off Victor's floor. Peter would just dump a smoke down Victor's toilet and Victor would go crook. Victor and Peter weren't that close. Peter reads a lot of transcripts and that 'cos he helps a lot of other prisoners with their cases.

Since her release after the drugs conviction, Kathy has occupied herself with her house and garden, her new dog Smokie, her ritual games of bingo and the making of quaint little ornaments. She brings home pieces of driftwood and other items she finds on the beach and paints and varnishes them, transforming them into the kind of novelty found in tourist shops and on mantelpieces everywhere.

When she has made sufficient numbers, Kathy takes her creations to a local weekend market and sells them, generally for between $2 and $5. Few of the purchasers are aware as they set off with their new acquisition that they are taking home a part of Granny Evil, the most notorious matriarch in Australian criminal history.

Kathy has lived at Venus Bay for more than fourteen years now and has formed a deep attachment for the place. It seems to provide her with the same sense of sanctuary and peace of mind she found alone in her cell in Pentridge.

In politics they talk about experienced hands 'knowing where the bodies are buried'. In the underworld it's better not to use phrases like that. But there's no doubting Kathy is privy to knowledge in a variety of areas that the average police officer would trade his freddy (badge) for. But there's never any sense that this weighs heavily on her soul. Kath, above all, is comfortable in her own company. Her fierce self-sufficiency may start to fade over the next decade as old-age creeps on, but there is little prospect of her sinking into a whining, guilt-ridden dotage. If she chooses to grow old in Venus Bay her last years are more likely to be characterised by a grin of defiance than a tear of remorse.

Index

285

INDEX

INDEX